Clothing: A Global History

For Janneke

with love

Clothing: A Global History

Or, The Imperialists' New Clothes

Robert Ross

polity

First published in 2008 by Polity Press

Polity Press
65 Bridge Street
Cambridge CB2 1UR, UK.

Polity Press
350 Main Street
Malden, MA 02148, USA

ISBN-13: 978-0-7456-3186-8
ISBN-13: 978-0-7456-3187-5(pb)

A catalogue record for this book is available from the British Library.

Typeset in 10.5 on 12 pt Times
by SNP Best-set Typesetter Ltd, Hong Kong
Printed and bound in the United States by Maple-vail

The publisher has used its best endeavours to ensure that the URLs for external websites referred to in this book are correct and active at the time of going to press. However, the publisher has no responsibility for the websites and can make no guarantee that a site will remain live or that the content is or will remain appropriate.

Every effort has been made to trace all copyright holders, but if any have been inadvertently overlooked the publishers will be pleased to include any necessary credits in any subsequent reprint or edition.

For further information on Polity, visit our website: www.polity.co.uk

Contents

Acknowledgements

I owe thanks to a number of people for their help in the writing of this book; first to the Netherlands Institute for Advanced Study, Wassenaar, its Rector, Wim Blockmans, its executive director, Wouter Hugenholtz, and its staff, particularly in the library. The half-year fellowship I enjoyed gave me the opportunity to break the back of the research and to begin the writing; to my own employers, Leiden University, and in particular to the department of African languages and cultures for their forbearance with work which does not centrally deal with the concerns of the department; to Anna Beerens, Jan-Bart Gewald, Mieke Jansen, Rudy Kousbroek, Kirsten McKenzie, Giacomo Macola, Mina Roces, Anjana Singh, Nettie Tichelaar, Ruth Watson, and Thera Wijsenbeek for references and comments on a number of sections; to seminar audiences in Basel, Sydney, Pretoria and Canberra who have heard, and made useful comments on, various of the chapters; to Polity for suggesting a topic which I would never have chosen myself and for their patience in awaiting the manuscript; to their anonymous readers for informed and helpful comments from which I have taken confidence and advice; and to librarians in a number of places, particularly in Leiden, for their help.

Above all, I have, and want, to thank Janneke Jansen, for continual encouragement, for constructive engagement, for her critical reading of the various chapters and her valuable advice and for much, much more. And that is only the academic side of things. The rest is far more important.

Leiden

Illustrations

Picture Credits

The publisher would like to thank the following for permission to reproduce the images in this book:

AFP/Getty Images (World leaders in Evian, 2003; Rati Sir Kamisese Mara and General Rabuka, Fiji)

Koninklijk Institut voor Taal-, Land- en Volkenkunde (A village headman from the Moluccas, Indonesia, 1919; The De Vries family, Batavia, 1915; Indonesian nationalists)

Getty Images (Corset advertisement; Mustafa Kemal Atatürk; James Dean in *Rebel Without a Cause*)

Time & Life Pictures/Getty Images (Girls in Mother Hubbards; Kwame Nkrumah (left) with a member of his cabinet)

Museum voor Volkenkunde, Leiden (A Christian village near Marianhill, KwaZulu-Natal)

The Namibian National Archive (Herero woman dancing, Windhock)

© Bettmann/Corbis (Jawaharlal Nehru and Mahatma Gandhi)

Rex Features (The New Look)

Jamie Jones/Rex Features (Girls in Islamic dress, Birmingham, 2002)

Powerhouse Museum, Sydney (Woman in a *qipao*)

Every effort has been made to trace all copyright holders, but if any have been inadvertently overlooked the publishers will be pleased to include any necessary credits in any subsequent reprint or edition.

1

Introduction

Take the meeting of world leaders known as the G8, which met in Evian, France, in June 2003. It was a gathering which had important discussions to conduct, and important decisions to make. What is intriguing, though, is the fact that as they emerged to have the collective photograph taken, the political leaders of the eight most powerful countries in the world – though the Chinese were not there – all of whom were men, all wore basically the same outfit – dark suit, light shirt, tie, polished shoes. The Presidents of Russia, France and the United States of America, the Prime Ministers of Japan, Italy, Great

1 World leaders in Evian, 2003

Britain and Canada and the Chancellor of Germany had all adopted this uniform. So had the leaders of lesser nations who were allowed to put their case to the mighty, with two exceptions, the President of Nigeria and the representative of Saudi Arabia. Prince Abdullah Ibn Abdul Aziz Al Saud was in flowing Bedouin robes, Olusegun Obasanjo was in equally flowing Yoruba costume. But the South African, Thabo Mbeki, wore a suit as well-tailored as that of any of his confreres, as did the presidents of India, Malaysia and China.

It is instructive, as a thought experiment, to wonder what a gathering of their predecessors four hundred years ago would have looked like. If it had been possible to gather the Kings of France and Spain, the Ottoman Sultan, the Shah of Persia, the Mughal Emperor, the Emperor of China, the Shogun of Japan and whoever might be given the eighth place, perhaps already the Stadhouder of the Netherlands, then there would have been no uniformity in their dress, even though, as in 2003, they were all men. Representatives from lesser powers, say the Alafin of Oyo, the Mwene Mutapa, leaders of the Iroquois confederacy, any remaining Inca notables, would only have added to the sartorial diversity on show. Moreover, none would be dressed as their successors now are.

Or take Hluhluwe, a small country town in northern Zululand, in a poor area of South Africa, living off sisal, pineapples, timber and rhinoceroses (via tourists), on a cold winter's weekday in 2003. It could have been anywhere, except that I happened to be sitting outside the supermarket for half an hour or so. The men there were dressed in cotton trousers – occasionally jeans – shirts and jackets, often of leather. The women generally wore skirts reaching halfway between the knee and the ankle, though a few wore cotton trousers. For the rest, most wore jerseys and woollen jackets, although a very few had blankets round their shoulders, generally to carry a baby. Both men and women wore socks and mass-produced shoes, often sports shoes. A number of men wore woollen hats – it was June, after all – and the women generally had some sort of headscarf or other covering on their heads. The few boys who were not at school, probably because they had no one to pay for their fees and school uniforms, wore knee length trousers and shirts. I saw no girls hanging around there.

The sight was, somehow, South African in its details, in the way the headscarves were tied, in the woolly hats, in the length of the skirts, but even in this politically most ethnic, most Zulu, of areas, there was no one who wore anything which was in any way obviously ethnic, except perhaps for the rather too fat man who had on short shorts and sandals as only a white South African can, and two dancers in Zulu warrior gear who were attracting tourists by the game reserve. For the rest, the people of Hluhluwe had long been accustomed to dressing in a casual version of Western clothing. And no doubt, if they could afford it, the men would wear suits and ties to church on Sundays, and to other important events, and the women smart dresses.

This scene, simple enough, could be replicated in tens of thousands of shopping centres across the globe. There are of course all sorts of minor variations, and often quite substantial ones. In general, I would imagine, the women are more likely to diverge from the standard western norm than are the men.

These two vignettes from the early twenty-first century raise a question that is profoundly historical. How has this cultural homogenization come about? How has it come to be that when the President of France and the Prime Minister of Japan meet they are wearing essentially the same clothes, while their predecessors, say Henri IV and the Shogun Tokugawa Ieyasu, would not have been? What process has resulted in the people of Hluhluwe wearing clothes that are basically the same as those worn by men and women in Leiden, the Netherlands; in Salta, Argentina; in Bangkok; in Charleston, South Carolina; and indeed in most towns in most countries in the world? Just as importantly, why was it was the President of Nigeria and the first minister of Saudi Arabia who held out against the trend, if that is what they were doing? Where, and why, do large proportions of the population not wear variations of the common mode? Why are bodies covered, almost everywhere? Even in winter, there would have been much more bare flesh in Hluhluwe a century and a half ago. Is it true that women are more constrained by "tradition" than men, and if so how has that come about? Is it true, as Ali Mazrui commented thirty-five years or more ago, that "the most successful cultural bequest from the West to the rest of the world has been precisely Western dress"? He continued: "Mankind is getting rapidly homogenised by the sheer acquisition of the Western shirt and the Western trousers. The Japanese businessman, the Arab Minister, the Indian lawyer, the African civil servant have all found a common denominator in the Western suit."[1] It is to these sorts of question that I hope to give some answers in the course of this book.[2]

These answers can obviously be subsumed under the term "globalization", itself a consequence of North American and European technical prowess, economic growth, imperialism and sense of cultural superiority.[3] For all its potential modishness, this term does refer to a phenomenon which is real and important. Among many other things, notably in the speed of information movement around the globe, the material culture of the world has become (partially) homogenized. But to demonstrate this obviously requires a global approach, one in which the courts of King Chulalongkorn of Siam and the Meiji

Emperor are as central as that of the King-Emperor Edward VII, in which, if it is necessary to find individuals, the most important are perhaps Kemal Atatürk, the Mahatma Gandhi and Jawaharlal Nehru, not Christian Dior, and in which the Herero long dress is as important as the New Look, probably more so because it has lasted much longer.

It should be obvious that I have not approached the writing of this book as a professional student of clothing, nor even more of the history of cloth. I was amused to discover Max Beerbohm's comment on Thomas Carlyle, who wrote one of the first treatises on clothing, to the effect that "anyone who dressed so very badly as did Thomas Carlyle should have tried to construct a philosophy of clothing has always seemed to me one of the most pathetic things in literature."[4] In stereotypical gendered behaviour, it was my sisters, not me, who, when we were young, would regularly visit the costume galleries of the Victoria and Albert Museum in London, and I cannot remember having done so until I was well on the way to completing this book.[5] Rather I am an African historian, and have taken pleasure from the idea that the continent will no longer be seen as a site of naked savagery. Specifically, I have long worked on colonial South Africa, and in that context I have written about the ways in which aspects of European culture were adopted, and put to their own uses, by the colonized. In this sense, I hope, this book is an extension of that work. If so, it must depart from the assumption that what people wear, like what they believe, can only in part be imposed from above, or outside. Rather, in the long term, the rules for external covering have to be internalized. This book is about how that has happened.

It should be clear that this approach is not the usual one in the history of clothing and dress. While I am in this a "lumper", generally those concerned with dress and clothing are what would be termed "splitters", if we were engaged in the study of natural, rather than social, history.[6] In other words they emphasize the differences between the various costumes which they study, just as some taxonomists are more likely than others to see the organisms they study as belonging to different species. The reasons for this lie both in the most common reaction of almost anyone, at least in my experience, towards clothing and dress, which is to look for and to stress the particular, and also in the history of the discipline of dress history. On the one hand, the history of textiles has tended, naturally and rightly enough, to be about questions of production and, to some extent, distribution, in other words on the classic subjects of economic history, most notably of course with regard to the origins of the Industrial Revolution but also much more widely. On the other, dress history as such had its origins first in antiquarianism, both temporal and spatial, and then within the broader field of art history. Initially, the study of apparel was one of the ways by which art historians attempted to date, and perhaps to place, paintings.[7] The finer the distinctions which could be made between what was being worn in a given year, and the next, and between the costume of one town, and the next, the better this task could be accomplished. As the discipline began to claim a higher status and to establish itself, this was primarily on the basis of work with collections, and on the basis of research into objects. There are of course dangers in such work. In general only the clothes from a tiny minority of the population, primarily from the highest strata, and in the relatively recent past, have survived. Moreover there are on occasion reasons why, even within this selection, certain sorts of clothes are overrepresented (for instance, silk, unlike wool, cotton or linen, cannot be recycled, and therefore garments made of such material are much more likely to have survived). I have the highest regard for the professionalism of such practitioners, who possess skills to which I cannot aspire. It should, however, be evident that their investigations into individual objects – their dating, provenance, manufacture and so forth – must lead to a concentration on the particular, and an avoidance of discussions of long-term similarities. In addition, many such scholars have been trained in schools of fashion, or are in other ways associated with them. The result can be an emphasis on the ephemeral, which fashion, important though it is and has been (as I hope this book will emphasize), of necessity is.

On the other hand, the drive towards the study of dress in general, and indeed dress history in particular, has been fed by ethnographic and anthropological enquiries. At their best, these are concerned with the structures of meaning which are given to dress codes. Thus one of the first, and probably still one of the most innovative, works in this genre, by Petr Bogatyrev on folk costume in Moravian Slovakia, took its inspiration from structural linguistics. However, in order to lay bare the structures in question it was necessary again to stress the differences between the dress worn by individuals of specific statuses – how the headgear of married women differed from that of the unmarried, and how the shame of unmarried mothers was marked sartorially, so that they married in other dress than putatively virgin brides, and so forth.[8] Even without the structuralist arguments within which Bogatyrev was working, most ethnographic work on costume was long either in some sense ethno-nationalist or effectively "othering" its subjects. It was rare for the student of ethnographic material culture, in which dress should be included, to follow the admonition – admittedly made only in 1996 – of Claude Lévi-Strauss that "if we really wanted to display the ethnography of New Guinea, we should display a Toyota alongside the masks".[9]

In one respect I am attempting to follow the conventional definitions.[10] In these, distinction is made between, on the one hand, "dress", which refers to the complete look, thus including for instance hair styling, tattooing and cosmetic scarification as well as items of apparel, and, on the other, "clothing", which refers to the items of apparel, generally but by no means always made of some form of textile, leather and so forth. Further, "costume" is used sparingly, and to refer to dress which is donned in order to demonstrate, unambiguously, a specific identity. Finally, there is "fashion", which of course is not specifically related to dress, but which refers to those things, material or otherwise, which at any given moment are, according to the *Oxford English Dictionary* the "conventional usage in dress, mode of life, etc., especially as observed in the upper circles of society". This is a definition which only holds good if the "upper circles of society" are taken very widely, to include, for instance, pop singers just as much as – currently much more than – duchesses. Who sets the fashion can change as quickly as the fashion itself, but the whole point of fashion is that it changes fast, and works to include and to exclude those who do, or do not, adhere to its dictates.

What is clothing for? The Germans describe the uses of clothing as *Schutz*, *Scham* and *Schmuck* – protection, modesty and ornament. These are all relative, even the need for protection against the elements. The inhabitants of Tierra del Fuego, which would seem to be one of the harshest climates in which humans have lived, were usually close to naked, and presumably coped with their need for warmth without clothing. Of course, it is in general much better to be scantily dressed when wet, as the cooling effects of water are exaggerated by soaked clothes. As for the rest, modesty is close to a human universal, and the end of innocence was signified, not only in the Book of Genesis, by the putting on of clothes. What constitutes modest dress, however, could vary from the leather cap covering the glans of the penis, with which a Zulu gentleman, in the past, was decently dressed, to the full body veil, the burqa, of Afghan women. There are equally those who, at a given moment, may wish to flaunt their bodies, rather than conceal them. And as for ornament, the malleability of fashion over the centuries has been extreme. Universals of male and female beauty simply do not exist, nor are there ways to predict what will be seen as enhancing that beauty.[11]

Though clothing then protects our bodies against the elements and against the unwanted gaze of our fellows and attracts the wanted gaze, it nevertheless does more. It is one of the ways in which we make statements. It forms a language, if a restricted one. There are relatively few things that can be "said" through clothes, but they are very important things. Essentially, people use clothes to make two basic statements: first, this is the sort of person I am; and secondly, this is what I am doing. Such claims, for that is what they are, need not necessarily be true – a sign has after all been defined as something through which it is possible to lie[12] – and often include a considerable degree of wishful thinking. They may also be forced upon the wearer of the clothes by some other people, as in the case of those slaves who were not allowed to wear shoes or a hat or, in parts of the Arabian peninsula, a full facial veil, and the choices are almost always constrained by economics. Furthermore, like every language, verbal or otherwise, clothing at any given time and place has a grammar, usually constructed out of a set of oppositions, and can always be analysed as a semiotic system.[13] This requires, though, that clothing systems be treated, for the purposes of analysis, as static, while in fact, like the grammars of all living languages, they are in continual flux. Indeed sartorial grammars are likely to change faster than those of many other sorts of language because one of the things that people often want to make clear through their clothing is that they are up to date and in fashion.

They are also languages which have to be learnt, either as a child or as a (young) adult. This may lead to a situation of bilingualism, and potentially interesting moments of "code-switching", or to the fairly complete replacement of the one code by another. There are two points which need to be made on this: first, individuals can make clear statements by wearing clothes from one sartorial idiom in circumstances which would really call for another; and, secondly, like all those who learn a language, they can make mistakes, which may lead to embarrassment. This may, of course, be a consequence of the fact that dress codes, indeed like verbal and all other codes, are not necessarily constant across all sections of even a "monolingual" society. There are, in other words, usually interacting dialects. And just as it is necessarily possible to understand the meaning of even the most personal piece of verbal art,[14] so individual choice in clothing – what I feel happy in, what suits me – can only exist within the contours of the total system, one which may be more or less restrictive of that choice.

There is of course another side to this. As with all language it is possible to be misunderstood, wilfully or otherwise. Indeed it is probably easier for mistakes to be made with non-verbal languages than with verbal ones. There are circumstances in which people do not realize what the message they are sending out may be, or even that they are "saying" anything at all. The failure of communication can cause major difficulties. As against this there are moments in which people are making claims through their clothes which are simply thought presumptuous, and are not accepted. Such occasions can lead to ridicule, to great embarrassment and to considerable social tension.

The things that people say, or are forced to say, through their clothing are thus above all statements about an individual's identity, which is of course continually shifting, being manipulated and reformulated, by clothing as much as by anything else, and which is likely to be dependent, in part, on the situation in which people find themselves. They are thus about gender, social status, age, occupation and so forth. Like the axes of multivariant statistical analysis, these may be stronger or weaker, and are, to a greater or lesser extent, correlated with each other, so that it may be possible to determine which is dependent on which, and to what extent. Within these, however, one axis is ever-present, namely that of gender. It is hard to conceive of an outfit worn by an adult, anywhere in the world and at any time, which does not in some way, blatantly or subtly, pronounce the gender of its wearer, and this even when the cut of the clothing is ignored.

In this book, I have attempted not to be lured into value judgements on either the aesthetics or the economics of clothing (or indeed on the political or other statements which the wearers of clothes use them to make). There has, however, been a strong streak of puritanism within the analysis of matters sartorial. Thomas Carlyle, in his *Sartor Resartus*, commented that the "first purpose of Clothes . . . was not warmth or decency, but ornament".[15] So far as can be judged, given the structure of this work, in which it is difficult always to be certain which opinions are meant to be seen as Carlyle's own, this was something to be deplored. Marx, as we shall see, was equally critical of the styles of clothing of his day. Again, and more explicitly, Thorstein Veblen saw extravagant clothes as part of the ways in which those who could afford to do so demonstrated that they did not need to labour. It was not a tendency of which he approved.[16] More recent authors, notably Pierre Bourdieu[17] and Mary Douglas[18] from among the canonical theorists, have analysed the ways in which particular societies – what is known as Western, in Bourdieu's case that of France – have used clothing in the creation and the marking of social differentiation. This is of course a process which is in fact universal, and was never uncontested, although as Mary Douglas commented, consumption was not necessarily competitive but could also be used to allow inclusion. However much those who wished to determine the structure of society might wish it otherwise, the establishment and marking of status gave opportunities and goals for those who wished to take on a better position, as well as for those who wished to deny them the possibility of social mobility. In this sense, the history of most, though not all, hitherto existing sartorial regimes has been the history of struggle – class, gender-based, ethnic or national.

Structure of the book

In this book, I will discuss the history of sartorial globalization from approximately the sixteenth century until the early years of the twenty-first. In chapter 2, I attempt to give a summary survey of the ways in which, some half a millennium ago, the rulers of societies from Peru eastwards to Japan attempted to impose rules correlating, by decree, social status with forms of dress. The regulations, which covered much more than just dress, are collectively known as sumptuary laws. The chapter also discusses how, particularly in Great Britain and the Netherlands, such laws came under fire, and slowly disappeared, allowing the development, much more than before, of a demand-driven economy, at least in clothing. In chapter 3, I discuss how, in England and France above all, the later eighteenth and early nineteenth centuries saw the emergence both of a culture of fashion and of many of the characteristic features of later European dress. In particular, this was the period of what is known as the "Great Masculine Renunciation", by which male dominance in the public sphere was signalled by sober, mainly dark clothing, and the exclusion of women from public affairs by the brightness of their clothing, and indeed the impracticality of much of what they wore.

Chapter 4 deals with the first expansion of the European sartorial regime outside the European peninsula. Particular attention is paid to how, on the one hand, the early English and Dutch colonists in India and the Indonesian archipelago began by accepting the mores and dress of those among whom they lived, but increasingly, as the colonies became further established felt, on their own skins, the pressure to conform to more general European norms. The further development of this process is described in chapter 6. On the other hand, in the great European colonies of the Americas, South and North, European dress styles were quickly part of the structure of colonial rule, although, as the movements for independence developed, the first forms of colonial nationalism in dress came into being, particularly in the British North American colonies, where resistance against imperial domination was signalled by the demonstrative wearing of "home-spun" cloth.

The spread of European-style clothing throughout the globe was a consequence, in the first instance, of European economic and political power and its associated prestige. However, this could only be achieved through the development of more efficient methods of production and, notably, distribution. In chapter 5, I discuss the introduction of various forms of new distribution and production techniques, notably new ways to provide efficient sizing of clothing, through the tape measure, the development of mail order businesses, the sewing machine and the paper pattern, all first used on a wide scale in North America. In addition, there was the large department store and the beginning of shopping as a leisure activity. Together with the establishment, in Paris, of a competitive market in women's haute couture (which paralleled the more understated London-based male tailoring industry), and eventually the introduction of ready-to-wear fashion, these trends created the conditions for the clothing market of the developed world in the twentieth century.

The following chapters deal with the uneven adoption of European clothing outside of Europe. In essence, they revolve round the paradox between, on the one hand, the assumption that modernity, in its many facets, and treatment as equals with colonial and other rulers required the adoption of European attire and, on the other, the potential use of African and Asian sartorial symbols to signify nationalist resistance. In chapter 6, I continue the discussion of the sartorial history of the major colonial settlements, arguing that in a number of places, notably in Australia and Latin America, modernity demanded the capture of costume by the suit and the dress, but that this was at best partial. In India and Indonesia, in contrast, European clothing rules might be used within the contexts of local political struggles, but very often it was some version of Asian dress which was employed to make the points of independence. Missionaries, who were among the major spreaders of European cultural norms to other continents, also mainly propagated the sort of dress they were themselves used to in their home countries, although there was often a distinction made between the dress of the missionaries, male and especially female, themselves and that which they allowed their converts to wear. As missionary converts were so frequently at the forefront of anti-colonial nationalism, this could only lead to considerable tensions.

It would be mistaken to believe that the adoption of European attire was inevitably or even primarily a consequence of colonialism. In many of those regions which avoided formal colonization, autocratic rulers required of their subjects that they adopt what was seen as modern clothing, on the assumption that by changing their outward appearance they would also change their habits of mind. As chapter 8 argues, this was the case in eighteenth-century Russia and in twentieth-century Turkey and Iran, and also, though in a less forcible way, in post-Meiji Japan. Perhaps it was the fear of modernity and its accompanying political message which kept colonial rulers from propagating European dress. However, as chapter 9 shows, the political desire for acceptance, an integral part of anti-colonial nationalism, generally led colonial elites to stress their own respectability, in part by adopting the dress of their rulers.

The clothing of the West, to which many outside Europe aspired in their various ways, was, of course, not static. In chapter 10, I discuss a number of the major shifts. While male formal clothing has remained relatively static, clothing for women has changed drastically, becoming much looser and much more revealing. In particular, the old prohibition on women wearing trousers has disappeared. In general, indeed, there has been a relaxation of rules and what was once considered informal wear – including the lounge suit for men – has become acceptable in settings where previously it would have been unthinkable. At the same time, the distribution of clothing in a whole variety of chain stores has become much more sophisticated and much more global, while the production of ready-to-wear garments, as always seeking out the locations for cheap labour, has to a remarkable extent relocated to parts of Asia.

Nevertheless, the globalization process has not been complete. In the last substantive chapter, chapter 11, I discuss how the assumption of Western clothing, or at least particular versions of it, has been tempered by forms of cultural nationalism, by the desire of men to control women and by religious constraints. As a result, in many parts of the world the extent of Westernization has been heavily influenced by considerations of gender. This has led, certainly among Muslims but also in much of Africa, to the creation of alternative modernities, in which a number of the precepts of the assumed homes of modernity, in Europe and North America, are at least partially rejected.

2

The Rules of Dress

Since clothing is inescapably a demonstration of identity, wearing clothes – or for that matter not doing so – is inevitably a political act, in the widest possible sense of that word. There are circumstances in which that politics is more blatant, or more contentious, than in others. Generally men and women say things, through their clothes as well as in other ways, that are acceptable to the mass of their fellows around them, and to the powers that be, and it is in the interest of those who hold power to make that daily practice an unexceptional and unthinking routine. In general, when we get dressed in the morning, we do not think of that as being as political as, say, voting or rioting. All the same, conservatism is just as much a political choice as any radical rejection of the status quo; it is just much more common.

Given this, power holders since the earliest recorded times have been concerned to regulate the dress of their subjects. In very crude terms, there are at least three main reasons why they have done this, although the reasons given here overlap enormously and cannot in practice be disentangled. First, dress can be a sign of political allegiance, or its converse, in a very direct sense, as for instance whether the portrait of a leader is worn on one's chest or one's arse.[1] Secondly, rulers and others with power may wish to use their power to impose what they consider to be moral behaviour on their subjects, however little they may feel inclined to practise such morality themselves. Morality, in this, is likely to be equated with frugality or with sexual propriety, which in its turn is all too often about maintaining male dominance and female subservience. Thirdly, clothing has been used to indicate rank, and thus regulations are frequently adopted to ensure that those who are considered inferior do not behave in ways unbecoming to their status, primarily by aping the behaviour of those who have considered themselves to be their betters.

Regulations of this type can be found throughout recorded history, going back, at least, to the Middle Assyrian laws of the fifteenth to thirteenth centuries BCE. These laid down, *inter alia,* that respectable married women should wear the veil, or at least some form of hair covering, and that slave girls and harlots must not.[2] Whether these were in fact the first such known laws does not in itself matter much. At the very least, they are an early example of the sort of regulations by which governments have attempted to control the sartorial behaviour of their subjects. Solon in Athens, Cato the Censor in Rome and the early Chinese emperors all behaved in similar ways, even though the powers of the former two were more restricted by the institutions in which they had to function.[3] Equally moralists, going back at least to the Prophet Isaiah, have railed against the excessive magnificence of dress,[4] and have urged the authorities to take action. However, what they complained about may not always have been the same. Juvenal, in ancient Rome, castigated male lawyers for wearing see-through chiffon in court, for instance.[5]

In the long term, of course, people are neither moral nor law-abiding. The very fact of historical change, which is continuous, demonstrates this. The fact that sumptuary laws were enacted therefore does not demonstrate that they were obeyed, rather the reverse. Certainly there were few governments which did not feel the need to reissue such edicts from time to time. Equally, what was complained of may not have been at all general. Neither laws nor jeremiads, therefore, can necessarily serve as proxies for practice, since there is always a discrepancy between the hopes and fears of rulers and propagandists and what people actually do. Nevertheless, for the purpose of this book, it is valuable to attempt a survey of the various measures which governments in the middle of the second millennium of our era took to regulate the dress of their subjects. These can then form the basis from which the further analysis can begin. The regulations and the complaints were attempting to control the world to an extent which was beyond the powers of any state, except sporadically and of course within the confines of its own court. As was argued above, in the end, people wear what their society, not their masters, thinks fit. However, it was out of the abandonment of this fiction that the modern world order of dress came into being.

Such a survey could begin almost anywhere. In the highlands of South America, to take one of the less obvious beginnings, it is clear that the Inca empire was able to use dress as a way of asserting its authority. There was an elaborate colour code, now apparently inde-cipherable, by which the Inca rulers asserted their power, and the textiles that were worn were also heavily regulated. Indeed, the unau-thorized wearing of cloth made from vicuña wool was a capital offence, and such cloth was used in royal sacrifices. Individuals who had done well were rewarded with cloth and with clothing, and those who were disgraced were stripped of both. Further, the tribute and redistribution systems which held the empire together were very largely organized around cloth, woven by the villagers as part of their obligations to the elite.[6]

As the empire expanded away from its heartland in Andean Peru, it both required its new subjects to wear clothing which approximated to Inca dress, particularly in Ecuador, where apparently the con-quered peoples were insufficiently, or at least inappropriately, dressed, and imposed upon them the duty to wear clothing which advertised their origin, thus providing an instant ethnic marker for the subordi-nate. As a corollary, the empire also equally limited the wearing of the highest-status apparel to those whose loyalty it wished to reward. In the Peruvian coastlands, the wearing of an Inca-style tunic, in its full glory, was restricted to those who had received such a tunic from the Emperor himself. However, when the Emperor visited such areas, he might wear the local clothing, as a sign of his favour towards his subjects.[7] These were practices which were repeated, obviously with variations, throughout the world.

The Aztec empire of the Mexica, for instance, marked its own bloody world on its own and others' bodies in a variety of ways. Out-siders in the capital city of Tenochtitlan were seen as such by their dress, as well as their language. Among the Mexica themselves, highly precise sumptuary laws distinguished the commoners, who in the street might not wear cotton, cloaks falling beneath the knee or sandals, from the nobles. Within the ranks of the nobles, specific orna-ments were reserved to individuals of particular status. These rules were laid down by Emperor Moctezuma the elder, so it was later said, so that

> all might live in their status, as it was reasonable to live with decorum and good manners, regimen and order that pertained in the city . . . also so that there might be given that respect and reverence, which was owed to the authority of his person and to the great lords of his kingdom, so that they might be known and respected as such.[8]

Warriors who were successful in the Aztecs' wars, taking captives for later sacrifice, were awarded what amounted to decorations – lip plugs and headbands with eagle-feather tassels, above all – to distinguish themselves from their less effective fellows. Indeed, such distinctions in ornamentation were to be found throughout North America. The marks of valour, or fortune, were hard earned and jealously guarded.[9]

It is not as easy to discover the rules of attire in those parts of the African continent which were not affected by Islam. Nevertheless, in the West African kingdoms along the Slave Coast distinctions were in place by the seventeenth, or at least the eighteenth, century. In Asante, there were many patterns of cloth which could only be worn by the King, and a number of others which were reserved to other individuals of high status.[10] In Whydah, for instance, only the King, his wives and members of his family were allowed to wear red cloth, while in Dahomey, to the north, the King was the only person allowed to wear shoes.[11] In seventeenth- and eighteenth-century Benin, to the west of the Niger Delta, the right to wear coral jewellery was granted by, and could be revoked by, the state's ruler, the Oba.[12]

In the great empires of the Old World, dress was primarily used as a way of signalling political allegiance. This was certainly something which had gone back to the early caliphates, as those who came to wait attendance on the Abbasid rulers in Samarra were required to wear black robes, and would otherwise be refused admittance.[13] The Ottoman sultans, from Mehmed the Conqueror (of Byzantium), laid down the headdress which was appropriate to all the ranks of his officials, in an ordinance which was apparently in force from the late fifteenth century until 1826.[14] Similarly, the Mughal emperors in northern India imposed Muslim dress on their Hindu courtiers, who

> were obliged to present themselves on state occasions dressed in the same fashion as their conquerors. The element of compulsion in this was at first distasteful. The innovation was accordingly resisted, and on their return to their homes they discarded the costume they had been forced to assume, and reverted to that to which they had been accustomed, and which they regarded as belonging to their race. Indeed, the wearing of Mahomedan costume would at first be looked on as an emblem of defeat and vassalage, a despotic interference with customs already sacred from their age. It must be remembered, however, that this change of costume was only imposed on those who were *in office* under the new rule – or those, in short, who were placed in some sort of authority; and hence, in course of time, the change of costume came to be regarded as an evidence of power in those who adopted it, and came to be valued accordingly. . . . The new costume, in fact, became an evidence that its wearer occupied a position of more or less importance and this reconciled him to a change which pride of custom and religious feeling would have led him to resist.[15]

All the same, in the later nineteenth century, a British historian, proud of the (temporary) distance which his people maintained from their Indian subjects, wrote of the Mughals that they had arrived as "ruddy men in boots" but had left power as "pale persons in petticoats", clearly in his eyes emasculated by Indianization.[16]

The dynasties could enforce the wearing of apparel which represented allegiance, and a change of dynasty could lead to a change of dress. After he had defeated the Safavid dynasty in Iran in 1736 Nadir Shar introduced a new four-peaked style of headgear, to represent his own control over the four lands of Iran, Afghanistan, India and Turkestan.[17] The Ming dynasty had abolished the code of dress imposed by its Yuan (Mongol) predecessors, and returned to what was considered to be a more properly Chinese style.[18] In general, the Ming railed against unwanted luxury among the lower orders, and reserved to itself and its officials clothes in the colours yellow, red, blue, black and white, leaving the common people only with greens and browns.[19] Once the Ming were overthrown, their successors the Qing, or Manchus, again required the signalling of allegiance to the new order through appearance, in part in terms of official dress,[20] and more significantly in men's hairstyle – shaven at the front, and with a pigtail – which was imposed on all Chinese; the Taiping rebels would become known as the long-haired because they rejected this symbol of subjection to the Manchu.[21] Both dynasties, however, were particularly concerned with the ceremonial and the dress at court, with the Qing emperors, for instance, laying down when their entourage should change from winter to summer clothing. What happened outside was less regulated.

Even though clothing codes and sumptuary laws are so widespread, there are two regions and places in which they were issued with particular frequency, namely Western Europe between about 1300 and 1700 and Japan under the Tokugawa shoguns, in other words in the two centuries subsequent to the battle of Sekigahara in 1600. These laws, moreover, had a structure which was rare elsewhere, in that they laid down that particular items of dress were forbidden to individuals who were not of suitable social status. In other words, they were, in effect, class legislation. The lawgivers divided the population into a variety of ranks, on whatever criteria, and proclaimed that only those in the higher categories might wear certain clothing. In this sense they differed from many other types of dress code which merely laid down the dress to be worn by the holders of specific offices (and thus only by implication was forbidden to those who might otherwise be seen as usurping the office).

It is not unusual to compare early modern Europe with Tokugawa Japan, on other grounds besides those of their respective sumptuary laws. Their elites faced decidedly analogous problems. To take Japan first, the Tokugawa family had founded its regime after it had emerged victorious from a long series of civil wars. During the course of these wars the social order of medieval Japan had been shaken up to such an extent that, for instance, a man of peasant descent, Toyotomi Hideyoshi, could become dictator of the country. As the Tokugawa established peace, they felt the need to re-establish the proper relationship between the orders, at least as they saw it. However, peace brought its dividends, so that over the centuries the prosperity of what was already a wealthy country continued to grow. In particular, some of the merchants, who were indeed thought of as the lowest rank of Japanese society (because useless, in comparison to samurai, peasants and artisans), were able to acquire very considerable levels of property and disposable income. They were not a challenge to samurai dominance in any direct sense, but they did represent a symbolic affront to the social ideas of the rulers. That the *chonin*, the townsmen, should threaten to outdo the samurai, whose income could only come from the peasants on their domains, was insupportable. Display had therefore to be curbed. Through the Tokugawa period (and indeed earlier), a whole range of laws were issued. In 1683 alone, at least seven laws restricted the clothing of townsmen and women to "ordinary silk, pongee,[22] cotton and ramie".[23] Specifically, the more labour-intensive (and thus expensive) methods of decorating cloth, by tie-dying and embroidering, were forbidden to them.[24] Equally, within the samurai class, there were all sorts of gradations. According to a decree of 1635, foot samurai and juniors were forbidden to "wear materials other than twill, crepe, *hirashima*, *habutae*, silk, pongee and cotton", archers and musketeers were to wear only silk, pongee and cotton, while pages and servants were only to put on cotton robes.[25] To our eyes, the most remarkable was the proscribing of gold and silver leaf on the costumes of puppets. "Only puppet generals may wear gold or silver hats." Indeed the manager of one puppet troupe was put in gaol for dressing his puppets too magnificently.[26]

Of course these rules did not work. These regulations were derisively described as "three day laws".[27] As Montaigne recognized long ago, sumptuary laws inevitably contained a basic contradiction. "To say that none by princes shall eat turbot, or shall be allowed to wear velvet and gold braid, and to forbid them to the people, what else is this but to give prestige to these things and to increase everyone's desire to enjoy them?"[28] A degree of control was possible. After the expulsion of the Portuguese, the fashion for dress modelled on their example fell away.[29] But beyond this the competitive display of fashion continued apace. In general, the forms of the clothing remained fairly stable, as the wrap-around *kosode* – in essence little more than a T-square of stuff – made up the basic garment for all, both male and female. For this reason the secretary to the Shogun was not entirely mistaken when he claimed in 1609 that for Japan he could show "by the evidence of traditions and of old papers that his nation had not changed its costume for over a thousand years".[30] All the same, at any rate in the later years of the Shogunate, there was competition in terms, first, of the material from which clothing was made, above all high-quality silk, and, secondly, of the ways in which the silk was dyed, painted and embroidered. The result was an art form of great magnificence, but also one which was in continual development. The leaders of fashion became the courtesans and the actors, particularly the *onnagata* (men who played women's roles), and even the imperial ladies themselves were tempted to follow such examples.[31] As a rule, though, fashions moved upwards through the social hierarchy, with the paradoxical result that samurai women, who were allowed to wear clothes coloured with the fiery red *beni* dye, tended to wear the greys, blues and browns which the merchants' wives had made popular.[32] They were the people of whom the moralist Ihara Saikaku complained, writing for instance in a work published in 1688 that:

> Fashions have changed from those of the past and have become increasingly ostentatious. In everything people have a liking for finery above their station. Women's clothes in particular go to extremes.... [I]n recent years, certain shrewd Kyoto people have started to lavish every manner of magnificence on men's and women's clothes and to put out design books in color. With modish fine-figured patterns, palace style hundred-color prints, and bled dapple tie-dye,[33] they go the limit for unusual designs to suit any taste.

Such extravagance on the part of a merchant's wife and daughters had impaired many family finances, and such clothes should only be worn when attending a wedding, a blossom-viewing in spring or a maple-viewing in autumn. Equally, "it is distressing to see a merchant wearing good silks. Pongee suits him better and looks better on him. But fine clothes are essential to a samurai's status, and therefore even a samurai who is without attendants should not dress like an ordinary person."[34] It is the plaint of a conservative hoping that the order which he believes once existed (but which in all probability never did) will return.

In Western Europe, over a rather longer period, sumptuary laws were common with regard to dress, and for that matter other forms of display such as the feasts allowable at a daughter's marriage and so forth. Such laws were issued in Carolingian times, but then not again until 1157, when the Italian city of Genoa banned the wearing of rich furs. Thereafter, such laws were issued with some regularity, both by monarchs, as in France (1188), Aragon (1234) and Castile (1256), and also by city governments, in Italy and, from 1304, in the German-speaking world, specifically Zurich. The Pope too fulminated against "immoderate ornamentation" in 1279, and from the later fourteenth century most of Western Europe had such laws, which were enforced with varying degrees of severity. They continued to be issued until around 1700, after which they died away in most of Europe.[35]

The content of the various laws was of course highly varied. One of the more imaginative methods was to restrict the wearing of sumptuous clothing to women of easy virtue. The Scots, for instance, issued a lapidary law in 1567 that "it be lawful to no women to wear above their estate except whores".[36] The Spanish, too, attempted to forbid the wearing of a particular type of hooped skirt, which jingled and clicked as the woman moved, to all except prostitutes, but the intentions of the rulers were defeated by the promenading of three daughters of one of Madrid's most influential judges in such garments.[37] The presumption of this tactic, which follows the solution provided (at least according to Diodorus Siculus) by Zaleucus, the lawgiver of the Locri in Ancient Greece, is that it would shame the respectable into modest restraint, to avoid being taken for the dishonourable. This was linked, at least for a while and in northern Italian cities, to the requirement that Jewish women should wear ear-rings, which had remained a widespread article of adornment in the Kingdom of Naples whence most had recently come. The assumption was that Jewish women were as unfaithful as the prostitutes. Within a few decades, however, ear-rings returned as items of high fashion, in the court of Ferrara above all, and in consequence Jewish ladies were forbidden to wear what had once been their distinguishing mark.[38]

More generally, though, attempts were made to restrict female clothing by decree in order to preserve their modesty and honour and limit their extravagance. In most Italian cities, certainly from the fifteenth century on, sumptuary legislation was primarily concerned with such matters. Many governments issued edicts on the amount of *décolletage* allowed, Savonarola in Florence, for instance, demanding that no more than two fingers of skin be visible below the collar-bone. Whether or not these laws were strictly enforced is uncertain, and in Italy prosecutions, at least for this form of indecent exposure, seem to have been rare; in seventeenth century Switzerland, in contrast, they were common. It is also not at all clear what the reaction of the women of these cities was to the essentially misogynist legislation imposed upon them. Nicolosa Sanuti, almost a proto-feminist from Bologna, did write that it was only through display that women could distinguish themselves from those lower in the social hierarchy. Magistracies, she wrote, "are not conceded to women; they do not strive for priesthoods, triumphs, the spoils of war, because these are considered the honours of men. Ornament and apparel, because they are our insignia of wealth, we cannot suffer to be taken from us." Given the regularity with which masculine governments attempted to curb female immodesty and extravagance, her ideas must have had resonances among many Italian women.[39]

Another regularly expressed reason for the legislation was strictly mercantilist, or at least protectionist. In 1615, the States-General of France petitioned Louis XIII to forbid

> the great luxury of cloth and trimmings of gold and of silver, pearls and diamonds, trimmings of Flanders and of Milan lace, stuff from China and other useless merchandise brought from the ends of the earth by means of which a quantity of gold and silver is taken out of your Kingdom.[40]

The ordinances of German towns, for instance Strassburg, also stressed the need to wear clothes, or more generally cloth, which were not foreign.[41] Equally, English legislation from 1337, in the reign of Edward III, to at least 1571, under Elizabeth, made it illegal for those who were not of sufficient class to wear anything but woollen cloth made in England – and latterly Wales, Ireland, Calais and Berwick-on-Tweed. In addition, they might, at least from the early sixteenth century on, wear rabbits' or lambs' fur, provided the animals in question had come from Britain. Since many dyestuffs also had to be imported, textiles in purple, scarlet, crimson and blue were also regularly forbidden. There were at least a dozen such acts, and hardly any attempts to regulate English clothing which did not in some way have a protectionist element.[42] Similarly the French edicts were generally highly protectionist, and it is no coincidence that twelve were issued as part of Colbert's mercantilist project between 1661 and 1683.[43]

There was an extension to this argument, widely used for instance in early seventeenth-century Spain, particularly under the *Junta de Reformación*. The Spanish had a long tradition of sumptuary laws, which stretched back to the *Reconquista* and would continue until 1766.[44] Thus, in a series of edicts, the Junta hoped to arrest the (relative) decline of Spanish power not merely by reducing Castile's dependence on foreign imports, but also by reforming manners and morals. Imposing proper clothing, in other words, was seen as a way to reverse the creeping decadence of Spanish society. The equation of simplicity of life-style with enhanced life-force, which has deep roots in Western thought, can rarely have been more clearly enunciated. It was not, however, a line of policy which was able to survive the challenge offered by the arrival of the Prince of Wales (the future Charles I of Scotland and England) and the Duke of Buckingham in Madrid in 1623, hoping to arrange a marriage of the former with a Spanish princess. Their own opulence required a Spanish counterbalance.[45]

In general, though, as in Japan, the point of sumptuary laws in late medieval and early modern Europe was to protect hierarchy, ensure deference and in general maintain order. Social change is in general problematic for those in power, or at least with an established stake in society. When those who were considered underlings displayed their newly acquired wealth, they were in all probability making a claim for improved social status, and increased participation within the structures of power. Clothing could thus be used as a challenge to the social order, particularly when what was worn was newfangled and fashionable. As such it had to be regulated, since the threat to established and generally landed elites from increasingly prosperous mercantile and other bourgeois groups was continuous, or anyway was thought to be so. That in the event the aristocracies were generally able to absorb these bourgeoisies, until the early twentieth century, if not later, is an irrelevance when set against their fears. Equally, of course, where mercantile groups were established in power, as in the cities of Northern Italy, they would want to maintain their position against the incessant threat from elsewhere. In part, they could do this, so they hoped, by regulating at least the outward signs of rank. As Hughes commented on Renaissance Italy, in "a society that dreamed of orders while facing the daily consequence of class fluidity, they had to be controlled by legislation".[46]

The degree to which the attempt at regulation could go can be exemplified by the proclamation issued by Elizabeth in England in 1575–6. To take men's clothing first, cloth of gold, silver tissue and purple silk could only be worn by dukes, marquesses, earls and knights of the Garter. Barons, viscounts and privy councillors might wear such clothes as contained mixed and embroidered cloth of gold and silver, and might also wear foreign woollen cloth. Their sons, those who had been on embassies and those with an income of 500 marks (£367) a year might wear gold, silver or silk lace. Knights and all with an income of £200 might wear velvet in the cloaks and upper garments, those with an income of £100 might do so in their jerkins, hose and doublets and might also wear satin, damask, taffeta and grosgrain in their cloaks and outer garments. There was also an elaborate code for how each group might adorn their horses' tackle. Similar restrictions were placed upon the women, largely on the basis of their husband's or father's rank, except that those women who were in attendance on peeresses were considered to be the equivalent of the wives of knights and their eldest sons or of those with an income above £100 a year. Thus, while the restrictions on cloth were largely the same as for the men, women below the rank of baroness were not allowed to embroider their clothes with pearls. Further distinction was made between the kirtle, or outer petticoat, which might be of somewhat higher-status cloth than in the cloak or gown.[47]

These sorts of edict were common throughout the monarchies, and many of the city-states. Some of the north Italian republics used sumptuary legislation in an attempt to curb aristocratic display, and thereby power. Savonarola's Florence was the most fervent in its attempts to make such laws "symbols of republican virtue", and, even after a generation of Medici rule, his edicts were reissued during the short-lived revival of the republic in 1527.[48] These were the exceptions. Far more common was the perceived need to maintain the world of order, and of orders (*Stände*). The usage survived in some places well into the eighteenth century. The Polish government issued such an edict as late as 1776.[49] In Germany, the last such ordinance, in Bavaria, was issued in 1818, though the last such regulations in the German cities were several decades earlier. The practice until such a date, if not longer, was informed by the ideology of order.[50] But by then the practice had totally died out in more Western and urban parts of the European continent.

In the later sumptuary laws, certainly in the German cities, much of what was attacked was "fashion". The newfangled was superfluous, dangerous and a threat to ordered society, and certain articles, notably pointed shoes, were a regular target. Indeed, both Frenchmen and Germans believed that their nation had no national dress – unlike all others – because of the dominance of the madness of continual change.[51] This was highly deprecated. From the end of the seventeenth century, if not earlier, the English, the French and the Dutch, at least, had given up all hope of controlling fashion.

Since sumptuary laws were often designed to bridle excess, it is of importance for the understanding of the later development of fashion to describe how the laws themselves came to fall out of fashion. First, however, it is necessary to point out that in one part of Western Europe, namely the Low Countries, dress codes had not existed – and for that matter other sumptuary laws were very rare. One edict had been issued in Flanders in 1497, late in relation to the surrounding countries. Moreover it was speedily withdrawn.[52] Evidently, the relative impotence, politically, of a landowning aristocracy, in comparison to the power to the merchant elites of the cities, meant that the pressure to curb the display of an increasingly wealthy bourgeoisie was absent. The Reformation, which led eventually to the creation of a

Protestant-run republic, the forerunner of what is today the kingdom of the Netherlands, did not lead to a change in the policy. On one occasion, the States of Holland, the legislative body of that province, did issue an edict in which it summed up the dangers of the wearing of costly materials of fur and gold thread – pride, the confusion of orders and so forth – but did not go so far as to forbid their use. Rather, in what may be seen as a modern solution, it imposed a tax on such goods, from which those above a certain status were exempt.[53] In a colonial context, as will be shown below, the Dutch were less circumspect, and quite prepared to issue an edict "for the control of magnificence and extravagance".

In England, in 1604, an act was passed abolishing all dress codes. The intention of the legislators was that it would be replaced by another, more attuned to the current situation than its predecessor, the law of 1575 described above. However, neither in 1604 nor in any subsequent years could the English House of Commons come to an agreement with the House of Lords – and increasingly not within its own ranks – as to what such a law should entail. Primarily, the members who opposed such legislation were concerned to ensure that they themselves were not subject to restrictions, but there was an increasing tendency to see such matters as display, ostentation and expenditure as matters for the individual conscience, and thus not something in which the state should be involved.[54] This was an attitude which survived even into the rule of the Commonwealth, generally seen as the high point of governmental regulation of individual behaviour. It was, however, John Milton, a leading official in that government, who argued for freedom of dress in the course of his famous plea for freedom of speech.[55]

During the late seventeenth and eighteenth centuries the argument was developed, in England and in Scotland, that luxury, and consumption in general, was good for the totality of society, immoral though it may have been for any given individual. This was a shift in consciousness of great importance, not just for the history of dress but much more widely, as it forms the intellectual basis of the economic transformation of the world since then. Fashion, in that sense, matters, and has mattered ever since the seventeenth century.

The development of this idea has been traced back to the writings of Nicholas Barbon, in the 1680s, and most notably to Bernard Mandeville in the first decade of the next century. Barbon was apparently the son of the Praise-God (Barebones), after whom one of the Parliaments under Cromwell was named. He had studied medicine in the Netherlands, but came to prominence as a building contractor in London in the aftermath of the Great Fire, and is best known as the initiator of fire insurance schemes. In his *Discourse on Trade* he argued, among many things, that it is spending on "cloaths and lodging" that did most to promote trade, that fashion served to "Dress a Man as if he lived in a perpetual Spring; he never sees the Autumn of his cloaths" and that therefore fashion is to be commended as providing a "livelihood for a great part of Mankind". Thus, prodigality is "a Vice that is prejudicial to the Man but not to Trade".[56] Mandeville, too, was trained as a doctor in the Netherlands, before settling in London in the 1690s, probably because he had written scurrilous verses attacking a government official in his native Rotterdam.[57] Mandeville wrote, in the "Remarks" on his verses, *The Fable of the Bees,* in praise of Pride that

> If we had no Vices, I cannot see why any Man should ever make more Suits than he has occasion for, tho' he were never so desirous of promoting the good of the Nation. . . . In such Golden Times no body would dress above his Condition, no body pinch his Family, cheat or overreach his Neighbour to purchase Finery, and consequently there would not be half the Consumption, nor a third part of the People employ'd as now there are.

In the anonymity of the great City, where only one in fifty of those passed in the street is known, people "are generally honour'd according to their Cloaths and other Accoutrements they have about them; from the richness of them we judge of their Wealth, and by their ordering of them we guess at their Understanding". Further Mandeville was to show how members of each social group attempted to ape that above it, as soon as they had the wherewithal to do so, and at the same time to set themselves off from those below them. The result was a continual renewal of fashion in the heights of society, and of expense throughout it: "It is this, or at least the consequence of it, that sets the Poor to Work, adds Spurs to Industry, and incourages the skilful Artificer to search after further Improvements." In our terms, Mandeville was explaining how a demand-driven economy came to work.[58]

It is difficult to say whether their shared background – at once medical and in London and the cities of the Dutch Republic – had any effect on their argument. In the later seventeenth century, outside the country, the Dutch, so it was said, "furnish infinite luxury which they themselves never practise, and traffic in pleasures which they never taste".[59] Simon Schama's cultural history of the Netherlands in its Golden Age is predicated around the angst deriving from the difficulty of being both rich and Calvinist,[60] although against Schama Jan de Vries (who knows even more about the history of the Dutch Republic) has argued that "luxury consumption" was not "even a more than ordinary source of anxiety or embarrassment". Nor did the stereotype of Dutch abstemiousness equate with the consumption patterns that were to be found in the Republic, much more widely spread though without a peak of old high aristocratic luxury. The Netherlands in the seventeenth century saw a spread of a democratic consumerism, in a whole variety of fields including clothing, which was the forerunner of much which followed elsewhere in Europe in the following century. However, this did not lead to a refashioning of economic thought such as to justify these changes.[61] Only elsewhere was it possible for Barbon and Mandeville to make the development from Calvinism, by which luxury, as Berry has put it, was de-moralized.

Barbon was an obscure writer and Mandeville was treated as immoral. Nevertheless, their ideas were taken up later in the eighteenth century by a number of authors who are squarely in the canon of Western thought, including Montesquieu, Voltaire, David Hume and, particularly, Adam Smith.[62] It was of course Smith, in attempting to solve the problem of theodicy – how can there be evil and poverty in a world created by a benevolent God – who came to the conclusion that liberty of trade and the relatively unrestrained pursuit of individual interest would provide the optimum conditions for the growth of prosperity and the reduction of poverty and suffering.[63] One corollary of this is, of course, a radical rejection of sumptuary laws, the "highest impertinence and presumption on the part of kings and ministers in the effort to watch over the economy of private people", as he wrote in *The Wealth of Nations*.[64] Another is that at an intellectual level fashion and display on the part of everyone in society were accepted as never before. The history of fashion, and of modern clothing, can begin from that point.

3

Redressing the Old World

Between sometime in the mid-eighteenth century and sometime in the course of the nineteenth – the precise dates do not matter for current purposes – a qualitative shift occurred in the economies of north-west Europe, and in the first instance that of England. It has come to be known as the Industrial Revolution, and it formed the basis for the European dominance of the rest of the world, which had already begun to take shape and which would last into the twentieth century, and longer if the United States and Russia are considered to be part of Europe (which in this book, for a number of reasons, they are generally not). It would form the basis, though perhaps to some extent derive, for the economic, and thus cultural, dominance of the "West", which lies at the basis of the spread of its clothing styles. The reasons for, and the course of, this process have become, naturally enough, one of the staples of economic history. Even to write about the Industrial Revolution as an entity, let alone one that can be discussed as such is no doubt something which not everyone would accept. Nevertheless, it would, I think, be generally acceptable to claim that what was going on was a substantial growth in productivity as a result, in the short term at least, of technical innovation which allowed the harnessing of various forms of non-animate power in the production process. At least in the old heroic myths on the Industrial Revolution, which may not be the whole truth, but are all the same true, this was in the first instance played out in the production of cotton thread, and above all in Lancashire.

It is at least arguable that the development of mechanized factory-organized production, though not the use of inanimate power, occurred earlier, and in London to the south of the Thames, rather than in Lancashire, with the large-scale production of hats. One leading manufacturer, who died in 1722, was probably employing seventy journeymen in his Southwark works. By the 1730s, England was exporting over 700,000 (men's) hats, of which 65 per cent were made of beaver or castor (by this stage, probably an imitation beaver created from rabbit's fur), and the rest from wool felt or rabbit. These figures are exclusive of the numbers being consumed within Great Britain itself, a figure which Gregory King in 1688 estimated at over 3 million a year (for both men and women).[1] It would only continue to grow as the century wore on. In time the centre of production moved from South London to the Lancashire–Cheshire border. In order to produce these nearly 80,000 beaver pelts were being imported annually, primarily by the Hudson's Bay Company by 1750. The consequences both for the beaver population of North America and for the economic development of wide areas of what was to become central and western Canada, which was hereby opened to world trade, were enormous.[2]

Clearly, the increase of production, and of productivity, must have occurred within the context of a market in which there was some relation between the growing supply of goods and the demand for them. How far supply was able to create demand, or how far the Industrial Revolution was in some sense demand-driven, as indeed the world economy of early twenty-first century seems to be, is a matter of debate among economic historians, with the consensus at the moment seeming to be in favour of the older and traditional former option.[3] What is, however, clear is that the changes in British attitudes towards consumption, adumbrated at the end of the last chapter, mirrored changes in the actual practice of large masses of the British population. There was a sharp rise in the levels of consumption, both of what had been seen as necessities and of "luxuries", again from the early eighteenth century, or perhaps slightly earlier, on. Moreover, the rise began from a high base; in 1688, Gregory King estimated that over 79 million articles of apparel – clothes, hats, shoes and a few accessories such as swords – entered the English stock, and that these were worth nearly 11 million pounds.[4] In these shifts, clothing was of great importance. That, after all, is what much of the cotton thread spun on the newfangled Lancastrian jennies was used for.

Part of the problem is that the manufacture of clothing was not subject to labour-saving techniques, at least until the invention of the sewing machine in the mid-nineteenth century.[5] There were, of course, skilled tailors organized under the guild system, who were responsible at least for the outer garments of men. In Paris, from 1675, there was also a guild of Mistress Dressmakers, registered by the King over the protests of the tailors. As the royal proclamation put it, it had become clear that "many women and girls [have] shown us that they have always worked at dressmaking, to clothe young children and persons of their sex", and that "women and girls of all sorts and conditions" have been going to "dressmakers for their skirts, dressing-gowns, bodices and other informal garments". It was, moreover, "convenient and appropriate to the decency and modesty of women and girls to allow them to be dressed by persons of their own sex when they judge this to be appropriate".[6] However, needlewomen in general did their work within the household, and were no doubt heavily exploited in the process. There were evidently very large numbers of them, and their work could be coordinated to produce great quantities of goods when necessary. In England, for instance, during the Seven Years War, a merchant and contractor called Charles James supplied the Royal Navy with 269,600 linen shirts in two years, that is to say over 10,000 a month, in addition to tens of thousands of pairs of drawers, trousers, in cotton duck, and other goods. For this he charged the Navy nearly £45,000.[7] The organization of production on this scale was a major undertaking, based on a putting-out system. One contractor at the end of the eighteenth century claimed that he and his partner employed more than a thousand workers each week sewing the shirts he was to sell to the Navy, but precisely how many, even to the nearest 500, he could not say, merely that they spread across "a great number" of London's parishes.[8] It is, however, significant that both around 1700 and in 1851 about a fifth of the working women in London were engaged in making or mending clothes.[9] This proportion would undoubtedly have increased if account were taken of the work in this field done by the 25 per cent of working women who were domestic servants, or indeed by that proportion who were not considered to have any occupation at all.

Among these, of course, there would have been the knitters. The proportion of fabric which is knitted, as opposed to being woven, has always been higher than is generally supposed, currently running at just under 50 percent. It was also the part of the industry which was first susceptible to mechanisation, with the framework knitting machine being invented in the 1580s, and from the 1670s becoming an economic proposition. At this period, the knitting frame was probably the most sophisticated piece of machinery in the world, containing over 2,000 parts. It lead to a level of production that was, in its way, quite remarkable. By the later eighteenth century, Great Britain was exporting around 2.5 million pairs of stockings a year, mainly woollen and machine-knitted, but also including many knitted by hand, and many made of silk or cotton.[10] At about the same time, every Parisian who left an inventory of his or her possessions at death owned on average 13.5 pairs of stockings, which would, of course, have almost all have been French-made.[11]

There were thus a number of ways in which clothing could be acquired in eighteenth-century England and France, at least. First, clothing could be made within the household, largely by women, including, of course, the servants. The skill to transform cloth into clothes was one of the major tasks in the education of women. A charity school in London allowed one of its (female) teachers to arrange that the schoolgirls might "work for the persons who want needle work and such things done". It was undoubtedly a perk for the teacher, but part of the education for the girls, just as the girls who came into Coram's Foundling Hospital were taught needlework as the first, and thus perhaps the most important, skill which they needed to survive as a poor woman in eighteenth-century London.[12] Secondly, and certainly for the outer garments, clothing could be ordered from a tailor or dressmaker, and produced to measure and individually. It would seem that in general the heavier outer garments were produced by the village or small-town tailor, and the lighter garments of linen or, increasingly, cotton, by the women of the household.[13] Thirdly, there was the second-hand market, which was very extensive, and of course provided an outlet for the clothing which had been stolen, a major branch of eighteenth-century criminality. These clothes would no doubt have to be altered to fit the purchaser, so that the skills within the household remained opportune in such cases. Finally, there was the ready-to-wear section of the market, which would of course grow with great speed but which was initially developed for the supply of the army and the navy.

These various sources of clothing were to serve a market sector increasingly concerned with fashion. Now, fashion as such is of course old. Ovid in 8 CE had complained that he could not keep up with the vagaries of daily changing styles,[14] and, as we have seen, from the later Middle Ages on many governments railed against the vagaries of fashion and attempted to curb them. It was also an old phenomenon that the royal courts provided the models for what was to be worn. What happened from the later seventeenth century on, at least in England and in France (and at one remove in the Netherlands[15] and no doubt elsewhere in Europe), was a much faster circulation of fashion away from the courtly centres, a much wider social dissemination of what was in fashion and, at least for men, the introduction and spread of the style which has come to dominate the world since then, at least in terms of formal wear.

To begin with the last, the introduction of the modern three-piece suit can be dated to 7 October 1666, when King Charles II of England

and Scotland announced his intention of henceforth only wearing an outfit consisting of a long jacket, a vest – later to be known as a waistcoat, but only after its length had declined – and breeches. At the time it was seen as "the Eastern fashion" and the vest was "after the Persian mode". What he put off was the cloak, doublet and hose which had been generally worn by men, and which had come to be seen as the French style. Indeed, Charles's actions were intended as a challenge to the King of France, Louis XIV, who recognized it as such and responded by putting his footmen into the new English style of dress. Nevertheless, although Charles's animosity towards the French did not last, and even in 1666 was probably dissimulated, his sartorial innovation did. With many changes – the breeches became trousers, the jacket and the waistcoat both shortened, the waistcoat lost its sleeves, colours changed – the ensemble is still with us.[16] Moreover, from then on until into the twentieth century, at least, London became the centre for male fashion. Paris, on the other hand, perhaps because of the presence there of the (female) dressmakers' guild, was the female equivalent.[17]

Charles's actions in putting on the suit have been seen in a number of ways. On the one hand, the cloth his suit was made of was best British wool, and in that sense wearing such an outfit – as opposed for instance to one made of silk – was seen as a patriotic and economic nationalist act; on the other the supposed Eastern form of his clothing might be considered to have been a boost for the East India Company, which at this stage was beginning to import calicoes from the Indian subcontinent, in direct competition with British wool.[18] The tension between the protectionist impulses and the interests of the cotton merchants continued into the eighteenth century, leading to a number of riots against calico printers and the, totally ineffectual, ban on the wearing of cotton in England in 1721.[19] The long-term trend, however, was clearly in the direction of the lighter fabrics, as had been evidenced by the introduction and spread of the New Draperies over the previous century.[20] The banning of cotton was, in any event, a dead letter, as there was no way in which the English East India Company was going to cut itself off from a market in which it made good profits, and which was well served by its Dutch competitor. The Dutch, of course, had no such scruples, as the trading interest of the Dutch East India Company, the VOC, could always trump the woollen manufactures of Leiden and elsewhere, which were entering into a period of long-term decline. In England, as in Paris, the eighteenth century saw a steady rise in the proportion of clothing made of cotton, and a decrease in the proportion of wool.[21]

It is to be feared that the attempts to ban calico-wearing in Britain only led to an increase in its popularity. As Montaigne had made clear, what was made illegal was thereby made greatly to be desired, particularly as the mechanisms for enforcing the prohibitions were in effect absent, and, in the very year after the passing of the banning act, the fashions at court, at least for men, were of a coloured opulence which would have required the wearing of imported silk and velvet fabric.[22] The fads of the court were always going to outweigh those of popularity-conscious politicians.

Moreover, the fashions prescribed in London would quickly have spread throughout the country. The eighteenth century saw the rise in England, and perhaps in Great Britain as a whole, of a country-wide network of information as to what was, this year, to be considered fashionable. From 1750 on, the *Ladies Diary or the Woman's Almanac* published woodcuts to tell its readers what was the current style of dress, hair, bonnets, accessories and so forth. By the end of the decade, the *Lady's Magazine*, edited by Oliver Goldsmith, was putting out monthly plates depicting what was in. Local newspapers, of which there were many, recorded what was being worn at London gatherings. Elizabeth Shackleton, a member of the Lancashire gentry, cut out the prints from the almanacs and pasted them into her diary, as well as pressing her correspondents to learn what should be worn, though she might reject that advice if she felt it unsuitable for a woman of her station and posture. There was no excuse, except perhaps poverty, for a woman wearing outmoded apparel.[23]

At the same time there was an extension of the market to cover the whole country. In 1727, Daniel Defoe described the dress of a hypothetical "country grocer's wife", an "honest townsman's daughter . . . not dress'd over fine". Her gown and petticoat were of silk woven in Spitalfields, her binding came from Bristol or Norwich, her petticoat of callamanca came from Norwich, but the quilting cotton from Manchester or from abroad, her stockings "from Tewkesbury if ordinary, from Leicester if woven", her lace and edgings from Stony Stratford and Great Marlow, her muslin was foreign, and her fine linen might be Dutch, her wrapper was of Irish linen printed in London, her hood was "a thin English lustring", her lambskin gloves from Northumberland or Scotland, her (few) ribbons from Coventry or London and her riding hood of English worsted made in Norwich. In other words, the products of some ten counties went into a single ensemble, even without taking account of the work done in her own town to sew her dresses and make her shoes. The country had undergone an act of sartorial union.[24]

It should not be imagined that the twin nationalizations – if the word be allowed outside its normal meaning – of fashion and of apparel were restricted to the feminine. A manufacturer and wholesale dealer in hats, Thomas Davies, wrote to his suppliers in 1785, for instance, that

> I am sadly afraid of our being lurched with our present stock for though the fashion at the time is very scarce yet I am inclined to think it will be very large again which God forbid for we have not a hat scarce in the house that runs more that 3″ and 4″ broad unless some very stale old Fashion'd taper crowns.

He had to wait for the London season to get going in the spring before he knew what was needed, and then ensure that his manufacturing plant (in Stockport, Cheshire) could produce the required goods fast enough.[25] Men's fashion could lead to vehement debates. In the 1770s, the young aristocrats were dressing in an exaggeratedly overstyled way, in "flowered and plain velvets, embroidery and orice". At the same time, they sported vast wigs, described, by hostile commentators, as weighing five pounds and standing nine inches above the head. It was a Frenchified, or perhaps Italianate, extravagance.[26]

What is in a sense remarkable about the short-lived Macaroni fashion is that it was a mode of aristocrats in reaction to that worn by the gentry and the bourgeoisie, and further that it was not in any way imitated lower down the social scale.[27] By the 1770s, English male dress, among those who could afford it, was becoming plainer. From the Glorious Revolution of 1688 onwards, equations of effeminacy with foppishness and with extravagance in dress, which were themselves very old, began actually to influence what was worn. The rulers of Whig-run Britain presented a model of themselves as sober and responsible. They "generally go plain, but in the best cloths and stuffs and wear the best linen of any nation in the world; not but they do not wear embroideries and lace on their clothes on solemn days, but they do not make it their daily wear as the French do".[28] Forty years later, the "man of business" was seen as wearing "a plain suit of super-fine cloth with excellent linen".[29] Masculinity, simplicity and Britishness came together to produce a style which was understated, though not cheap.[30] It remained important to patronize the best tailors and use the best cloth, though increasingly the distinctions between the truly well-dressed and the also-ran were visible only to connoisseurs – an added benefit of distinction, of course. Fashion was increasingly, and erroneously, seen as a matter for women, and for the French. Englishmen were above such fripperies.

Across the Channel, things went differently, at least in part because the political history of Bourbon France was so different from that of Hanoverian England, and also because the rise in real incomes which began in England from the middle of the eighteenth century, or earlier, did not occur in France at that stage to anything like the same extent. Massive social inequalities were made visible in the clothing that was worn. A noble's wardrobe in 1789 Paris might be worth 6,000 *livres*, the equivalent of about 250 *sétiers* of corn; a wage-earner's just over 100 *livres*.[31] Equally, the entrenched privileges of the guilds were far greater than in England. High fashion at the centre of power became for the first time a matter of individuals, and thus an art form to rival that of painting or sculpture. Rose Bertin, "marchande de mode" – in the invective of the time "ministre des modes" – to Queen Marie-Antoinette from the 1770s, was the first dressmaker, or indeed tailor, whose name and creations are known as deriving from a specific workshop, and thus the forerunner of the line which was to run from Worth to Dior and modern haute couture.[32] At the same time, the eighteenth century saw the steady rise of a consumer market, at least in Paris, and the spread of goods to an ever wider range of French men and women.[33] Certainly for the male members of the bourgeoisie fashions simplified much as they did in England. Matters did not always run parallel. The Macaroni fashion, considered to be Frenchified and thus politically suspect in Hanoverian England, was thought to be a sign of Anglicization in Paris.[34] More importantly, a sharp sartorial division between the court, with its attendant aristocracy, and the wider populace remained, and was expressed in the externals of appearance as much as in the ferment of political debate.

Both came to a head after the breakdown of monarchical and court-led government which has come to be known as the French Revolution. The Revolution was set in motion when King Louis XVI was forced to summon the States-General so as to be able to raise the taxes he required to maintain his rule. Within the States-General, clothing came to be a matter of great contention. The ladies of the court ordered great new creations for the Opening, and Marie-Antoinette appeared in a gown of violet over a silver skirt. The Master of Ceremonies, the Marquis de Brezé, issued an order for the correct dress during meetings.[35] The First Estate, the Clergy, were to wear their appropriate clerical dress, and the Second, the aristocrats, a black silk *habit à la française* with gold braid, a lace cravat and a plumed hat. The problem came with the Third Estate, who represented the (male) population of France who were neither clergy nor aristocrats. They, in the words of Mary Wollstonecraft, were "stupidly commanded to wear the black mantle that distinguishes the lawyers", thus being set off against the "gaudily caparisoned" nobility. As Aileen Ribeiro pointed out, it was not that this style of clothing was out of fashion; it was indeed the current trend. Rather the deputies resented the imposition on them of an outfit by royal decree, and moreover one in which their junior position was stressed. In the engraving which Jacques-Louis David made of the Tennis-Court Oath, the moment when the Third Estate declared themselves to be the National Assembly, only about three of the men are wearing the official costume as laid down, and one of these, the Comte de Mirabeau, was doing so to demonstrate his choice of an Estate to which he, as an aristocrat, did not have to belong.[36]

Over the years that followed, dress, as the most visible expression of self, and thus of opinions, remained highly politicized. So-called liberty caps and cockades in the hat – *tricoleur* for the Revolutionaries, white for the monarchists – were the clearest badges of party. On 5 July 1792 the Legislative Assembly proclaimed that all men, but not all women, must wear such cockades. Rose Bertin, Marie-Antoinette's former *marchande de mode*, earned her living for a while assembling such favours. There was, however, an attempt made a year later by some Revolutionary women to enforce the wearing of such badges on all those of their sex. This led to great protests. It was seen as a trick of the counter-revolutionaries "to attack the strongest passion of women, that is their attire", and the women themselves were not prepared to wear "a costume that they honour but which they believe to be reserved to men". Those women who attempted to enforce the wearing of the cockade were seen as leaving the sphere appropriate to their sex, and the National Convention, which by now had replaced the Legislative Assembly, ruled that "no person of either sex may constrain any citizen or citizeness to dress in a particular manner, each individual being free to wear whatever clothing or attire of its sex that pleases him". All the same, there remained limits to licence. In defence of a decree in April 1792 forbidding the wearing of monkish habits by former members of the suppressed religious orders, it was argued:

> Would it be permitted to one sex to wear indistinctly the clothing of one or the other sex? Do not the police prohibit masks and cockades that might be a sign of a party opposed to the Revolution? Do not the police prohibit clothing that undermines morals? And if the simple clothing of a citizen is susceptible to a multitude of wise regulations, would religious costume, which can entail so many abuses, then not be submitted to any police rule?[37]

The Revolution could determine much, but not, in the eyes of at least its male leaders, the hierarchies of gender. They were probably right. It is not chance that between 1789 and 1793 the first French journal, the *Journal de la mode et du goût*, was published in Paris, three times a month each with three coloured engravings. It only ceased at the height of the Terror, a wise precaution on the part of its editor, Lebrun Tossa, who was no friend to the Robespierrean regime.[38]

At the same time, the struggle in the streets of Paris was being played out in clothing. In the succession of *journées*, the demonstrations which ran from the storming of the Bastille till the establishment of the Committee of Public Safety under Robespierre, and the concomitant Terror, the radical forces were known as the *sans-culottes*, "those who do not wear breeches". The loose-legged trouser was the sign of radical, revolutionary Paris, in contrast to the breeches, tightened below the knee, and stockings of the aristocrats and the bourgeoisie. Attempts were made at this stage to design a French national costume, to be worn by all men equally, and to give liberty, at least to the limbs – in other words no constriction below the knee.[39] In the aftermath of the Thermidor coup of 27 July 1794, which sent Robespierre to the guillotine, those who could afford it and wished to demonstrate their pleasure at the end of the Terror went round the streets of Paris dressed in breeches and with shaggy locks and buckled shoes. They were known as the *muscadins* or *incroyables*, or indeed as the original *jeunesse dorée*. One of their songs included the line "Remettez vos culottes" ("Put your breeches back on", or equally "pull your pants up"). If they were caught by those who in their heart still supported Robespierre, they risked having their finery pulled off and their hair shaved *à la Titus*, the approved short crop of the Revolution.[40]

In some respects, the simplification and levelling of the Revolution did not last. Napoleon not only wore extravagant costumes himself, notably at his coronation,[41] but replaced his trousers with aristocratic breeches.[42] He also issued numerous decrees (re-)introducing official dress into a great range of offices, including one for members of the Legislative Corps.[43] In other respects, though, the fashionable styles of the first decades of the nineteenth century came to reflect the gains won by the Revolution. For women, the Empire style – generally in white muslin, high-waisted, with a low neckline, minimally corseted, if at all, often with a Kashmir shawl and frequently portrayed barefoot – demonstrated both an association with Grecian, and thus Republican, models, and in its studied simplicity maintained the reaction against the sartorial extravaganzas of the *Ancien Régime*. Equality was not to be seen in such dresses, in which any form of labour was going to spoil them, but liberty from physical constraint could be. For men, too, the "trend toward masculine sameness" of tailored suits in dark colours continued, in Paris as much as in London.[44] While the Empire style would not last, the trend to dark, often black, clothing among men would continue, effectively up to the present day.

As long ago as 1930, J. C. Flügel noted this phenomenon, which he termed "the Great Masculine Renunciation". In his words:

> Men gave up their right to all the brighter, gayer, more elaborate and more varied forms of ornamentation, leaving these entirely to the use of women, and thereby making their own tailoring the most austere and ascetic of arts ... Man abandoned his claim to be considered beautiful. He aimed henceforth at being only useful.[45]

The temptation is to assume that this process had to do with the French Revolution, and in particular with the sartorial chaos surrounding the calling of the States-General.[46] Although these may have prevented European elites from succumbing to the temptation to resume gaudy apparel, these arguments do not hold in their totality. First, dark, particularly black, clothing for men had a long history, going back at least to Philip the Good, Duke of Burgundy, in the early fifteenth century, and being the preferred colour of both Philip II of Spain and his Dutch opponents.[47] Secondly, the trend towards simplicity and away from gaudy colours in male clothing had begun well before the Revolution. Those who lived through the "great masculine renunciation" saw it as a gradual process, which was largely complete by the 1780s.[48] Thirdly, the greatest propagandists for the new style were not French, but English, nor for that matter middle-class but at the peak of society, namely the Prince Regent, later King George IV, and his adviser in matters of clothing George "Beau" Brummel. Brummel, dressed in dark clothing, blue in the daytime, black in the evening, with tight-fitting pantaloons, scrupulously clean linen and a saturnine countenance, stood out because of the elegance and simplicity of his clothing, rather than for its opulence. He was at the birth of the principle of English masculine clothing which proclaimed that "the great art in dressing well is to do so without making yourself conspicuous".[49] Shortly thereafter, the books of conduct were proclaiming that in town men should wear black, grey or navy; in the country brown and dark green were permissible.[50] Only men in service, thus in livery, or serving His or Her Majesty in the armed forces, where they could glory in full-dress uniform, were able to display like birds of paradise on a lek.

It was, of course, a style in which the distinction between the sexes, and between the spheres which the sexes should inhabit, was maximized. The men were drab, understated and powerful; the women fluffy, decorative and without a place in the public world. Men were fully covered, except for the head and the hands; at various periods, and on suitable occasions, women might display their shoulders and parts of the upper chest. Men might wear sumptuous, embroidered and gorgeously coloured dressing gowns, made of silk and quilted, but only in their own houses, and he who came to visit would be in a dark suit.[51] The world of business was for the soberly dressed, and women's exclusion from that world was thus further stressed. This was what was to be exported across the globe.

4

First Colonialisms

From the late fifteenth century, Europeans, first Iberians and then above all those from the north-west shores of Eurasia, and the attendant archipelago, spread out by sea throughout the globe. The era of modern colonization was beginning.

There were of course a whole variety of forms which the interaction between the Europeans and the inhabitants of the rest of the world took. In the long term, there were few areas which managed to keep the new arrivals out. The Holy cities of Islam are the most evident, although there were numerous others where Europeans were held at bay for many decades or indeed centuries. There were also those areas, notably much of the interior of Africa and central Asia from the Himalayas north, which Europeans simply could not reach until much later, although signs of their material presence on the coasts preceded them far inland. Elsewhere, through the subsequent few centuries, European presence at any given time and place can be thought of in terms of three extreme scenarios (in practice of course any given situation contained a mixture of the three): first, acceptance as more or less privileged foreigner into the host society; secondly, the conquest and domination of that society; and, thirdly, the clearing of the land of its original inhabitants and the plantation of a new society, often with the aid of slaves brought from some third part of the world. Each of these possibilities had its own specific sartorial consequences.

Close to one point of this triangle were the Europeans in much of mainland Asia, particularly China and India, and also in Japan. The Catholic missionaries in China, for instance, mainly Jesuits, were quite prepared to take on Chinese dress. In about 1581, Michele Ruggieri was taken to the governor of Kwang-tung province in southern China, who asked him "to dress in the fashion of their priests, which is a little different from ours; now we have done so and, in brief, have become Chinese in order to win China for Christ".[1] His colleague, Matteo Ricci, quite consciously developed this practice to make a sartorial claim not to be treated as a (Buddhist) religious specialist, and thus he and his colleagues stopped shaving and after a time began to appear as Confucian literati. In 1595, Ricci described his new robe:

> The formal robe, worn by literati and notables, is of dark purple silk with long, wide sleeves; the hem, which touches my feet, has a border of bright blue silk half a palm in width and the sleeves and the lapel, which drops to the waist, are trimmed in the same way. . . . The Chinese wear this costume on the occasion of visits to persons with whom they are not well-acquainted, formal banquets, and when calling on officials. Since persons receiving visitors dress, in accordance with their rank, in the same way, my prestige is greatly enhanced when I go visiting.[2]

This strategy, taking on the clothes of another society in order to gain respect, and a hearing, within it, was one which was to be widely used by later nationalist movements in colonial contexts.

The Jesuits, with their desire to convince the Chinese of the truths they proclaimed and their strategy of attempting to work from the elite down, were perhaps extreme in their adoption of Asian dress. There were certainly those who were happy to maintain the external markers of their origin. The Dutch, on their annual visit to the Shogun of Japan, wore their best costumes from the Netherlands, at least when they were not required to demonstrate to the court, and to the Japanese ladies concealed behind a screen, what were the current European fashions for women.[3] However, there were also those Europeans who took on the habits, in the original as well as in the more recent, and more common, sense of the word, of the country in which they found themselves.

India was of course the most notable place in which these forms of acculturation went on. It maintained its ability to absorb its invaders, socially and sartorially. By the later sixteenth century, the Portuguese in and around Goa were taking on Indian clothes, at least in the privacy of their own homes, for all that they had to be careful of the Inquisition which was likely to compound Indianization of dress with apostasy, not entirely without justification.[4] The English and Dutch, too, were described as dressing "according to the mode of the country", by a German traveller in the 1630s.[5] This was the way in which Englishmen in India continued to dress until the later eighteenth century. Even members of the Council of the East India Company met "in Banyan shirts, Long drawers . . . and Conjee . . .

caps".[6] This was a mode which lasted longer among those English who came to be posted to the Indian courts and towns away from the presidency capitals of Calcutta, Bombay and Madras. There an Anglo-Indian life style, complete with Indian wife and/or mistress, hookah and the loose clothes of the country could survive until the early years of the nineteenth century.[7] In the coastal cities, as colonialism developed, pressure was imposed to set Europeans at a distance from the Indians. James Johnson, a doctor who propounded the acceptance of tropical behaviour in a tropical clime, noted in 1813 that

> The necessity which tyrant custom – perhaps policy, has imposed on us, of continuing to appear in European dress – particularly in *uniform*, on almost all public occasions, and in all formal parties, under a burning sky is not one of the least miseries of tropical life! It is true, that this ceremony is often waived, in the more social circles that gather round the supper-table, where the light cool, and elegant vesture of the East, supersedes the cumbrous garb of northern climates.

There were always a few newcomers, Johnson continued, who held out against the adoption of Indian dress, even in informal moments.[8] It was a trend that was to continue and intensify as the nineteenth century wore on.

This process seems to have occurred rather earlier in the Dutch colonial settlement in what was to become Indonesia, at least in its capital Batavia (Jakarta). As early as 1656, a man who returned to Batavia after an absence of a few years was surprised to see how modest and undecorated costumes of Chinese silk had made way for outfits of costly European cloth with much gold and silver.[9] Throughout the period of Dutch East India Company rule, European men in Batavia dressed in European dress, at least in public. For women, matters were more complicated. Female society in Batavia during the seventeenth and eighteenth centuries was heavily mestizo, much more than that of the men. There were many comments that the womenfolk of the elite, often of at least partially Asian descent, were almost in sex-specific seclusion, only appearing to go to church and at weddings. When they did go out, they would generally be dressed at least partially in European clothing, displaying their diamonds and other jewellery, and it was so that they had portraits of themselves taken, as did their husbands.[10] Cornelia van Beveren, a Dutchwoman, described the clothes in which she married Juriaen Beck on 27 October 1689 as follows:

> My bridal gown was of black velvet with a train one and half yards long. The underskirt was of white satin embroidered from top to bottom with gold lace, and the undersleeves were of the same material and lace, with

bows of pearls and diamond buttons. The crowns that I married with were made entirely of mother-of-pearl and diamonds which my bride-groom had given me for the purpose. Seven ropes of pearls were twisted through my hair, and the jewels at my throat and bosom were also very costly.[11]

Nevertheless, behind this public face was a private world in which even the great ladies would wear a *kebaya* and a *sarong*, which visiting Europeans would see as merely a chemise and a petticoat.

The Dutch in the Indonesian archipelago, where they held power, were using dress to set themselves aside from, and thus above, their subjects. In South East Asia in general, the distinctions of dress between the various ranks of society were in general fairly small, although there were a number of sumptuary laws limiting particular patterns to the various grades of nobility and yellow cloth, which resembled gold, was forbidden to foreigners.[12] This changed after the Dutch arrived. European-style dress was henceforth reserved for the Dutch, and for the Indonesians who had converted to Christianity. They were allowed to wear European-style hats, shoes and stockings.[13] The allies of the Dutch in the wars of seventeenth-century Java might also wear Dutch clothing. Thus Mangkurat II of Mataram is said to have dressed himself for battle against his adversaries in "stockings and shoes, short knee-breeches with buttons at the knee, a tripartite velvet jacket, open in front, [trimmed] with gold lace, adorned with jewels, and a cap".[14] From a distance he could be mistaken for the Dutch Governor-General. This usage continued until into the twentieth century when an official from Ambon, the partially Christianized island in the Moluccas, wore eighteenth-century European clothing, complete with sword, as his official uniform.[15]

Reserving European clothing to the Dutch and their allies had a corollary, namely that individuals of other nationalities in the multi-ethnic setting of Batavia were also required to wear dress which signalled their origin. In order to prevent coalitions against them from developing, the Dutch laid down that each of the Indonesian "nations" were to inhabit specific areas of the town and to wear the clothing that appertained to their origin. The Javanese, for instance, were forbidden to wear the costume of the Balinese. In particular, the Chinese might not wear any form of Indonesian dress, but had to remain distinctively subjects of the Middle Kingdom.[16] At the same time, the Dutch rulers of Batavia did what their confreres in the Republic never did, by issuing, in 1754, a major sumptuary law, aimed at the colonial community itself. This summarized and replaced no fewer than six previous edicts issued over the previous century. It was presented as a measure to reduce the "splendour and display" (*pracht*

2 A village headman from the Moluccas, Indonesia, 1919

en praal), in other words the extravagant living, in Batavia and the other towns under the control of the Dutch East India Company. In fact, the effect was to emphasize the distinction in status between the higher ranks of the company and those below them. Thus, for instance, only upper merchants and above were allowed to wear golden buttons, camisoles of gold or silver cloth or clothes embroidered with gold or silver thread, and only those women who took their status from that of the upper merchants were allowed dresses of velvet or gold and silver cloth – and only those one stage higher in the hierarchy might have their clothes so embroidered.[17] The world of Batavia was one in which status was worn, at least in theory, according to the dictates of its Dutch rulers.

As in British India, though, a concerted campaign was eventually begun to reduce the colonial elite to the behaviour that their masters from Europe thought appropriate. Indeed, this campaign began during the period between 1811 and 1816 that the British ruled in Batavia. An attempt was made to bring the mestiza women out of seclusion, and to dress them as befitted the wives of the rulers of empire. As a British officer wrote, with their arrival, "the younger ladies, and those who mix much in society with them, adopted the fashionable habiliments of our fair countrywomen, and in their manner as well as dress they are improving wonderfully". The *Java Government Gazette* even printed articles under such titles as "Female

Fashions for April", describing what was being worn in London and Paris. It was a campaign which was continued by the new Dutch rulers, after they regained the island of Java. The wife of the Governor-General in the 1840s, for instance, "spares no pains ... to persuade the ladies to adopt a more suitable and less bizarre costume". A woman who arrived from Europe was expected to parade in Batavia in the latest European fineries, for the benefit of her fellows.[18] As in British India, taming the old colonial order entailed taming its exterior.

The European conquest of the Americas, from around 1500 onwards, led to a fairly comprehensive social remodelling of the two continents over the subsequent centuries. The Europeans, of course, brought with them a number of diseases which exacted a terrible toll on the unresistant populations of the continents – they also took a few, notably syphilis, back with them to the Old World. These, combined with the technological advantages of steel above stone, ensured the fast subjection of most of the Amerindian societies, at least except for those which were able to take over certain items which the Europeans brought with them, notably the horse. In some areas, in particular the woodlands of the eastern seaboard of North America, in the hinterland of the Rio de la Plata, and in parts of what were to become Brazil and Chile, the consequent destruction was so total that social orders were created as if from new. Elsewhere, in the highlands of Mexico and the Andes and in the lowlands of the tropical isthmus, colonial societies proper began, with foreign rulers lording it over, and exploiting, the indigenous, and attempting to recreate their worlds. They had after all come to the Americas to acquire wealth, for which they needed people from whose labour they could profit, and to extend the Kingdom of Christ, for which they needed souls.

The new society which European colonization was bent on creating entailed new social skins. This redressing of the Americas from the early sixteenth century onwards had two main facets. On the one hand, there was the attempt to cover those bodies which had been partially naked or, in the eyes of in particular the clergy who accompanied the colonists, inappropriately decked. In certain places, particularly in the highlands of Mexico and the Andes, what was needed to meet the norms of the Spaniards was relatively minor. In Michoacán, to the west of what became Mexico City, for instance, all the friars required from the women was the lengthening of their skirts to around the ankle, and the addition of some head covering, which is described as a *toca*, a head scarf.[19] Women seem to have continued to wear upper garments that were basically unshaped shifts reaching well down below the waist, known by the Nahuatl name *huipil*.[20]

Clothes for men were somewhat more distinct from the pre-colonial versions, as they made use of the possibility of cutting cloth with steel shears, which had not been present before the arrival of the Spanish. Thus, men in Mexico came to wear "fitted and buttoned" shirts very early. *Camisa*, chemise or shirt, is indeed one of the first words to have been taken into Nahuatl from Spanish. Wide-legged trousers seem to have become popular slightly later, and certainly in the sixteenth century the old loincloth was still worn, even with a Spanish-style shirt.[21]

In the warmer parts of the Americas, the efforts of the clergy to ensure that their flock was decently clad met with greater resistance. As late as the end of the eighteenth century, parish clergy in Yucatan, for instance, among the Maya, could enforce the wearing of what they considered to be decent dress in church, but had much more difficulty in persuading the village men to wear more than a loincloth, or the village women to cover their upper bodies, on other occasions. Even the women's blouses, when they were worn, were often embroidered with floral motifs, apparently as a replacement for the tattooing with which their ancestors would have decorated their bodies before the conquest.[22]

In much of lowland South America, the process of conquest was if anything even more brutal than in Mexico, Yucatan and their surroundings. Amerindian societies were far too often seen primarily as sources of forced labour, and slave raids, or *razzias*, above all in the deep hinterland of São Paulo, were frequent. In such a situation, the interests of missionaries and the indigenous population could easily coalesce. For this reason, it was in the upper reaches of the La Plata river system, in what is now Paraguay and the areas of Argentina, Brazil and Uruguay to the east of the Parana river, that the most far-reaching programme of acculturation during the colonial era of America was enacted.[23] Between 1610 and their expulsion in 1767 from Spanish territories,[24] the Jesuits controlled some dozens of mission towns and some tens of thousands of primarily Guarani adherents, in what was a fairly stringent theocracy. Within the communal economies built up on what were known as the Jesuit "reductions", so-called because they entailed the forced concentration of population, growing cotton, and then spinning and weaving it into cloth, were among the major economic activities of these settlements, and on occasion the artisans were highly skilled. As so often, the demand that people be properly dressed had created a significant economic sector.[25]

As always, modesty was combined with display, undoubtedly of individual attraction and certainly of status. This was the second facet of colonial clothing. The Spaniards felt the need to maintain their status, even to the extent of importing woollen cloth into Yucatan, and the Mayan nobility of the area were prepared to adopt what must have been a most uncomfortable costume in the heat and humidity of the lowland tropics.[26] Such practices might lead to conflict. In Quito at the end of the sixteenth century, so it is reported, attempts by the indigenous to "imitate the Spanish 'nation' ", by wearing fancy shirts and silk scarves on feast days, led to the perpetrators of this transgression against the colonial order being dealt with by the local authorities who "strip them naked, take their clothes and tell them they should wear only cotton".[27] It was of course a futile exercise, in the long run. Those who had money would use it to display that fact. The barbers and bloodletters of the same city, certainly not of Spanish descent, are, rather later, described as able to "set [themselves] off from the others as they make their breeches out of a fine cotton, wear a shirt bordered by lace four fingers wide and wear shoes with a silver or gold buckle".[28] A royal edict "to moderate the scandalous excess of the clothes that Negroes, mulattos, indios, and mestizos of both sexes wear" was torn down from the wall of the court on which it was posted by two slave women belonging to one of the court's judges.[29] The only recourse which remained to the creole and Spanish elite was to outdo their social underlings in magnificence, in what Schwartz and Salomon describe as "sumptuary tail chasing".[30] The Quito rich are described as wearing gold and silver cloth, and by the mid-eighteenth century they were ardently following Paris fashions. Observers well used to the opulence of European courts were amazed at the richness, particularly of women's dress, on display in the major cities of Latin America. At the other end of the social scale, people were being identified as "Indian", and required to pay taxes accordingly on the basis of their clothing – although the official criterion was racial descent and there were those who argued that only poverty, and not their proper status, forced them to wear "Indian" clothing.[31]

That clothing was, of course, not static. Clothing maintained its function as a marker of ethnic and of regional identity. Modern researchers in highland Ecuador, for instance, have been able to identify a whole range of dress styles which differ in subtle or gross ways between the regions, and indeed between the villages of a region. Costume, indeed, has been considered to be one of the major exceptions to the general rule that "with respect to any major cultural category, Spanish America tends to show less variety than Spain". This was obviously a consequence of the colonial past – although the process of folklorization, or the invention of local traditions, which underlies such diversity may have developed in the post-colonial nineteenth century. Certainly one element of what became the stereotypical folk costume – at least for men – of Andean South America, the poncho, was only invented in the seventeenth century in Chile, and from there it spread north at least to Colombia. It is of course a very simple garment, consisting of two rectangular pieces of (usually woollen) cloth sewn together, with a split for the head, but, like the Lesotho blanket, is highly appropriate wear for horse-riding, and thus only came into existence after the introduction of the horse into South America.[32]

The colonial history of America north of Mexico consists of two, not entirely integrated, streams: on the one hand, it is about the progressive conquest of Native American societies by the invading Europeans, although the teleology involved in this comment was not necessarily obvious to the participants, nor was the process as unidirectional in the large scale as it is in the small; on the other, it is about the creation of settler societies, British and French and often supported by slave labour of African origin, in the wake of the expropriation of the land. The sartorial consequences of these two processes, conquest and colonization, were at least as interrelated as the processes themselves, not least because, as was pointed out in chapter 3, one of the most important elements in question was the fur trade, an economic activity which had as its end-product a commodity used as a raw material for the production of clothing.

The frontier was, of course, a zone of sartorial exchange, as well as being one of political and economic, and for that matter sexual and religious, exchange. By around 1700 the male Indians of the eastern forests had largely taken on European coats – they called them matchcoats in a bastardization of the Algonquian root *majigoode*. This was a replacement for the fur mantles they would previously have worn, and presumably it was more economic to trade products of the hunt for European-style cloth or made-up clothes than to transform them into articles of dress. There were of course variations, regional, in terms of status and from the Euroamerican norms. In general though, few Indians wore the breeches of the Euroamericans, preferring long leggings and a breechcloth. The Creeks and Seminoles of the far south-east, for instance, took on variations of the Scots dress worn by the Highlanders, often soldiers, who had been located in Georgia, in part because it was easy to accept Scotsmen into what were matrilineal societies, so that a Creek chief could be known to the British as William McIntosh and be dressed much like his patrilineal clansmen near Inverness. Further north, the *sachems* of the Mohawk valley were by the 1750s wearing frilled shirts under their matchcoats to demonstrate their status.[33] Similar strategic appropriation of European dress as a means of claiming status, towards both Euroamericans and other Indians, was long used much further west, for instance by the various Blackfoot chiefs in the mid-nineteenth century. There were also moments when it was precisely the rejection of European-style clothing which marked the resistance, and it became dangerous for those who did not want to confront the American government and settlers to be seen such dress.[34]

The sartorial traffic was not entirely one way. On the frontier, there were many Euroamericans who took on items of dress more associated with the Indians, such as hunting shirts, at times made of deerskin, moccasins, leggings, even breechcloths, scalping knives and tomahawks.[35] Nevertheless these were the outsiders. There was no shift in dress codes among the colonists of the eastern seaboard, and the St Lawrence valley, towards something which might be seen as Native American dress. On the contrary, except for occasional protests, such as when the citizens of Boston dressed as Amerindians threw cases of tea into the harbour, the aim was to be appear as little American as possible. With its own idiosyncracies, colonial North America attempted to look as like Europe as possible. It was important not to qualify for "the Epithet of Buckskins, alluding to their Leather Breeches, and the Jackets of the Common People; which is all over Virginia, as great a Reproach as in England to call a Man Oaf, or Clown, or Lubberkin".[36]

Initially, of course, the class and status divisions of the Old Continent were replicated, or reconstructed. The sumptuary laws of Massachusetts show this process at work. In the years after the establishment of the colony, "fancy" dress was outlawed for all persons indiscriminately. In 1651, however, the General Court expressed its

> utter detestation and dislike, that men and women of mean condition should take upon them the garb of gentlemen, by wearing Gold and Silver lace, or Buttons, or points at their knees, or to walk in great Boots, or Women of the same rank to wear Silk or Tiffany hoods, or scarfes, which, though allowable in persons of greater Estates, or more liberal Education, yet we cannot but judge it intolerable in persons of such like condition.[37]

It was as always impossible to impose such distinction by legislation. Rather it was the economics of early American life on which sartorial differentiation was based. As in Europe, the rich were able to wear fine, or smooth, fabrics – silk for women, velvet and superfine wool for men, best linen at neck and cuff for all. At least in winter, the planters of tidewater Virginia, and their families, were able to approximate to the clothing of the English upper gentry and aristocracy, though in summer they might capitulate to the climate, wear linen waistcoats and breeches and go wigless. The poorer members of society had to make do with coarser stuff, notably osnaburg (a coarse linen), fustian (a mixture of cotton and linen) and the varieties of cloth made of home-spun yarn, which were necessarily less perfectly finished than those imported from England.[38] Slaves, too, were apportioned rough cloth for their clothes. The South Carolina legislature in 1735 went so far as to prescribe that slaves only be allowed to wear the cheapest cloths and importers specified that the material they imported was fit for "Negro clothing". One man is described as wearing "an old white negro cloth jacket and trowsers". The women, at least among the field hands, were provided with simple bodices and long skirts, and apparently no shoes.[39] A Mr Kidd in the West Indies imported checked woollen cloth in bulk from Wilson and Son of Bannockburn, Scotland, for his slaves; later the pattern would be transferred to become Macpherson clan tartan.[40]

This, of course, was only half the story, at the most. Like those who were excluded from the highest ranks of society everywhere, the slaves and the non-elite free of colonial North America contested their oppression and exclusion, and did so through their dress as much as any other way. To begin with the slaves, most were constrained to wear the clothes they received from their masters. Many of the ex-slaves interviewed decades after the abolition of slavery commented on the rough clothing which they received from their owners, although those who worked as house servants generally were much better dressed than the field hands.[41] The advertisements describing runaways generally describe them dressed in the standard apparel of North American labourers, as much from necessity, it would appear, as from a hope to blend into the free population. Nevertheless, there were those who had been able to acquire a considerable wardrobe, by fair means or foul. In 1777 two slaves, known only as Dick and Lucy, escaped from their master in Anne Arundel County, Maryland. Dick had with him

> a green cloth coat, with a crimson velvet cape, a red plush d[itt]o, with blue cuffs and cape, a deep blue camblet jacket, with gold lace at the sleeves, down the breast and round the collar, a pair of Russia drab overalls, a white shirt, two osnabrig do, a pair of pumps and buckles, with sundry other cloths,

and his companion

> had with her two calico gowns, one purple and white, the other red and white, a deep blue moreens petticoat, two white country cotton do, a striped do, and jacket and black silk bonnet, a variety of handkerchiefs and ruffles, two lawn aprons, two Irish linen do, a pair of high heel shoes, a paid of kid gloves and a pair of silk mitts, a blue sarsanet handkerchief

trim'd with gauze, with white ribbon sew'd to it, several white linen shirts, osnabrigs for two do, hempen rolles petticoat, with several other things that she will probably exchange for others if in her power.

Clearly, these two people had a concern for clothing, and for their outward appearance which far exceeded the opportunities provided by their master. Equally, in Charleston, "there is scarce a new mode which *favourite* black and mulatto *women slaves* are not immediately *enabled* to adopt".[42] There are certainly hints that even in the eighteenth century a specifically Afro-American sartorial aesthetic was beginning to develop, with a much greater celebration of the juxtaposition of bright colours than was general among the whites. Certainly, well before the middle of the nineteenth century this was the case. Fanny Kemble described slaves on Sundays as dressed in

> the most ludicrous combination of incongruities that you can conceive – frills, flounces, ribbons, combs stuck in their woolly heads ... filthy finery, every color in the rainbow and the deepest possible shades blended in fierce companionship round one dusky visage; head handkerchiefs, that put one's very eye's out from a mile off; chintzes with sprawling patterns, that might be seen if the clouds were printed with them; beads, bugles, flaring sashes, and above all, little fanciful aprons, which finish these incongruous toilets with a sort of airy grace.... One young man ... came to pay his respects to me in a magnificent black satin waistcoat, shirt gills which absolutely engulfed his black visage, and neither shoes nor stockings on his feet.[43]

In many ways this aesthetic was to outlast slavery.

There was another form of resistance to the sartorial hegemony of the colonial aristocrats, not on the part of the unfree but rather on that of the religious. For those of evangelical persuasion, plainness of dress was great good, as the alternative was indicative of the sins of pride and vanity (if not more). The costumes of the eighteenth-century pious have survived into the modern United States in the dress of the Amish and other Mennonite communities, particularly in Pennsylvania, complete with the rejection of buttons which had once been made of precious metal and formed the main way to display wealth.[44] In the past, such dress was much more widely used. Quaker men not only famously kept their hats on when others removed them to honour their superiors;[45] they also enjoined "all that profess the Truth [to] ... keep to Plainess in Apparel as becomes the Truth and that none wear long-lapped Sleeves, of coats gathered at the Sides, or Superfluous Buttons, or broad Ribbons about their Hats, or long curled Periwiggs", and the women were not to wear scarves nor, as far as possible, "strip'd or flower'd Stuffs, or other useless &

superfluous Things". The Methodists, too, disciplined dress. For John Wesley, "the wearing [of] costly array is directly opposite to the being adorned with good works". When he preached to a congregation in Savannah, Georgia, he drove home his message to such an effect that thereafter "I saw neither gold in the church, nor costly apparel; but the congregation in general was almost constantly clothed in plain, clean linen or woollen." The children of Jonathan Edwards, the instigator of the Great Revival, are described as "not dressed in silks and satins, but plain, as become the children of those who in all things, ought to be examples of Christian simplicity". And in 1810 a fashionable man attending a Methodist camp meeting was overcome by the message he had heard to the extent that "with his hands he deliberately opened his shirt bosom, took hold of his ruffles, tore them off, and threw them down in the straw; and in less than two minutes God blessed his soul, and he sprang to his feet, loudly praising God".[46] The rejection of the worldly life was clear.

In the end, though, it was the claiming of a world, rather than its rejection, which was of major significance. As the eighteenth century wore on, the British American colonies became increasingly wealthy. To the extent that they had not already done so, the inhabitants of New England and the Middle colonies, in particular, began to participate in the "Consumer Revolution". British exports to the mainland colonies in the Americas grew by 50 per cent between 1720 and 1770, and particularly sharply in the latter half of this period. As Benjamin Franklin told the House of Commons in 1766, the colonists had "a fondness for [British] fashions, that greatly increased the commerce".[47] At about the same time the Lieutenant-Governor of Virginia commented that "the common planters" of the colony usually dressed themselves "in the manufactures of Great Brittain [*sic*] altogether".[48]

The consequences of this were multiple. In the first place, the spread of wealth and of fashion meant that the distinctions which were to be made on the basis of clothing became exceedingly subtle. A gentleman could no longer be recognized by the splendour of his apparel, but rather by the quality of the cloth he wore, the skill of its tailoring, and also by his posture and general mien.[49] Secondly, the adoption of British clothing throughout the colonies made it more possible for there to emerge a degree of consciousness that their inhabitants belonged to a single nation, even if the most northerly, Nova Scotia, did not join the others in revolt. The fact that the people dressed alike made it more probable that they would act alike.[50]

This should not be exaggerated. Take Sam Adams, whose visit to the Continental Congress in Philadelphia was his first trip out of

Boston, except to cross the Charles River to attend Harvard. He was notoriously so slovenly in dress that his friends clubbed together to buy him a new wardrobe, including the necessary wigs, so that he would not disgrace Massachusetts at the Congress.[51] He had, however, elevated plain dress to a principle, not so much religious as republican. With many others, he hoped that the newly independent United States would become a republic of virtue, and despaired of the foppishness which he saw returning to Boston after the heady years of the Revolution.[52] His problem was that what he saw as a principle had been for others merely a temporary tactic. In the years preceding the Revolution, plain dress had been a patriotic duty. As the British began to increase the taxation on imports into the colonies, so their inhabitants began to retaliate by boycotting – not, of course, described as such, the word had not yet been coined – British goods, and by stressing the wearing of "home-spun" American cloth. Students at Harvard and Yale, for instance, had appeared at Commencement in the late 1760s in suits of homespun cloth, and various colonies had passed non-importation motions through their assemblies.[53] Franklin described his ideal republican man as appearing "in the plainest Country Garb; his Great Coat was coarse and looked old and threadbare; his Linnen was homespun; his Beard perhaps of Seven Days Growth, his Shoes thick and heavy, and every Part of his Dress corresponding".[54] This was, of course, what Michael Zakim has described as a "consciously levelling" movement, and one which was to symbolize democracy and – within the limits set by slavery and gender – equality. The Revolution after all celebrated Yankee Doodle, whom the British had satirized as the country bumpkin who tried to dress in the elaborate Macaroni fashions of the aristocracy, but at the same time the Revolution made Yankee Doodle's attempt to imitate the aristocracy both unnecessary and politically inopportune. Sartorial simplicity, allowing for economic nationalism, had driven the American colonies' drive for independence.

It could not last. George Washington appeared at his inaugural as the first President of the United States in "a complete suit of home-spun cloaths; but the cloth was of so fine a Fabric, and so Handsomely finished, that it was universally mistaken for a foreign manufactured superfine cloth". He completed the outfit with American-made silk stockings and plain silver-buckled shoes.[55] The rich of even Boston were soon once again flaunting their finery, and the respectable were again accusing those farmers who rioted against unfavourable economic conditions of bringing their troubles on themselves by acquiescing in their wives' love of luxury. Nevertheless, democracy and sartorial egalitarianism – relatively speaking in both cases, of course – was maintained in what had become the United States, not by levelling down, as during the Revolution, but by levelling up. An ever increasing quantity of ready-made clothing, of substantially improving quality, began to spread through North America, probably before it did in Europe. It was the beginning of a new era of dress.

5

The Production, Care and Distribution of Clothing

The development of clothing on European styles, and its dissemination across the globe, was not merely a consequence of the power Europeans had to impose their own dress, and the prestige which made it attractive for such dress to be worn, even if it was not as such imposed, as was indeed generally the case. It was made possible only because of the developments in the techniques of production and distribution of clothing, so that the beginnings could be made towards a single market of items of dress. Globalization thus depended on economic organization, while, to a large degree, it was that very economic organization which allowed Europe and the neo-Europes across the oceans to dominate the world.

The production of clothing, or for that matter of other products based on textiles such as bed-sheets and blankets, entails a very large number of processes, which are, of course, continually in development. In all of them there were, in the course of the eighteenth and nineteenth centuries, significant technical and organizational improvements. These processes would begin, in terms of the production process, not in terms of historical time, with the breeding of new races of sheep, or varieties of cotton, and their adaptation to new climatic conditions and regions.[1] The increase in the world supply of wool through the introduction of merino sheep to Australia is a clear example of this. This was then linked to organization of the production of crops, most evidently in the adaptation of techniques of labour organization – plantation slavery – in use in the sugar industry to the growing of cotton in the Southern states of the USA. There were undoubtedly improvements in the production techniques of cotton and linen, for instance through new understandings of fertilizer, although mechanized ploughing, harvesting and sheep shearing were matters for the twentieth century. The fibre obtained had to be cleaned. The most notable advance here was Witney's cotton gin, which eliminated the need to separate by hand the cotton fibres from the seeds they naturally surround and protect, but the mechanical washing of wool, for instance in the South African karoo or the Australian outback, is conceptually equivalent.[2] The cotton, and to a degree the wool, would be baled or put in sacks, mechanically or by hand. The fibre would then be shipped to the location of further production, thus benefiting from the general improvement in transport consequent upon the introduction of the steamship and the railway, although in places, notably in the US South, the demands of the cotton industry led to the construction of railroads or the introduction of river steamer services. Once arrived at one of the industrial centres, the fibre was further cleaned, wool carded and then spun to produce continuous thread. This was the location for the most spectacular early mechanization, with the development of spinning mills driven by water power and operating various jennies and mules. From then the yarn, as it had become, was woven or knitted into cloth, again increasingly mechanized, although, as we have seen, mechanical knitters were an invention of sixteenth-century England. After this, woven woollen cloth needed to be fulled, sheared and dressed, to make it presentable – cottons and linens needed less post-weaving manipulation. Either before or after being woven, the yarn or cloth was dyed, or indeed printed, and throughout the nineteenth century new chemical dye-stuffs were being introduced, increasing the palette of colour available and cheapening the process (though undoubtedly causing difficulties for the cochineal producers of Mexico, for instance, long the prime suppliers of red dye). However, while a stocking could be sold and worn straight from the knitting machine, a bolt of cloth is not a suit of clothes. In Europe and its colonial and ex-colonial extensions, such as the United States, though not in for instance India, the stuff had to be cut to shape. Moreover, no two human beings are exactly the same size and shape. Thus cloth had to be cut to measure, or at the very least the sizes of the garments had to be standardized. They then had to be sewn together. Once the garments had been made up, they had to be distributed to the customers and sold.

In all of these sections of the process whereby eventually clothing was produced, there was innovation, and very often an increase in the scale of the units of production. Moreover, at all stages at which value was added to the product, by transportation to a more favourable location or by its further manipulation, the organs of credit and financing were involved. There is in principle no reason why any one stage in the process should be considered more important than any other, why for instance the introduction of the spinning jenny should weigh more than, say, that of the sewing machine in the measurement of industrial progress, although there may be reasons in terms of the labour saving involved, or the possibilities for the rationalization of economic organization to favour the one over the other. In this chapter, however, I will concentrate above all on the later stages of the production process, by which cloth was turned into clothes, an area, it seems to me, to which the economic historians of Europe and the United States have paid less attention than to that which happened earlier in the process.

Take, for instance, the introduction of the tape measure. It comes as a surprise to realize that this seemingly simple piece of apparatus has not been around for ever. However, until around 1820 it was normal for tailors and dressmakers to record the relevant measurements of a customer's body – chest, waist, inside leg and so forth – by making marks on or nicks in a long strip of parchment which had been held to the customer's body. This strip could then be given a name and hung up in the workshop as a reference for future purchases, just as a shoemaker would carve and hold the models of his customers' feet – the brads – around which he would make the boots and shoes as required. With a tape measure, the same battery of measurements, for which there were, as the nineteenth century wore on, a whole range of systems,[3] could be recorded on paper in feet and inches, or in centimetres in those areas where Napoleon had once held sway. It then became possible for a salesman to gauge which of the clothes in his stock would fit most precisely the figure of the customer before him. The result was that for the first time ready-to-wear clothing could be offered for sale which could in some way meet the demands of respectability.

In order for this to be possible, it was first necessary to adapt the techniques of large-scale production, which had already been developed primarily for the supply of army uniforms and equivalent institutional customers. While an army officer would have his uniform made, at a cost to himself, by a tailor, recruited men were dependent on what was provided for them. The US army maintained its own establishment, with 300 to 400 women on the books, to provide uniforms for its soldiers, but these tended to be of the "one size fits all" variety. In 1831, an officer wrote that

> very many of the pantaloons issued to the soldiers are too small and short. In truth but few exceptions to the contrary, the men of 6 feet high have to compromise the matter between the coat and stockings in the arrangement of the pantaloons, which if properly drawn up shew the leg above the stocking and if not so drawn up expose some portion of the shirt between the waistband and the coat.[4]

Civilians, obviously, would not tolerate this, if they could afford otherwise, and the military would also not think that this was conducive to the image they wished to present on the parade ground.

The shift to an acceptable quality of ready-to-wear clothing was primarily a question of marketing. For this reason it is not surprising that the first major centre of the industry was New York. From around 1820 a number of men began businesses in the city manufacturing men's coats and suits in large numbers and a variety of sizes. In this they were aided by the measurements of male figures provided by the US army, so they knew for the first time how men's shapes and sizes were statistically distributed. The most famous of these were the Brooks Brothers, who eventually came to build an emporium on Broadway for half a million dollars. None of the Brooks family actually knew how to cut a suit. What they could do was organize the labour of those who had the skill, and arrange for the marketing of the products. They themselves seem to have maintained the sale of the clothes which they had made in their own hands, but New York could also provide the clothing for provincial North America. Michael Zakim has shown how the clothing merchants of Augusta, Georgia, had each developed very close ties with particular clothing manufactures in New York City. Within three weeks of an order being laid, the relevant goods could be delivered to the customers in this centre, where the elite of upland Georgia regularly came. At the same time, of course, these same merchants were selling cheap clothing – what in England was known as slops, or the working clothing of the farmers – which were sold to the poor, or to dress Georgia's large slave population. The top end of the ready-to-wear sector could only flourish because it was integrated with the lower levels of the market.[5]

Something similar occurred in Great Britain, again in the second quarter of the nineteenth century. The first really important firm were E. Moses & Son, East End tailors, whose initial capital was compiled in the 1840s from the supply of chests, complete with bedding, washing and eating gear as well as suitable outfits, for emigrants to Australia. To this they added first a good line in mourning clothes, a costume which was suitably uniform in style, and also one that had to be acquired at great speed by the newly bereaved. On the basis of this, and given great entrepreneurial skills, the firm was able to open a major emporium in Aldgate, in the City of London, which by 1846 covered the surface of what had been seven houses – and a number of others were later added. From here they sold choices of coats, trousers and waistcoats in a number of different colours, at very sharp prices. They were in time able to open other outlets, in London's West End, in a couple of Yorkshire towns and even, for a while, in Melbourne, Australia. They clearly aimed at a specific sector of the market – what would best be described as the lower middle class, or at least those above the level of manual labour – and had a scheme whereby individuals could buy two suits a year, and, on return of the previous year's suits, receive a new one for a very low price. The profit was probably made by selling on the old suit on the second-hand market. This does not mean that respectable labourers might not on occasion purchase a suit, for instance to go to church. There was a problem in this, though, as the figures of those who lived by manual labour were more muscly than those of the clerks, and even the best ready-made suits tended not to fit them.[6]

A whole variety of other garments were also being made in batches for sale as ready-to-wear. Hosiery and such like was of course long produced by the framework knitters, and underwear was also produced in much the same way in the English East Midlands. Shirtmaking moved away from London to become a major source of female employment in Ireland, particularly in Londonderry, no doubt as a result of the proximity of Irish linen and cotton cloth from Lancashire which could be shipped across the Irish Sea. By 1860, E. Moses & Son claimed that 80 per cent of the British population bought their clothes ready-made,[7] and an increasing proportion of these bought their clothes new, and not from the second-hand market. By this date, it has been claimed, "the transition from bespoke to ready-made clothing was largely complete", at least for male clothing.[8] Equally the beginnings of the transition had also been made in France by this stage, again centred on the capital. By 1847, there were 233 manufacturers of ready-to-wear clothing active in Paris, with some 7,000 workers in their employ.[9] In Germany, in contrast, the shift occurred later, except perhaps for the production of uniforms.[10] In the Netherlands, ready-made clothing was almost all imported, largely from Germany, although a few manufacturing firms were established from the 1870s on.[11]

That this transition had occurred so early is in some ways remarkable, since it was a consequence of developments in organization and marketing, not in the first instance of technical advances. The first patents for the sewing machine had been taken out in the 1840s, but until around 1860 the machines could sew only in straight lines, and were thus of limited use for the production of clothes. Rather, the cut pieces of material were distributed to women and, to a lesser degree, men in order to be made up into garments. By 1841, complaints were made that it was impossible to find a pair of pantaloons in New York City which had been made by a man. To a degree this was done in workplaces provided by the contractor; more often, in the dwellings, typically the garrets, inhabited by the women themselves. There was obviously a concentration of these workers in the major cities of New

York, London and Paris, but at least New York clothiers had developed a system by which seamstresses were found over a radius of several hundred kilometres. A cutter could cut in a week the cloth it would take 300 sewers to make up in the same time. The merchant would bring the pieces round, and return a few days later to pick up the made-up clothes, or the seamstresses would collect the stuff from a manufacturer, and return them to claim her payment. The result was a level of exploitation of the needlewomen which was very considerable, and which attracted a substantial agitation from the respectable, both because respectable women often ran the risk of themselves becoming dependent on needlework for subsistence, if they were widowed or otherwise impoverished, and also because seamstresses often found that prostitution was the only way to acquire an income sufficient to still their hunger. At all events, they were forced to work exceedingly long hours in order to keep body and soul together. This was what was – and still is – known as sweated labour, at the basis of most clothing industries throughout the world. But the numbers involved were very large. In London in 1851, 125,000 women over the age of twenty (16.3 per cent of the age group) earned a living in the clothing and shoemaking industries, almost as many as were in domestic service. Even this figure hides all those married women who did some sewing to supplement the family income which the census takers saw, rightly or wrongly, as being primarily brought in by the husband.[12]

Once that "decisively revolutionary machine", as Karl Marx described it,[13] the sewing machine, was introduced, from around 1860, the organization of production began to change slowly. Since a man's coat was calculated to contain 25,243 stitches,[14] the room for improvement was very considerable. There was of course no technical reason why, with the introduction of the sewing machine, the labourers should be brought to the place of production, rather than the goods put out to where the labourers lived, as had long been the case. The sewing machines were driven by the muscle power of the operator, just as the needle and thimble were. To establish a factory required a very substantial concentration of capital, while individual operatives could purchase sewing machines relatively cheaply. However, these could apparently not weigh against the advantages in terms of quality control, cleanliness and labour discipline which work in a factory system could provide. Paternalist employers could also claim that in this way they looked after their largely female labourers much better than under the old sweatshop system.[15] Furthermore, it became much easier to divide the production of clothes into a whole variety of separate processes, which could be assigned to workers who had been trained to perform only one of these tasks, unlike the old apprenticed tailor who had mastered them all. By 1905, the making of a man's coat in New York had been split down into thirty-nine separate operations, only one of which – making pockets – required more than a few months' training.[16] The industrial use of the sewing machine allowed what might be thought of as assembly-line organization for suits of clothes well before it was the case for automobiles.[17]

The ready-to-wear clothing business was, of course, in no way a monolithic industry. It obviously flourished first in those sectors of the clothing market where a degree of uniformity could be expected. In Germany, the first area to be so treated was apparently that of lady's coats, followed by jackets, undergarments and blouses, and only at the end of the century by dresses and women's suits.[18] Elsewhere, though there was little difference between the ready-made production of men's and women's underwear, in general outer garments for men were mass-produced earlier than for women. The reasons for this have to do with what is known as the "Great Masculine Renunciation".

As was pointed out in chapter 3, the Great Masculine Renunciation is a description of male clothing through the nineteenth century, and indeed up to 1930, when J. C. Flügel coined the term.[19] The argument inherent in the term is that throughout this period men wore monotonous clothing in order to emphasize their seriousness, while women had their essential frivolity forced on them by means of the dress they were expected to wear. As Flügel put it, with the French and Industrial Revolutions, "Man abandoned his claim to being considered beautiful. He henceforth aimed at being only useful." The corollary is that women were no longer to be useful, only beautiful. Flügel himself, as a Freudian and a leading member of both the Federation of Progressive Societies and Individuals and the Men's Dress Reform Party in London, was concerned to change this pattern.[20] In so doing, he was involved in an attempt at the reformation of what would later be described as gender.

There are a number of caveats which have to be placed around the general concept of the Great Masculine Renunciation. Most importantly, it remains a question whether respectable male dress was as boring, conservative and demonstratively undemonstrative as Flügel would have us believe. There are certainly those, most notably the art historian Anne Hollander, who would argue that the male suit, as it has developed, is the most sexy of garments, and above all one which is most appropriate to the modern world, whatever that may be. For her, male fashion has always been ahead of that of women.[21] Less controversially, there were always dandies, men who attempted to stand out by their clothes, and not follow Brummel's precept that the essence of good dressing was understated elegance, so that a man was badly dressed if heads turned as he walked past. Throughout the nineteenth century, there was male fashion, just as there was female fashion. In London, Paris and New York, perhaps in that order, the cut of the coats, the tightness and colour of the trousers – or seriously tight-fitting pantaloons – and the form of the cravat continually varied. However, it was not the customers who followed these fashions. Rather the burgeoning fashion magazines were aimed at the tailors, who were, in a sense, responsible for ensuring that their men were dressed as the season demanded.[22]

On the other side of the sex divide, matters were slightly clearer. There can be little doubt that the clothes which middle- and upper-class European and North American women wore during much of the nineteenth century had the effect of confirming, and to some extent enforcing, their subservience to men. Once the body-clinging muslins of the Empire style had followed Napoleon to the sartorial equivalent of St Helena, women went about increasingly dressed in long skirts, concealing all the lower leg, and generally the ankle as well, which were draped over great swathes of petticoats. In the early 1850s, many of the petticoats were replaced by the hooped construction of the crinoline – in its way a harking back to the hooped skirts of the eighteenth century.[23] By around 1868, these had become passé, and the silhouette, symmetrical in all directions which this ensured, gave way, after a short interlude in which length was stressed, with relatively tight skirts, to one in which the fore-and-aft of the body was emphasized, with a protruding bosom and a bustle above the backside to exaggerate steatopygia,[24] to create the fashionable S-shape. At about the same time the ideal Victorian woman ceased to be a frail creature, and came to demonstrate a much sturdier, better padded figure.

Under these clothes, whatever the fashion was, Victorian women wore corsets, cages of whalebone and stuff which surrounded the body from the waist, or slightly lower, to the breasts. These were standard from the highest reaches of society – Queen Victoria herself prescribed a decolleté and bare shoulders as court dress, which would have been impossible without a corset supporting the bosom[25] – to the lowest – corsets in drab brown were part of the standard clothing issued by workhouses. Some employers, though, thought it against the proper order of society if their domestic servants wore corsets, even hand-me-downs from the mistress.[26] They were for a long time worn for all activities, even, till deep in the twentieth century, to play tennis, so that the locker rooms of the tournaments might be adorned with blood-stained corsets. These corsets had a function. In the first place

3 Corset advertisement

they allowed the attachment of the crinolines and petticoats which were worn under the skirts. For this they had to be fairly tight about the waist, as otherwise the corset with its attachments would ride up the torso.[27] Secondly, they allowed women to conform more precisely to the body forms which were most desired, smooth, round rather than oval and without unseemly bulges at the waist.

There has been considerable controversy as to the role of the corset in gender relations. Leigh Summers, perhaps as outspoken as any, has claimed that it was "a powerful coercive apparatus in the control of Victorian women, and ... was instrumental, indeed crucial, in the maintenance of Victorian hetero-patriarchal dominance".[28] There have been claims that the corset was responsible for the low birth rate of middle-class women in the nineteenth century by constricting the uterus, with consequences for fertility; this might, in some circumstances, be seen as an escape from "hetero-patriarchal dominance", were it not that the same corset was also seen as causing women considerable pain during sexual intercourse.[29] Certainly, women wearing tight corsets were likely to be short of breath, and physiologically more likely to faint, thus encouraging the myth of the frailty of fashionable females. If this is the case, then the corset, and more generally clothing, was partly responsible for the continuation of gender norms whereby women were held out of the public sphere and subordinated to men. It is a commonplace that such norms did exist – although as with all commonplaces it is important to realize that matters were much more complicated and less universally applicable than might be thought. The question is how far clothing, and more specifically the constricting corset, did more than reflect these norms, but actually enforced and strengthened them.

It might be claimed that such an argument would be negated by the fact that corsets were also worn by some men. Much as Victorian ideology might have wished it to be otherwise, vanity was not a vice confined to the female sex, and corsets, to achieve a suitable figure, were the nineteenth-century equivalent of liposuction and spinal support. Furthermore, it is by no means certain that such men as wore corsets were as restricted in their movements as women were. It is also not sufficient to point to the fact that extreme tight-lacers, who reduced their waists to well under 20 inches (51 cm) were relatively rare, and in general limited to the lower sections of society, not those who set the tone, although Elizabeth, the Empress of Austria (Sissy), was a notable exception. What can be made clear is that, from their childhood, the great majority of French, English and North American women, at the very least, of the more affluent sections of society, forced themselves, or were forced by their mothers, into exceedingly uncomfortable and restrictive undergarments. It was thought that their femininity and their attractiveness depended on it, although there were many in the medical profession who considered that the wearing of corsets, laced too tight, was thoroughly injurious to women's health – although this last might be seen as a typical reaction of the male establishment against women asserting their independence.[30] Moreover, above their corsets women wore a remarkable number of petticoats, up to a dozen until the introduction of the crinoline made the numbers required many fewer, but at the same time greatly increased the danger of clothes catching fire and immolating the unwary. The quantity of such underclothes was literally staggering. In 1888, Lady Harberton, first president of the Rational Dress Society, recommended that the maximum weight of underclothes, worn at any one time, should not exceed 7 pounds (3.2 kg).[31] Presumably many women actually carried much more than this around with them, and it has been calculated that at times the petticoats contained up to thirty metres of stuff.[32] Both the weight and the circumference of the skirts, which by the 1850s were reaching 4 metres at the hem, greatly reduced the mobility of women, and there are numerous cartoons lampooning the fact that women were so ridiculously dressed that they could not enter street-cars, or even pass through the aisles of the department stores. In order to bear such clothes, women often had to have straps across their shoulders added to their corsets, which, together with tight sleeves, made it difficult for them to raise their arms above the horizontal. Full participation in public life was effectively ruled out. Around 1850, the early feminist Susan B. Anthony asserted that "I can see no business avocation, in which woman in her present dress *can possibly* earn *equal wages* with man".[33] In modern terms, there is little more to be said.

What had to be done was to reform women's dress. At mid-century, a number of American women, mainly in New York State, and to some extent in the Upper Mid-West of the United States, began to develop new forms of dress as part of their general drive towards women's rights, itself of course linked to other arenas of reform, of which the struggle for the abolition of slavery was the most important, but which included hydropathy, with the water-cures allowing women to take exercise, and various degrees of vegetarianism. It had already led to the adoption in the state of the Married Women's Property Act and would eventually lead to calls for the franchise. In these circles, some women took to wearing long trousers, sometimes gathered at the ankle, below a knee-length dress, apparently in imitation of the clothing worn at Oneida, a Utopian religious community in the neighbourhood. The first to do so was apparently Elizabeth Smith Miller, but it came to be known after another of her circle, Amelia Bloomer, who advocated it in the newspaper she edited, *The Lily*. Trousers, or rather pantaloons, worn by women came to be known as Bloomers.[34]

The reaction was perhaps predictable, but certainly vehement. Female dress was above all to be distinguished from that of the males, as was enjoined in the Bible.[35] This had come to mean that women should wear skirts, and that bifurcated lower garments were reserved for men. Women wearing trousers were seen as challenging what had come to be the natural order of things. They were further ridiculed, with women in bloomers being portrayed in cartoons as smoking cigars, proposing marriage and generally usurping what were thought to be male prerogatives. Therefore, the wearing of trousers was seen to be immoral, perhaps because trousers were thought to reveal the shape of a woman's lower body, and certainly because they were seen as a symbol of male supremacy. It did not matter that Amelia Bloomer's attire was too voluminous to do this, and after all this was a period when the female attribute of the upper torso – the bosom – was often exaggeratedly evident. It was even considered shocking that women engaged in manual labour, for instance Lancashire pit-girls, who sensibly wore tough trousers for their work. The shock was in their bifurcated garments, not in the coarseness of their work.[36] The ladies of the women's rights movement in the United States generally moved back into skirts, afraid that their clothing would detract attention from what they saw as the more important parts of their message. For one of them, Lucy Stone, woman's "miserable style of dress" was "a consequence of her present vassalage not its cause". Admittedly, there were those who saw the women's movement as a "moral war", which could only be won by those with the individual strength of character to sustain the struggle, and thus to wear reform dress.[37] In general, though, when between the 1850s and the last decades of the nineteenth century, with the development of bicycling as a female activity, women wore bifurcated garments, they did so as underclothes, and thus in principle in the most private of spheres.[38] Even there the proprieties had to be observed. For most of the nineteenth century, when women wore drawers – in themselves a recently introduced garment – these consisted of two tubes of stuff joined together at the waistband, but with the gusset, and thus the crutch, left open.[39]

The later nineteenth century saw two major trends, apparently contradictory but in fact largely complementary. The first was the establishment of a commercialised haute couture for women, in the first instance in Paris. The major figure in this was Charles Frederick Worth, an Englishman who had moved to the French capital in the 1840s and who gained fame and position as the couturier of the Empress Eugénie and the rest of the court during the Second Empire. However, unlike his predecessor Rose Bertin, his business survived the fall of his main patroness, when she and Napoleon III were driven into exile in 1871. He had become the first dress-designer to convert his prowess as a couturier and as a businessman into the creation of a fashion house. His great skill was to combine English tailoring, till them only applied to male clothing, with French feminine luxury.[40] Worth was thus at the beginning of a line of designer-businessmen and women, who determine what is known as haute couture for women. This is the line which runs via Jeanne Paquine, Coco Chanel and Elsa Schiaparelli to Yves Saint-Laurent, Christian Dior and Karl Lagerfeld. There was to be much innovation in the high regions of the fashion industry – Paris has always in its way dominated, but there have been other centres including Milan, London, and New York; clothing for men has been treated in the same way as that for women, though the tailored suit has never been ousted as the summum of elegance; the catwalk and fashion show was developed as a way to advertise; fashion houses since 1910 also market perfumes, to name but four. Nevertheless, the basic structure of the high industry, which stresses dress as a form of applied art, has survived surprisingly unchanged.

The second trend, in both Europe and North America and for both men and women, was a steady democratization of dress, coincident with the steady embourgeoisement of society. Three processes were at work here, two rather well-hidden and the third fully evident to all the inhabitants of the big cities. To begin with the last, the second half of the nineteenth century saw the development of the great department stores, which of course sold many things besides clothing and dress accessories. They began as mercer's and draper's stores, selling cloth, ribbons and so forth, but soon developed into much broader enterprises, notable, among other things, for the fixity of their prices – discounts and haggling were not to have any place in their operation. The Bon Marché in Paris, founded in 1853, is generally held to be the first such, but it may have been preceded both by at least one store in London, W. Hitchcock and Co., and by similar establishments in Manchester and Newcastle.[41] Such stores generally sold both ready-to-wear and made-to-measure clothing, and had a large staff of seamstresses ready to make up the orders that were taken by the salespeople. In 1863, for instance, Shoolbreds in Tottenham Court Road in London, probably the largest such establishment at the time, had 400 counter and clerical employers, but they were backed up by around 100 mantle makers and 11 milliners, as well as 95 upholsterers and 40 carpet seamers for the other parts of the store's business.[42]

The great stores – the Bon Marché in Paris, Harrods in London, Macys and Bloomingdales in New York, Marshall Field in Chicago and many others – provided the middle-class women of the cities with the opportunity for pleasure outside the home to a degree which was not general at the time.[43] There was, famously, no obligation to purchase anything on entering the store, although of course once customers were lured into such an environment, one made as attractive and seductive as possible, then the temptation to buy was great. The restaurants of such stores became the first places were women could take tea and other refreshments, perhaps not alone, but certainly not necessarily in the company of men.[44] Shopping became an accepted form of recreation – and female kleptomania one of the fashionable diseases of the era.[45] The choice of clothing available in these stores allowed a range of choice and of sartorial self-expression which was relatively new. Worth himself complained of the department stores that they took away his custom and devalued his creativity.[46] His successors would embrace the opportunities they offered to allow the direct sale of designer-labelled *prêt-à-porter* clothing.

The department stores, at least in the United States of America, were often linked to substantial mail order businesses, also a development of the late nineteenth century. From 1872, when Aaron Montgomery Ward issued his first catalogue, it became possible to purchase clothing, and other goods, through the mail. The business burgeoned after 1913 when the US mail upped the permitted weight of parcels from 4 to 20 pounds. The major firms, all located in Chicago whence they could best serve the great mid-Western rural market, ensured that ready-made, relatively fashionable clothing could reach all those who could afford it, who formed the great majority of the population, very quickly. The catalogues of these firms were vast. By 1921, Sears, Roebuck and Co. issued a book of 1064 pages, including ninety of women's wear, many printed in colour, and forty pages of men's and boy's clothing. The turnover of these great establishments was remarkable. In 1896, Sears Roebuck is said to have sold 9,000 men's suits in a single day. The blue serge suit had conquered America.[47]

The second major innovation was the commercial paper pattern. Until the 1860s, those women who were not trained dressmakers could only produce a fitting garment by unpicking one they already possessed and cutting the new stuff to the same pattern. This obviously made it harder to innovate and follow fashion closely. Systems had been developed whereby dressmakers could scale up patterns from published paper diagrams, but it was a highly complicated and skilled process, beyond the reach of an amateur. It was thus not possible for the mass of women to take advantage of the opportunities offered by the introduction and quick dissemination of the sewing machine into a great many households, other than as outworkers for clothing manufacturers.[48] However, by the second half of the nineteenth century, dressmakers had developed a number of systems by which clothes could be made to fit the vast majority of forms – the forerunners of the "sizes" in which clothes in the shops today are sorted. It was thus not a difficult step for businesses to distribute patterns to the various dressmaking outlets, in conjunction with information on the latest high, Parisian, fashions. The first to do this with some success was "Madame" Ellen Louise Demorest, whose business, based in New York but with agents throughout the United States, began to flourish from 1860. Madame Demorest, however, continued to concentrate on the top end of the market, and on professional, if small-town, dressmakers, who could in such a way provide their clientele with the most fashionable attire. The clear innovation came from Ebenezer Butterick, a merchant tailor from Worcester, Massachusetts, who began in the early 1860s to distribute graded patterns for, first, men's shirts and, then, children's clothing, printed on tissue paper. In 1867, Butterick moved to New York and began to concentrate on the market for women's clothing. Within a remarkably short time the firm established itself, creating a vast market for a commodity which as yet people did not realize they needed. On the basis of an extensive advertising campaign, by developing agencies throughout the country – usually draper's shops or sewing-machine merchants, in a natural symbiosis – and through mail order, Butterick was able to sell 6 million paper patterns a year within four years of opening his business.[49]

The sale and distribution of dress and other clothing patterns, which allowed women – it was almost invariably women – to make their own and their family's clothes to a considerable degree of sophistication and at home, went in tandem with a further democratization of fashion journalism. It was important for the purveyors of paper patterns that they reached as wide a market as possible. Both Butterick and Demorest had their own journals in America, and in Britain at least Butterick worked closely with the various sectors of fashion journalism. Often, indeed, patterns were distributed together with the magazines.[50]

As the nineteenth century progressed, another major change in the technology of clothing began to come into use. According to the received, probably somewhat apocryphal, account, in 1825 a French dyer, Jean-Baptiste Jolly, first discovered that kerosene could be used to remove dirt from fabrics. From then on, various firms began to develop new liquids which could do the same job, preferably without the risk of explosion which was inherent in a process which consisted of sloshing petrol around. Dry cleaning, as the process has come to be known, was developed on a commercial scale from the 1860s onwards, but could only be done in large factories. Indeed, the most important company in Britain, Pullars, a Scottish firm of dyers based in Perth, used the burgeoning railway system to collect and redistribute clothing from across the country. Nevertheless, it was only in the twentieth century that the process became general. The consequences for how outer clothing looked, and smelt, and for the colours which could be worn, were evidently huge. It is, however, symptomatic of the state of historical writing on such matters that a generation ago Kenneth Hudson could write that "No-one ... has yet written and published even an adequate history of dry cleaning", and to the best of my knowledge this is still the case.[51] It is only when the technical processes of clothing production, care and distribution are taken into account that the development of clothing styles, and their spread across the world, can be fully understood.

6

The Export of Europe

In the course of his inspiring and justly renowned enquiry into the consequences attendant upon the invention of the sewing machine, Karl Marx noted, more or less in passing, that the exploitation of labour in the clothing industries, where by 1861 in Britain as many labourers worked as in agriculture, was enhanced by the "constant extension of the market", particularly in "England's colonial market where, besides, English tastes and habits prevail".[1] As usual his insight was correct, even if he did follow the prejudice of his time by railing against the "murderous, meaningless caprices of fashion", though as an economic disaster – he was after all not a supply-side economist – rather than a moral one. Through the course of the nineteenth century, the styles of clothing which had been developed in Europe and the United States of America began to be spread throughout the globe. Clearly the processes of production and distribution pioneered in England and in New York aided in this dissemination of the specific forms of costume which were then considered to be the most modern.

This process obviously went fastest in the areas of white settlement, although each of these areas had its own particular history, and by extension its own history of costume. Thus, the history of white Australia's foundation as a convict colony lasted long.[2] It had indeed begun two oceans away. Before the British convicts were put on the ships which were to carry them to Australia, they were stripped of their own clothes – which were then sold to an old clothes merchant, or appropriated by the Quartermaster – and dressed in the drab greys and blues of their new convict status and uniform.[3] An attempt was made by the first Governor of the penal colony of Botany Bay, in what was to become New South Wales, to have cloth sent out with a distinguishing stripe, so that convicts' clothes did not find their way into the pawn shop, but apparently the shipment never arrived. Occasionally, those who were further sentenced to hard labour in the gaol gangs were forced to wear jackets which were garishly particoloured in primrose yellow and black, as a further sign of their ignominy. In general, though, the main mark by which the convicts were distinguished was the length of their coat. On at least one occasion, the magistrates ordered the tails of a frock coat to be cut off. However, in the wearing of short jackets of a dull blue stuff the convicts were scarcely distinguished from the mass of working men. Convict women, too, wore clothes which hardly differed from those of their free counterparts.[4] They were, of course, not supposed to wear finery. When they did so, it was, naturally enough, a form of "everyday resistance", against the conditions of their sentence, or indeed more generally against their situation. One group of convicts in Hobart, Tasmania, who were known as the "Flash Mob", took to wearing ear-rings and silk scarves as a protest against the rules of the factory where they had to work.[5]

The result, at least in the early part of the nineteenth century, was that those who were not convicts, and could afford it, made a very definite effort to demonstrate their distinction from those they considered their social inferiors. In a society where domestic service was available and opportunities for respectable women to work outside the house non-existent, particularly the women of the elite, stereotypically engaged in charitable work, made it clear to those who were forced to accept their charity how the relations of power and status truly lay. There was, however, always a degree of tension involved in this. Those whose sentence had expired, the so-called emancipists, might rise in social status, until a few of the children of those who had come to Australia as convicts on the First Fleet were among the leading citizens of Sydney by the 1820s. In addition, it was not always easy for the colonial elite to acquire either the materials or the information required to dress in the latest fashions, much as the elite women attempted to follow the trends of Paris, or to a lesser degree London.[6]

The dress of white Australian males, in contrast, is not described as being heavily influenced by fashion, and was often claimed to be rather shabby. In the early days of colonial society, it was often modelled more on the practices of Europeans in tropical countries, particularly the British in India. White suits, without waistcoats in summer, with silk shirts, could be seen in the towns, at a time when the Great Masculine Renunciation was clothing the men of European elites in drab blacks.[7] Eventually though, the pressure for conformity to the norms of Europe, and the need to demonstrate the maturity and the respectability of colonial society, drove the male bourgeoisie of Melbourne and Sydney into top hats and frock coats. It is said that this happened quickly, during the period of prosperity caused by the gold rush of the early 1850s.[8] However, there were countervailing pressures which maintained a degree of sartorial informality impossible in Europe. First, the Australian ideologies of "mateship", of the equality of all (white) men, which had been begun among the convicts and which was transferred to all those who were not part of the elite, militated against excessive outward distinction of those who could afford it. Remarkably, and exceptionally, the ideology of equality trumped individual hankering for status, although there was always a countervailing move towards social distinction, particularly in Sydney and Melbourne. Secondly, real prestige and economic power in Australia remained long among the sheep-farming landowners, who, even when they came to town, saw no need to accommodate to the modes of the city. Australian informality began early in the history of the colonial society, and has continued ever since.

In Latin America, the interplay of nationalism, cosmopolitanism and elite formation produced a distinct sartorial regime in the decades after independence from Spain and Portugal. The revolutions themselves produced, at least in the imagery, specific forms of attire. Simón Bolívar and José de San Martín, the great leaders of the movements for independence, were portrayed as wearing windswept capes to separate them from the constricted dress of the colonial Spanish ruling class.[9] In the years after independence, some ladies in Buenos Aires sported a most extravagant head piece, known as a *peinetón*, built up from oversized combs. This has been seen as a means by which women could claim a – temporary – place within the public arena, and was, not surprisingly, condemned by those who did not feel that the shifts within the political order should be continued into the sphere of relations between men and women.[10] But such revolutionary expressions of dissidence soon died away among the elite.

Increasingly the cultural orientation of the Latin American elites was directed towards northern Europe, and later the United States. While they were political nationalists, the elites were concerned both to set themselves off from the mass of their fellow countrymen and women and to demonstrate their connections with the world of high culture in Paris and London. By the 1840s, the British were exporting 10 yards of cloth a year for every inhabitant of the continent.[11] Ready-made clothing was less prominent among the imports, since there were still many tailors and seamstresses to do the work of making the cloth into garments. Nevertheless, the more specialized parts of apparel were not manufactured locally. In 1859, for instance, a merchant in San José, the capital of Costa Rica, advertised that he had received "150 crinolines of all kinds for ladies and girls".[12] Few concessions to the climate were made by those who wished and were able to demonstrate their cosmopolitanism. By 1890, the Brazilian businessman in Rio de Janeiro, so it was reported, "walks about in a black frockcoat, capped with a top hat, imposing martyrdom on himself with the most perfect lack of concern". They also wore highly polished shoes, as indeed South Americans have continued to do to this day. The point for this largely white ruling class in their "black wool topcoats and vests, in narrow corsets and thick skirts" was to distinguish themselves from the "darker, cooler, poor who went about half-naked, openly proclaiming uncouth inferiority".[13] It is not surprising, as Arnold J. Bauer pointed out, that the best-selling book of etiquette in Latin America was particularly concerned with sweat and the attempts to remove it. Correct clothing, together with the mastery of the body, was a major element of the "central axiom of modernization, the passage from barbarie to civilization".[14]

Away from the port cities and capitals, the capture of costume by the suits and dresses of Europe was selective and incomplete. Nevertheless, as the nineteenth century progressed, even in the Andean regions of Peru and Bolivia, the local notables did all they could to appear as if they were Europeans, even if visitors might scorn their inability quite to match European standards. In hard times, the right sort of shoes would be a priority above meat for dinner. The ladies might become the subject of unwelcome gossip if they copied Parisian fashions too closely, as the rules of sartorial propriety were sharper. The creoles of Cuzco and Arequipa were close enough in dress to Lima, and indeed to Paris, for this to be a potential problem, and even the Amerindian chiefs of the Bolivian lowlands demonstrated their prestige through donning clothes in the fashion of Europe, and rejecting lip plugs. However, in this, as elsewhere, there were specific local variations even with the assumption of more universal patterns. Certainly, mass-produced clothing did not reach these areas until deep in the twentieth century, in part because of wearers' desire for individuality, and the concomitant dislike of dress which might be identical to that of someone else.[15]

Within the two great tropical colonies of the nineteenth century, British India and the Dutch East Indies (Indonesia), sartorial politics were of particular sharpness and complexity. The two lands had much in common, not merely a climate which made the unthinking, or rather unfeeling, transfer of European garb virtually impossible. They also had histories of dress in which the Hindu ideas of the greater purity of uncut cloth were being overlaid by the Muslim ideas of propriety and of garb long before the arrival of the Europeans.[16] The result was an uncertainty as to the level of bare flesh which might be displayed, almost inevitably more when cloth is draped around the body rather than tailored to fit it. Even when an Indian woman wore a bodice under her sari – and current opinion, probably incorrectly, suggests that this was introduced by the missionaries[17] – she would probably take it off to cook, so as to be pure for the most ritually important act.[18] There were also many circumstances in which it would have been highly impolite, and insulting, for a Javanese man to cover his torso.[19] In South India, specifically in the modern province of Kerala, the rules of dress before the coming of British hegemony were clear. It was considered most improper to appear before a superior with the breast covered. A Brahmin would appear in the temple with a naked chest; a Nayar, from the landowning groups, would uncover his or her chest when a Brahmin appeared. At other times, a Nayar woman would drape a cloth, the continuance of that which she wore around her lower body, across her breasts. Lower-caste individuals, both men and women, who thus had to show respect for everyone above them, were forbidden to wear any clothing above the waist or below the knee, including shoes, or to carry umbrellas. Also they had to remain at a certain distance from their superiors, as otherwise they would pollute them.[20] Equally, both regions – they can only be called countries after colonization, and with India, once again not after independence – were cursed with colonial rulers who were determined to find ways of setting themselves off from the populations which they hoped to control, and who used dress as one of the clearest ways of doing this. At the same time, both regions began through the nineteenth century to develop Asian elites who were striving for political and social acceptance from the colonial rulers, and used their apparel as one of the ways of so doing, generally without a great degree of success.

There were also clear differences between the two regions. Indonesia is proportionately more heavily Islamicized than India, even when, as was the case under colonial rule, Bangladesh and Pakistan are considered part of India. It also has areas, notably in the Moluccas and northern Sulawesi, which are predominantly Christian, while in India Christian communities are always regional minorities. Equally, of great importance was the way in which ruling colonial society dealt with those whom its menfolk had begotten on Asian women. In India, from the early part of the nineteenth century, Eurasians were generally considered beyond the pale; in Indonesia, they remained classified as part of the European population, and at least until the early twentieth century seen as the lower echelons of

European colonial society. The distinct forms of interplay between race and gender, and the levels of contact between the British and the Indians, on the one hand, and the Dutch and the Javanese, on the other, were widely expressed in the clothing of the various groups.

From the early nineteenth century, the British official class began to set itself off from the Indians, and in a un-"oriental" way. No longer was prestige to be gained from the display of colour, or for that matter from being carried around in a palanquin. Lord William Bentinck, Governor-General, was described as thinking and acting "like a Pennsylvania Quaker", riding on horseback and plainly dressed.[21] Men began to wear black suits – the nickname at times for officials – and black top hats. At least for a while, this became what was universally required. Where white jackets had been generally worn, even to dinner, and white trousers had been universal, by the 1840s black broadcloth had become universal, even in the hottest weather. For a while it was customary to appear at dinner dressed in black, and then change into more comfortable whites, but even this died out by the 1860s. Their clothing, according to the magistrate Frederick Shore

> affords an additional proof of an opinion I have seen great reason to entertain: viz. that the English are nationally the most bigoted and illiberal people I have ever seen or heard of ... I think the climate of India is quite debilitating enough without our giving it adventitious aid by wearing a dress unsuited to it; and I act on that principle.[22]

The discomfort was accentuated, perhaps invisibly but certainly not unknown to those around, by the perceived medical need to wear flannel underwear at all times, and indeed not to take it off in the hottest weather, so as to prevent chilling. As E. M. Collingham pointed out, it was precisely the unsuitability of the Britisher's attire by which he maintained his nationality and his distance from the peoples he was governing.

Shore himself, safely away from the gaze of his fellow countrymen in a remote station in Upper India, employed older techniques, as part of a campaign against the systematic degradation of the East India Company's Indian subjects. He continued to wear Indian-style clothing even in court, and at the same time insisted that those who appeared before him did so barefooted. This he claimed was in line with Indian custom, and that respect should be shown either by removing the turban, in the English fashion of baring the head, or by removing shoes and stockings, as an Indian would show respect. He claimed that he did not mind which of the two disrobings was applied, so long as one or the other was. However, in both cases he was out of kilter with the developing spirit of colonial rule. In 1830, the East India Company, still ruling from Calcutta, felt impelled to issue an Ordinance, directed specifically at Shore, banning the wearing of Indian dress by its officials in public functions. Twenty-four years later, it issued another allowing Indian gentlemen "on official and semi-official occasions ... to appear in the presence of the servants of the British government" in European boots or shoes, as such had become the general practice of the sort of man who came to plead in the courts of Calcutta.[23]

The most pronounced symbol of Britishness in India was, however, the sola topi. Made from the extremely light pith of the sola tree (hence its alternative name of pith helmet), this uncomfortable and much hated headgear was worn when out of doors in the midday sun by all Britishers, male and female, adults and children, from the mid-nineteenth century up to Independence. It was supposed to protect the wearer from sunstroke, and may indeed have done so, but its clear function was above all to provide a sign of difference, and of superiority. It is thus not surprising, first, that British soldiers were put on a charge should they go out without it; secondly, that many of the Eurasians of British India wore the topi to claim their place in the colonial sun; and thirdly, that hardly any Indians ever wore what was so evidently a foreign and an imperial article of clothing.[24]

The Dutch in Indonesia accentuated their dominance without subjecting themselves to the sartorial torture of the British in India. This they did primarily by wearing white clothing, which in Indonesia, with its rich traditions of printed batik cloth, has been primarily the colour of mourning, or of the *hajj*. Dutchmen would wear white trousers and a jacket buttoned up to where the torso joined a stiff, raised collar. Such jackets, made of cotton drill, or, for those who could afford the best, Russian linen, were made to be washed, but before being ironed they were starched so stiff that, it was said, they could stand up on their own. Obviously, various forms of braid and other decorations were added by which those in colonial service could demonstrate the rank they held in the colonial hierarchy. Members of the colonial civil service (*Binnenlands Bestuur*) wore specific caps, as did members of the armed forces, while private citizens could don any form of hat that took their fancy. All, though, wore socks and leather shoes.[25] The only concession to Indonesia was in the leisure wear, when Dutch men might on occasion wear trousers of batik, or even a sarong, but these were clearly different in form from those worn by the Javanese. Moreover, the wearing of "Indisch" dress was seen as the prerogative of the sick. When a man was "undressed, that is to say dressed in *Indisch* clothing at a time of the day when everyone should be wearing European clothing, then it is said that he is sick".[26]

Similar, perhaps more accentuated, distinctions between the attire of the colonized and those of the colonizers could be discerned among the women. It was, after all, a first requirement of colonization that the male colonizers maintained a sexual monopoly over those women they had brought with them, and it was of equal importance to the colonized elites that colonial access to native women – which could never be prevented entirely – happened as far as possible on terms the elite could accept. Clothing was one of the ways in which such social distancing was achieved. Thus in Indonesia the Dutch women, including those who would have wanted to be considered Dutch, wore the full range of crinolines and bustles as prescribed by Paris through the nineteenth century, at least in public. In private, or at least on non-official occasions, they would wear the *kain kabaya*, a combination of a hip-length blouse and an ankle-length wrap-around batik skirt, which they had in common with the upper-class Javanese ladies. The main distinction between the two at this stage was that the European's blouse was most probably white, while that of the Javanese never would be.[27] Equally, the British in India did everything to ensure that they were set aside from the Eurasians, and above all the autochthonous Indians. They might do all they could to delay as long as possible the hour at which they had to be dressed in full glory, but when they did so, they had to appear in a costume as close as possible to that of Europe, with the exception that such Indian stuffs as might be in fashion in the metropolis were not allowed in India. In the 1820s, Mrs Fenton deplored that it was "the extremity of bad taste to appear in anything of Indian manufacture . . . when I wanted to purchase one of those fine-wrought Dacca muslins I was assured I must not be seen in it as none but half-castes *ever* wore them. These dresses sell in London as high as £7 or £10."[28] The version she wished to wear, though, was probably too transparent, as Bengali muslins were still being worn, even by the sister of the Governor-General, a decade later.[29] As in Java, and indeed everywhere, "a loose and careless toilet carried a suggestion of loose and careless morals".[30] It was with this in mind that one European woman living in India in the nineteenth century proudly wrote to her mother in England that she had always worn her stays.[31]

If European women were constrained from wearing the clothing of the Indian and Javanese, the converse was even more clearly the case. Indian and Javanese women remained in general outside the public sphere, or only appeared in it at moments of high ceremony, as did most of the Europeans. There was thus in the nineteenth century no occasion for the Asian ladies to attempt to emulate European styles, while the reasons for not doing so, analogous to those

4 The De Vries family, Batavia, 1915

which kept the *totoks* and the *memsahibs* in Dutch or English dress, were overwhelming. There were no apparent gains, and many losses, in wearing crinolines or their successors. To have done so would have been to advertise moral turpitude, as well as being peculiarly uncomfortable. It was neither something that the women wished to do, nor what their menfolk would have permitted.[32]

There were other ways in which the coming of colonial rule might affect the gender relations, and general hierarchies, of the colonized. The systems of hierarchy which had pertained were predicated upon, and designed to maintain, a high level of social stasis. However, some specific groups in South India were able to achieve upward social mobility and thus challenge this order. In particular some of the group of palm-sugar tappers, known as the Shanars, became richer and, changing their caste appellation to Nadar, began to claim status which had previously been reserved to their putative superiors. As part of this move, very many of them joined the mission churches of the London Missionary Society, which were first established in the region in 1806. The converts were expected to cover their breasts, in order to preserve their modesty in ways acceptable to the missionaries. From 1812 onwards the new Christians received permission to cover their torsos with long-sleeved blouses of cotton, as the Syrian Christians of the area had long done, but they were excluded from wearing an upper cloth as the Nayar women did. The LMS missionary women also created a form of jacket which could be worn in church, and elsewhere, with decency.[33]

This was precisely what was not intended. The converts who did appear in "decent dress displeased their neighbours, especially the Nayars, who began to mock, abuse and illtreat them in various ways in markets and way sides".[34] The missionaries were able to obtain court rulings that their convert women might cover their breasts, but the aim of the Christians was, first, to use their Christianity to free themselves from the oppression of the higher castes and, secondly, to take on the symbols of status of those above them. They were not social revolutionaries; when individuals still lower than them in status joined a congregation, they abandoned it.[35] The dress designed by the missionaries was thought of as equivalent to the badge of an English poorhouse, and one missionary even commented that his converts preferred the "upper cloth" to the jacket, for the same reason as English ladies wore crinolines, namely "to appear more respectable", even though missionaries complained that it did not provide sufficient cover.[36] In this challenge to social hierarchy, by a group who were attempting to rise in what was in principle a closed system, dress was of great importance, and it was recognized as such. Precisely for this reason, in 1858 a series of riots broke out throughout Travancore.[37] Nadar women were publicly stripped of their cloths. Twelve chapels were burnt down. The disturbances nearly brought about the full annexation of the state, for which the missionaries agitated. The British informed the Raja in no uncertain terms that the prohibitions on the wearing of a breast cloth were "unsuited to the present age and unworthy of an enlightened prince". Finally the state of Travancore issued a proclamation that

> there is no objection to Shanar women either putting on a jacket, like the Christian Shanar women, or to Shanar women of all creeds dressing in coarse cloth, and tying themselves round with it as Mukkavattigal [low-caste fisherwomen] do, or to covering their bosoms in any manner whatever; but not like women of high caste.[38]

The last clause of this proclamation was what it was all about. The missionaries were being used to achieve social advance within the contexts of a South Indian social system. A woman covering her breasts was conceptually equivalent to a man wearing a suit and tie in a colonial situation. The arena, and the sexual content, were different.

In general, men, and in particular those whose position or ambition took them into the public sphere controlled by the colonists, had to discover some acceptable sartorial compromise between the European and the Indian, or Javanese. For a number, things might be forced on them. The soldiers of the colonial armies, for instance, had to wear the uniforms decided for them by the colonial governments. Certainly, in the case of the British Indian army, this might include a degree of exoticization, producing uniforms which were obviously distinct from those of the British regiments.[39] In general, though, enlistment in a colonial army entailed forcing the new recruit's body into unnatural garb, at times quite literally. One of the major difficulties of the Koninklijke Nederlandsch Indische Leger, the army of the Dutch East Indies, derived from the boots which had been sent out from Holland, made on lasts for the feet of Dutchmen who had worn shoes since infancy. The pain which this caused the shorter and broader feet of the Indonesians, which had never been so constrained and malformed, must have been terrible.[40]

For others, the donning of European-style dress may have been no less painful, but was certainly part of a strategy around the assumption of modernity, as it was seen, and at the same time a claim to acceptance by the colonial authorities as equals, claims that were generally not accepted. For this reason, in both India and Indonesia, the wearing of European dress by prominent Indian or Javanese men was at the beginning, though not necessarily at the end, of anti-colonial nationalism.

Initially, the process of adopting European dress was far from complete. The first garment to be added to the various Asian costumes was generally a jacket, followed by a shirt. The result was a new combination, beginning in at least the 1870s, whereby, for instance among the *bhadrokok*, the Bengali elite,

> the European dress-shirt in its still version was by itself a recognized formal wear for men. Wealthy people went to visit and even to parties in these shirts, looking very imposing with their starched fronts, gold diamond studs and links, sometimes a gold chain, and a very fine crinkled dhoti as diaphanous as the finest muslin, and also patent leather pumps with bows.[41]

In Java, similarly, the combination of a sarong with a European jacket was normal attire at the beginning of the twentieth century, for instance for the students of the School for Native Civil Servants, in Bandung, who in 1903 had themselves pictured thus, with sarongs, jackets, watch-chains, head-cloths and a whole variety of neckties.[42]

The young men attending such a school are unlikely to have been the most politically advanced of their generation, or if they were they would at least temporarily have hidden their true feeling for the sake of their education, and of their careers. Those who were more stridently anti-colonial were more likely to be Westernized in their dress. At the first congress of the Sarekat Islam, held in 1916, the board were said to have been dressed either in tails with a white (bow) tie, or in a dinner jacket, presumably with a black bow-tie.[43] This was at

5 Indonesian nationalists

the beginning of the generation of nationalists who would lead Indonesia to Independence. It was a generation of which some of the elite had studied in the Netherlands and taken on the dress of the country in which they had stayed for a while. Sukarno himself was always dressed in immaculate European clothing, and those around him were known for their sartorial care. It was a way of acquiring prestige. The one exception in their usual costume, certainly on the part of Sukarno, was the *peci*, the black cap with which Sukarno in particular attempted to demonstrate his solidarity with the Javanese masses. At least in its name, though, this hat is Dutch, deriving from *petje*, the diminutive of the word which translates into English as "cap".[44] This is one of those many moments in colonial history when it seems appropriate to rephrase the comment in the book of Ecclesiastes as "Irony of Ironies: all is Irony."

In India, too, it was head covering which was the most likely to remain unchanged. As has been regularly pointed out, in the Indian subcontinent the head is generally regarded as the seat of purity, and headgear, in consequence, as the most unchanging mark of affiliation, to caste, to religion or to region. It was quite normal for men to wear immaculate European dress topped off by a turban or cap in the style appropriate for its wearer. Those who sported straw hats, or toppers, were often accused "of taking on superior British airs". The *sola topi*, as has been shown, was in its way the British equivalent, as a true caste mark of the British race.[45]

Even those Indians who did take on European clothing at a given moment in their careers seem never to have been totally at ease in so doing. European clothing was often seen as the garb of a particular situation, and once that situation was over it would be cast aside. In Europe, or in the office, they might wear European clothing; returning to India, or to their home, or to their region of origin they might put aside European things. Ramanujan remembered how

> My father, on his annual trip to his home state of Kerala, in the 1940s, felt compelled to remove his Western suit at the border town of Alwaye. On one occasion he forgot to take off his suit and ran into ridicule everywhere he stopped. People who waited on him made it clear that they found his suit an affront.[46]

By this stage, of course, Indian anti-colonial nationalism had reached a high point, and this was from the beginning a sartorial as well as a political matter. Such protests began, at the very latest, in 1905, in Bengali reactions and boycotts against the proposed (and effectuated) partition of their province. Motilal Nehru wrote of this movement that

The Bengali reigns supreme throughout Bengal. He goes to the office bare-footed in his dhoti and chaddar and refuses to use anything of English manufacture at the risk of losing his employment. His [employers] cannot do without him and give him free admittance. Bengali High Court judges, barristers, solicitors, noblemen, merchants, have all discarded English costume. Thousands of indigenous industries have sprung up. We are passing through the most critical period of British Indian history.[47]

As the agitation died down, so did the enthusiasm for the dhoti, and it was only a few Indian politicians, often fervent Hindu nationalists, who remained unwilling to wear European dress. Only with Gandhi's rise to prominence within the nationalist movement, from about 1920 onwards, did the wearing of European dress again become a major issue within the politics of the Raj.

7

Reclothed in Rightful Minds: Christian Missions and Clothing

The use of clothing to ensure bodily discipline was, and remains, clearest among religious communities. To concentrate on the Christians, the habits of monks and nuns were clearly designed to ensure that they were continually aware of their vocation. As the constitution of the Marist Brothers, approved by the Vatican in 1881, had it: "There must be entire uniformity in the whole costume of the little Brothers of Mary, both in the form of the clothes, and the quality of their material, as well as in the manner of wearing them." So could the brothers be protected, by the Virgin Mary, against "the worldly snares of the devil".[1] Protestant ministers of religion were generally to be recognized by their sober black clothing and in many denominations in the anglophone world by the wearing of the tie-less reversed white dog-collar – though this was initially seen as a papist innovation which spread slowly and with resistance from the High Church to the Low, and then to the Nonconformists. Out of function, this would be put off and there would be little to distinguish the clergyman from the rest of the conservatively attired middle-class male population. Dutch *dominees* in the nineteenth century wore a particular shape of hat, and often white bands, even when in not in church, but later would only be distinguishable from the other leading citizens of a town or village by the fact they always wore black suits.[2] Only when they went into the pulpit were they, or indeed Protestant clergymen in other lands, clearly dressed as religious functionaries.

Neither Catholics nor Protestants attempted to impose a specific uniform on the laity (except for very specific rituals such as a Catholic First Communion). Both, however, demanded from their adherents that particular forms of dress be worn. Religious adherence entailed a level of civilization, and that civilization was demonstrated in clothing. It was an outward sign of a virtuous life – although of course, like every other sign, it was something with which one could lie. The Protestant Evangelical concern with the dangers of finery has already been described. From at least the beginnings of the nineteenth century, the churches conducted a civilizing offensive within the heartlands of Christianity.[3] This entailed attempts to impose particular standards of behaviour on the masses of the population. In Britain, temperance movements, the Society for the Protection of Cruelty to Animals, Sunday schools, and in general attempts at moral and temporal uplift were part of a single package, one that was certainly decently clothed.[4] It was also a package which was to be exported to the rest of the globe, through the movement for the abolition of slavery and above all through the missions.

Missionaries are of necessity cultural imperialists, in the broadest and loosest sense of that expression.[5] Their prime concern is to convince those among whom they work of the correctness of the particular set of beliefs they themselves hold. It is to be expected that the acceptance of these beliefs entails, in some way or other, a change in behaviour. Exactly what has been acceptable to which group of missionaries varies enormously from place to place, and from denomination to denomination, but there have been few who have been able not to equate their own practices with true moral behaviour, and thus with the will of God. After all, missionaries base their own norms on their interpretation of the Bible and of the Christian tradition, both in some sense thought to be God-given. As a result, the missionary movement since the end of the eighteenth century has been one of the major ways in which European mores, and specifically European styles of dress, have spread across world.

It took a while from the beginnings of the modern missions before this came to be seen as an essential part of mission practice. In South Africa, the region where the early Protestant missions were as successful and as important as anywhere in the world, the cultural politics took a while to be worked out. On the one hand, there were the missionaries of the Moravian Brotherhood. These were politically conservative and in general humble men and women, who created, at a village which came to be known as Genadendal, around 100 kilometres from Cape Town, what was the first mission station in Africa. Here a strict discipline was imposed on the residents and converts, and every effort was made to ensure that such money as they earned by labouring for the European farmers in the region was spent on proper clothing. One visitor to the settlement within a few years of it being opened commented that "all barbarous customs [had] been civilised away" by the missionaries, and the Khoekhoe inhabitants were beginning to exchange their sheepskins for clothes.[6] Fifteen years later, a visiting English minister wrote of how at a service "all the communicants [were] in their Sunday's dress, neat and clean ... most of the women are dressed in clean white gowns. Both men and women save their best apparel, that they may appear decent at church on Sundays, but there is no affectation of finery among them."[7]

The alternative tendency was represented by the most remarkable of the first generation of missionaries, the Dutchman Dr Johannes van der Kemp. Van der Kemp was an unlikely missionary, from a much higher social status than almost all his colleagues and totally unconcerned with his own position in society. The evidence on his concerns is contradictory. On the one hand, he is said to have written to both the Netherlands and Britain for clothing for his converts at Bethelsdorp, near modern Port Elizabeth in the Eastern Cape, and to have bought merino sheep so that the inhabitants might be able to spin and weave the wool. On the other, there were regular complaints that Bethelsdorp did not do what it could to ensure the civilization of its inhabitants – by which was generally meant, by the surrounding farmers and the British and Dutch officials, that these people did not perform labour for the colonists at minimal wages. Van der Kemp, after his death, was recalled as having exclaimed that "I never wish to see them [the Khoekhoe] better dressed than in their greasy karosses, all civilisation is from the Divil [*sic*]."[8] Van der Kemp himself "pushed frugality, or rather abstinence, and the forgetfulness of all care for his person, to the extreme limits", never wearing a hat and believing that a missionary should "in the matter of clothes and linen ... possess only what he was actually wearing". His argument was that "in order to raise the natives to his own level [a missionary] must in everything which is not reprehensible go down to theirs". This was an argument which virtually none of the missionaries who came after him shared. Rather, so they claimed, "experience has demonstrated [its] falsity".[9]

The missiological basis for these ideas was provided by Dr John Philip, long-term superintendent of the London Missionary Society in South Africa. He had to defeat attempts to destroy the missions, and to continue the oppression of the Khoekhoe by challenging their detractors on their own ground. The missions, he claimed, promoted the interests of the colony by raising up the Khoekhoe as decent and above all hard-working members of society. As Philip wrote, "the meaning attached by many of our countrymen to the word 'civilization' is often extremely vague, signifying little more than a conformity to their own ideas in dress and manner of living". As he put it later, privately and succinctly: "The question between us and the government was one of civilisation. The criterion of a people's civilisation with Lord Charles Somerset [the Governor of the Cape from 1812 to 1827] was whether the people used knives and forks."[10] He could have added, also, whether they wore shirts, trousers, jackets and dresses. For Philip, on the other hand, civilization was inseparable from Christianity, and Christianity was an essential element in the civilization of the world and the bringing of material progress. The creation of wants was thus a necessary part of conversion. As he wrote:

> While I am satisfied, from abundance of incontrovertible facts, that permanent societies of Christians can never be maintained among an uncivilized people without imparting to them the arts and habits of civilized life, I am satisfied, on grounds no less evident, that if missionaries lose their religion and sink into mere mechanics, the work of civilization and moral improvement will speedily retrograde.[11]

In this, for reasons of morality, propriety and, in Philip's eyes, civilized behaviour, dress was vital. Indeed, he argued that much of advantage to building proper – in his eyes – houses was that otherwise clothes could not be kept in order, extravagance would ensue from the need to replace them, and needles and thimbles would get lost in the rubbish.[12]

The inhabitants of Bethelsdorp followed his precepts. By 1825, in Bethelsdorp, "the sheep-skin caross, with its filthy accompaniments, has disappeared, and the great body of the people and of the children are clothed in British manufactures".[13] Five years later, when a great dinner was held there to honour Philip and to celebrate the granting of legal equality in the Cape Colony to the Khoekhoe, the men, as a French Huguenot missionary who was present noted, wore cotton trousers and waistcoats of striped calico, or indeed cloth suits, and "arranged their cravats according to Parisian fashion with a square knot and the large corners crossed or held in place with a pin with a sparkling head". The women also "wore dresses of printed calico, with white stockings and small black shoes ... all had neat handkerchiefs of silk or red and yellow cotton on their heads". It is, however, symptomatic that when this journal was sent to Paris, the editors cut the parts of this passage in which the apparent extravagance of the converts was described. It was not the end which contributors to mission funds envisaged their subscriptions leading.[14]

Processes very equivalent to those in Southern Africa occurred throughout the Pacific, another area very heavily influenced by the London Missionary Society, and also by the Wesleyans. Modern historians of the mission, certainly those whose sympathy is clearly with the church, tend to be somewhat apologetic about the ways in which the churches imposed the Victorian ideals of dress and bodily cover on the inhabitants of the Pacific islands.[15] Nevertheless, it is clear that in many of the island societies the acceptance of Christianity was associated with the assumption of a variety of European dress. Since in time most of the inhabitants of the Pacific came to convert to Christianity in one form or another, and often became fervent and fundamentalist, this entailed a fairly total reclothing of the region.

Before the missionaries arrived, of course, Pacific islanders were, with few exceptions, no more naked than they were, in the normal sense of the word, savages. The main exceptions seem to have been among the Australians, who thus found the European habits of dressing to be ridiculous. They did, however, often wear fur cloaks, and there was a clear distinction between the body ornament of men and women.[16] To the British colonists fell the devil's task of teaching them that they were naked, and should be ashamed. A missionary who arrived in Sydney in 1817 remembered that

> It was the custom at this time for the Aborigines both male and female to parade the streets without a particle of clothing, and it struck me very forcibly . . . to observe such scenes in the midst of what was called a civilized community, and when walking one day with some colonial Ladies, and meeting a mixed party of undressed natives of both sexes, no slight embarrassment was felt as to how dexterously to avoid the unseemly meeting, but this was speedily removed by their claiming old acquaintance privileges, and entering into a friendly conversation with our friends.[17]

The initial attempts to "remedy" this situation did cause great problems, in part because the first attempts by officials to issue clothing without distinguishing between the sexes was a clear affront, and in part because the Australians had a clear preference for receiving, and wearing, a multi-purpose blanket rather than cut and sewn clothes.[18] These, of course, did not cover their nakedness to the satisfaction of the Europeans. Slowly, though, European clothes came to be accepted as ways in which Australians could express their status, though often in ways which surprised European observers. Around 1840, for instance, Louisa Meredith wrote that "great was the pride and grandeur of who could button his upper man in a dress coat, that alone being considered an ample costume".[19] There are other descriptions of the same sort of phenomenon, clearly seen as ridiculous by the Europeans, but not by the wearers of the clothing. The functions of protection from the elements and of the preservation of modesty were in this case not important; all that mattered was thus adornment of the body and the demonstration of status.

Elsewhere in the Pacific, the pre-contact traditions of body adornment were more elaborate than in Australia. In many of the islands of Polynesia, the art of tattooing – the word was introduced into English by the first British voyagers in the region, including Captain Cook, whom the *Oxford English Dictionary* credits with the first English usage of the word – was widely practised, and the consequent body art of high elaboration.[20] Given this, and the climate, little more was needed than penis wrappers made of plaited pandanus leaves which were generally worn in Vanuatu – and which men continued to wear even after they had come to assume trousers above them. Women in the islands which make up that state, known colonially as the New Hebrides, would wear skirts of such material, or of bark cloth, whose length indicated their marital status, dropping at betrothal and rising again after a woman had been widowed (and served her mourning period) and had once again entered the marriage market.[21] Bark cloth was often seen as imbued with sacred qualities. Its preparation, beaten out from the pith stripped from the trees, was above all women's work, and one that was undertaken by all levels of society, including the queens of Tahiti.[22] Perhaps as a result, the quantities of clothing which might be worn on ceremonial occasions were prodigious. In Hawaii, before the arrival of the Europeans, women wore a wrapper made of bark cloth, around the waist for commoners but higher, just under the bust, for royalty. This cloth, made by beating soaked fibres from the paper mulberry tree, was heavy, uncomfortable, and could not be washed, but nevertheless it is reported that Hawaiian queens, on very special occasions, wore up to 72 yards of the material, which was so stiff and thick that they were forced to keep their arms outstretched.[23] It did not need the Rational Dress Association to expound on the virtues of European and North American woven cotton cloth.

In a sense, though, the London Missionary Society played the role of the Rational Dress Association, not so much to free women from the burden of bark cloth, but rather to free them from sin. The problem, for the missionaries, was much more that the men, and particularly the women, were underdressed, not overcovered. They did not recognize that there were rules of decorum in the island societies, so that even young women swimming would ensure that their genitalia remained out of sight.[24] The problem was that the missionaries thought to be universal the particular rules which they had brought to the Pacific from half a world away.

From the point of view of the missionaries, the outward signs of conversion were clearly to be found on the bodies of the new converts.

Missionaries themselves were always thickly dressed – at least when anyone else could see – and their main gifts were cloth.[25] Missionaries arriving at an island where they might not have been for some time were happy to see the Christian congregation dressed in European type clothing. As the LMS missionary John Williams commented on one occasion, "all of them, even to the lowest, aspired to the possession of a gown, a bonnet, and a shawl, that they might appear like Christian women".[26] The men in Aitutakei in the Cook Islands wore European-shaped hats to distinguish them from the "heathen head-dresses" of the opposition party.[27] Again in Rarotonga, in the same archipelago, Williams noted that "compared with what they were when I first visited them [the community] 'were clothed and in their right mind'. All the females wore bonnets, and were dressed in white cloth, whilst the men wore clothes and hats of native manufacture. The change thus presented was peculiarly gratifying."[28] Again William Gill, on the same island, wrote a description of his charges, who lived in one of the more temperate climates of the Pacific, for the edification of those who contributed to the funds of the LMS:

> Their dress consists of light English and American cotton material, made up in loose European style: the women having a native cloth wrapper, as inner garment, over which is worn a long flowing robe; they have no shoes, but a bonnet of *finely wrought plait*, and neatly trimmed with foreign ribbon, is considered essential to complete their dress. The men wear shirt, trousers, waistcoat, and coat, most of them have strong rush hats, for common use, and finer ones for occasional service, and about 1 in every 20 completes his full dress by putting on stockings and shoes.[29]

It was accepted that a change of religion entailed a change of dress. In 1854, one of the Fijiana rulers, Cakobau, converted together with the mass of his subjects. As the Wesleyan missionary, the Rev. Joseph Waterhouse, wrote:

> It was then resolved that the religion of Christ should be substituted for the vain traditions received from their fathers. Bales of native cali-coes were opened, divided and distributed to those who wished to clothe themselves. . . . The change in the people was very striking. All had clean faces and were suitably clad . . . and previous to the commencement of worship, the chiefs respectfully removed their snow white turbans. . . . Next day the temples were spoiled of their ornaments. 'His new religion shall not save Thakombau,' exclaimed some. 'It is only a fresh scheme to gain time; and when he recovers his position he will throw off his dress.'[30]

The motives, and the sincerity, of the conversion are not at this stage of importance. What is clear is how closely associated were

Christianity and the adoption of European-style clothing. In Samoa, too, European dress was said – by the LMS missionary John Williams – to have been a major argument for conversion. Of the Europeans it was said, "you can see ... that their God is superior to ours. They are clothed from head down to the feet and we are naked." More generally, the technological advantage of the Welshman and his entourage was praised. "They have noble ships while we have only canoes. They have strong beautiful clothes of various colours while we have only ti leaves. They have sharp knives while we have only a bamboo to cut with."[31]

The clothing that was worn by the converts was to some extent specific to the region. Men, it would seem and with some important exceptions, wore shirts and trousers and hats, also jackets when they were being smart. Women, on the other hand, came to wear a thoroughly characteristic dress, the so-called "Mother Hubbard", a loose-fitting smock which has been described as "the most famous style of mission-inspired clothing", and which most evidently was designed to camouflage the woman's figure, in a remarkable example of convergent evolution with Islamic dress.[32] To the French, in New Caledonia, this was known as the "robe mission".[33] It was described at the end of the nineteenth century as follows:

> An ordinary native dress is made yoke shape. Something like a lady's nightdress, but shorter, with elbow sleeves. Galatea, or good print, makes nice gown – yoke lined. Two widths in skirt, three-quarters of a yard in length to come in under the knee. Plenty of room at neck *and arms* ... Turkey red frill, or red braid makes a nice gay finish. The natives dearly love bright colours.[34]

It was, it has been correctly pointed out, not a style of clothing which the European women in the Pacific would have worn themselves, whether or not they were attached to the mission. It was thus a dress for Christian "natives". How far it achieved its goal is far from certain. One observer, unfortunately not identified, noted that "the clothes the [Polynesian] girls put on became a source of allurement to men who all their lives had taken nudity for granted".[35] It is far from certain that the covering of bodies actually improved the "morality" of the mission's converts, even within the value system of the missionaries. It is likely, above all, to have made the missionaries, their wives and their European sponsors feel more comfortable. The broader process of bodily discipline, and for that matter the sewing classes, which many missionary wives held, may in time have had their effect, but that would be hard to quantify.[36]

As always there are ironies in this process. It was not merely that individuals wore the clothing appropriate to the situation in which

6 Girls in Mother Hubbards

they found themselves, so that the Queen of Tahiti would change from European clothing to bark cloth when the discussions in her assembly moved from matters concerning the mission to those internal to the island's politics.[37] Equally to this day, Samoan men will bare their chests, at least if they are tattooed, as a matter of respect, when attending the chief's gathering, which may indeed occur after church on Sunday.[38]

It was not always European clothing that was propagated, just as it was not always Europeans who were doing the propagating. As in most missionary fields, mass conversions were achieved only once converts were employed as the main evangelizers. In much of Polynesia, those evangelists were Tahitians, following the mass adoption of Christianity in the Society Islands during the course of the 1820s. The missionaries had asked those Tahitians who were to be baptized to cover themselves for the service. The men were to wear

> a *tiputa*, a wrapper reaching to the middle of the leg, and the women to get a *hu tipanoi*, a wrapper reaching down to the foot. In the above dress, the first 14 were baptised in 1819 ... more than a 1,000 were all in the old costume, except oiling the body all over on the Sabbath. But from that day they all adopted the dress of the 14 at least on the Sabbath day, and have continued to improve in clothing from that time to the present.[39]

As they brought their newly adopted religion to both the Cook Islands and to Samoa, they also brought new ways of dressing. In the Society Islands, it had been normal for men and women to cover the torso. It was general to wear a piece of bark cloth draped over the shoulders with a slit for the head, much as modern poncho. These then were widely adopted by the new Christian parties in the other islands.[40] In the Cook Islands, culturally very much under Tahitian influence, it has been suggested that the introduction of European calicoes, which could be acquired with much less labour than bark cloth, entailed "a democratization of prosperity". Previously the poncho had been a mark of rank, and of associated wealth.[41] In Fiji, on the other hand, what was introduced was a long bark cloth skirt, for men as well as women, known as the *sulu*. It replaced the simple loincloth which had been worn by men before the introduction of Christianity.[42] It is still worn as Fijian national dress, in one of the more obvious versions of invented traditions, though today the cloth will be cotton or other woven material. A Fijian aristocrat will even wear a pin-stripe *sulu* to accompany a dress coat and tie, as full court dress.[43]

There was a further twist to this in Hawaii. From the early nineteenth century European and American traders brought with them a whole variety of consumer goods, in particular cloth and a certain amount of made-up clothing. By 1820, when the missionaries of the American Board of Commissioners for Foreign Missions established their presence, they found that a male chief might be dressed, for instance, in "a neat white dimity jacket, black silk vest, nankeen pantaloons, white cotton stockings, shoes, plaid cravat and a neat English hat".[44] It was a way in which the Hawaiian aristocracy, newly enriched

7 Ratu Sir Kamisese Mara and General Rabuka, Fiji

by the sandalwood trade, was able to demonstrate its importance in what Marshall Sahlins has called "the political economy of grandeur".[45] However, the skill to turn the cloth which the traders had brought into clothing was lacking until the arrival of the missionary women, who were all trained as seamstresses, as well as to be wives. One of their first tasks was to make a dress for the Queen Dowager Kalakau, a woman of formidable proportions weighing about 130 kilograms, as indeed befitted a powerful woman in a culture where size and corpulence were much desired.[46] This was the sort of request which could not be refused. The New England ladies appreciated that the style of the period, with a tightly fitting bodice, would not, in their eyes, be appropriate for "the Polynesian figure". The result was that, in a few days, they invented a new style, which became known as the *holokū*. This was an unwaisted shift hanging from a yoke, which was in its loose, flowing lines thought better adapted to an island climate. The sleeves were fitted tightly, in a concession to the fashions of the North America they had left in 1819. The dress was made from a bolt of white cambric which the Queen had in her possession.[47]

While the dress of male Hawaiians has not remained in the fashion of 1819 New England, the *holokū* has become a symbol of Hawaiian ethnicity, to distinguish those of Polynesian descent from the majority populations, immigrants from Japan or Euro-America.[48] It is, of course, not at all unusual for articles of dress to become the markers of ethnicity, nor that those markers which are seen as "traditional" were created – "invented" – in the relatively recent past. What is relatively unusual is that the invention can be dated to the day, in this case 4 April 1820, and ascribed to specific individuals, Queen Kalakua and the missionary wives Lucy Thurson and Lucia Holman.

To return to Southern Africa, eventually, by the second quarter of the twentieth century if not earlier, all South Africans had taken on some variant of Western dress – shirts, jackets and trousers for men, blouses and skirts for women. But this was a long and differentiated process. The attempts which were made by the British conquerors of parts of the Eastern Cape to impose European attire on the Xhosa under their control came to naught.[49] Rather the change of fashion came with social change in its various ways, and particularly with the conversion to Christianity, a process which, except for the Khoekhoe and ex-slaves of the Cape and a very few Xhosa and Tswana, only began after the 1850s. In rural North America, revival services had an "anxious seat", where repenting sinners would sit; for an American missionary in South Africa "the shirt is the anxious seat of the Zulu".[50]

As graphic an illustration of this as any can be seen in two photographs taken by Roman Catholic missionaries around the Marianhill station in what is now KwaZulu-Natal in the 1880s. These photographs have as captions written into the print "a heathen kraal" and "a Christian kraal". There are differences in the architecture of the houses, as the Christian houses have walls, allowing the possibility of doors though which people can enter in a more or less standing position, as opposed to the low entries of the "traditional" bee-hive

8 A Christian village near Marianhill, KwaZulu-Natal

houses. The people, at least as the missionary photographer wanted them displayed, were also differently attired, with no bare flesh (except for face, neck and hands) displayed by the Christians.[51] For a time, in this area of the country, Western clothing had become a mark of Christianity. This was the case elsewhere as well. In the dreams of a potential convert at Ramaliane in the far south-west Transvaal, what is now North-West Province, heaven was full of people wearing "nice dresses".[52]

The clothing that Africans donned was at times a careful mixture of old and new meaning. Sechele, ruler of the Bakwena in what is now southern Botswana, had a suit, in European style, made of leopard skin, the ancient symbol of power through much of Africa.[53] Others transformed the skills which they had long had in the working of leather to deal with the new European cloth, often under the tute-lage of the missionaries' wives. In 1865 Behrens, a missionary of the German Hermannsburg Society, stationed at Bethanie to the north-west of Pretoria, described a scene which must have been common:

These baptised people want to wear clothes but do not know how to get them.[54] They gather patches and all kinds of material, and it is a lot of work to sell clothes to them or get them for them otherwise. Our Hermannsburg home board sent me material for about eight to nine dresses but within two days everything was sold out; even if they had sent me material for twelve dresses, everything would have been sold for sheep, goats and cash. It is such a pity that I cannot get hold of cheap clothes for I could really help these people. If I possessed worn clothes which people give away in Germany, especially in the higher ranks, I could really make my congregation look nice and cover their nakedness. After all the material has been sold, there is a hustle and bustle of tailors in front of my house. My wife is very busy cutting the material and teaching the women how to sew, and she gets quite angry with the stupid ones of the [African] women who simply do not understand how to make decent stitches. But she struggles back to work good-humouredly every day. Most of the people have succeeded in appearing for church quite decently. The men started to sew dresses for their wives, which they can wear during the week, and they really do a good job. In short, baptised people and baptismal candidates urgently desire clothes, they all want to get rid of their naked condition, their old stupid hides and whatever they might drape around their hips.[55]

The rituals of conversion and baptism were marked by dress. There are many stories of women putting off the ornaments they had received at their marriage, or their initiation, and taking on first the headscarf which had become the badge of Christianity, and then, at least among the Hermannsburg Lutherans, receiving a white dress from the missionary for the ceremony of Baptism.[56]

As long as the missionaries could control the access to cloth, and to European-style clothing, they were reasonably content with the attire of their charges. After about 1870, however, matters changed. From the 1870s, after the Diamond Fields in Kimberley had opened, the cash income of the African societies of the South African interior began to increase rapidly. There had been long a tradition of labour migration from what is now Limpopo province to the coastal ports, but the opportunities provided by the new bonanza towns far outstripped what had previously been available.[57] For a while, African miners were paid as well, if not better, than their fellows in Europe. The money went on guns and ammunition, to defend what were as yet unconquered polities, but also on consumer goods, above all clothing. Both in the mining towns themselves, and on the migrants' return to their home villages, men dressed expensively. There were those in Kimberley who wore trousers and tail coats, not necessarily together.[58] When Sol Plaatje married Elizabeth M'belle, both members of the Christian elite, Plaatje with his best man wore "bell toppers, morning coats, white waistcoats, light pants, and patent leathers", and this despite having been brought up on a Berlin mission station.[59] In the countryside, as the Berlin missionary Carl Benjamin Richter reported, "we might encounter a Mossuto in a black suit and in black trousers, a waistcoat which does not lack a brass watch chain ... and his head carries a hat", but his feet, like those of soldiers in the Dutch East Indian Army, could not cope with shoes. Some of the African chiefs considered that migrants should not take on the customs – the trousers – of the whites, and only those who had converted to Christianity were prepared to go against their wishes. Others, though, of a younger generation, "are more inclined to adopt outer European customs". In particular, colourful umbrellas had become a symbol of prosperity among these groups. "From early on until late in the evening one can see young gentlemen promenade with umbrellas put up, and the young man succeeds in what he wants: his presence demands attention, and all the world watches him."[60]

The urge to display was not, of course, limited to the young men. When they had the opportunity, which was particularly in the towns, the Christian women attached to the missions were also eager to show their sophistication. This was too much for the Lutheran missionaries. In 1875, the Rev. Friedrich Grünberger in Pretoria felt called upon to preach

> about the misuse of crinolines, which unfortunately are spreading among the blacks. Some of the women tried to get rid of this fashion article at once, but others hesitated. One of them even said, "if I prohibited them from wearing crinolines, she would convert to the English Church, where nobody would care about that." So I had to take tough action. I went with two elders from house to house, starting off with the house of this very reluctant woman and we confiscated all crinolines to burn them to death before their eyes with the others joyfully laughing.[61]

The bonfire of the crinolines was followed up by missionaries issuing their own private sumptuary laws, in an attempt, as vain as anywhere else, to maintain social order and prevent sinful extravagance. Silks and satins were forbidden. Brides who appeared in silk gowns would simply not be married. Clothing had to be prepared under the supervision of a missionary's wife. However, richer stuffs were allowed to the families of the missionaries, in a crude attempt to ensure the supremacy of the Europeans over those they had never really seen as their brothers and sisters in Christ.[62]

This was the danger of preaching the gospel of dress. Eventually those who took on European clothing would use it not merely for modesty, but also for an immodest display of extravagance. This was a problem inherent in the goals of Protestantism. On the one hand, missionaries preached diligence, and indeed the adoption of Western ideas of proper commercial relationships. But this had to be an end in itself, or at least the end was in the world to come, not in this one.

They did not know how to deal with the motivation of most people, most of the time, for working hard, namely the desire for wealth and the status which accompanies it. In the Hawaiian archipelago, there were missionaries who were aware of the dilemma by the late 1840s, if not earlier. One wrote

> Without new wants are created, industry can hardly be expected to increase to a very great extent; for who will work without a motive? There needs however in my opinion much vigilance on the part of the missionary to prevent their celebration from running to an extreme. At the last [temperance] celebration at Haula, I noticed an elegant youth, dressed in the perfection of good taste, from the ribbon in the shoe to the white glove. I marvelled to know where he could deposit his rich attire after the occasion was past.

The missionary was shocked to discover that the young man lived in a house which did not approach New England norms. The balance was wrong and indeed sinful, in his eyes.[63]

Two further examples may illustrate the question further. The first concerns Eweland, straddling the southern border between Ghana and Togo. This is an area which had, and has, a flourishing tradition of textile production, weaving *Kente* cloths. In these coloured and patterned strips no more than ten centimetres wide are produced on a narrow loom and then sewn together to produce large cloths of great beauty, which are worn draped in various ways about the body of both men and women. When the missionaries of the *Norddeutsche Missionsgesellschaft* arrived and began to create Christian settlements, often in the first instance by buying slave children in the market and liberating them, they were concerned to inculcate a particular view of civilization.[64] This entailed specific forms of dress, in which women would wear more than a cloth wrapped around the hips – above all the breasts had to be shielded from view – and the men were encouraged to wear Western-style suits. For teachers, above all, black coats, white shirts and ties became a badge of their profession. No doubt, as elsewhere, the outer clothes of the men were imported from great emporia of ready-to-wear clothes, while women's clothes, and men's shirts and undergarments, were produced locally. The missionary women were busy teaching women to sew – the stitching of the cloth strips had been a male occupation – and more importantly to cut stuff from which the clothes were made.

The first Ewe converts were likely to be more prosperous and more individualistic than the mass of their fellows. They did not have to worry that their personal accumulation would be seen as selfish, and thereby that they would be the targets of witchcraft. They also, to the satisfaction of the missionaries, were far from indolent. The problem, as the missionary D. Bavendamm commented in 1894, was that

> Their ideal and this is what they work for: *Beautiful clothes* and good food, or to speak with Augustine: 'Pleasure, worldly pleasure is their shibboleth, but instead of bread they receive stone,' because they do not look for the bread. Often, when I leave church service on Sunday, I go to them and try to talk to them. Then often in the midst of a spiritual talk somebody may ask: Master, how much is your hat, your dress-coat, your shoes? Or in a free hour they ask me to look at my photograph album. I allow it. They have submitted all pages to a precise examination and correctly found out the gentleman who wears the best collar and the best tie and now they come with this picture: Master, order us such a collar, such a tie for Christmas.

In a mission which, more than many, was predicated on opposition to the luxury of the world, this caused problems. On the one hand, in such a country dressing more demurely, which was a condition of Christianity, meant wearing "less simple, that is, better clothes than before". On the other, this entailed a level of worldliness which was not appreciated by those who brought that same message.[65]

The second example relates to what is now Namibia, and in particular to the Herero people who lived in the centre of the country. In many ways the sartorial history of the Herero was initially very similar to that of other Southern African groups. In 1846, sewing classes were begun by Emma Hahn, the wife of one of the pioneer missionaries. Although she and her husband initially made few converts, Emma Hahn and her fellows did succeed in inculcating European ideals of dress widely among those under their – partial – influence. Although, as elsewhere, the full import of European attire was not taken on board immediately, and on occasion men could be seen wearing the dresses they had captured in a raid, by the 1870s at least it was normal for those who belonged to the leading families of the Namibian central highlands to be wearing European clothes. Men had on jackets, trousers, shoes, shirts and hats of European manufacture, women long cotton dresses much as those throughout the rest of the region, at least while they were being photographed. These replaced the leather garments which had previously been worn, and which, for women, included characteristic headgear, with three upstanding peaks. In replacement of this, Herero women in European clothing initially wore headscarves, as did most Southern Africans, but later replaced this with substantial headgear.[66]

This is in no way unsurprising in terms of the history of clothing in those parts of the world influenced by the Protestant missions, and certainly not in Southern Africa. What is remarkable is that the dress styles of the 1880s are still worn today, and that they have been taken up totally into Herero "tradition". The various parts of the costume – bodice, skirt, apron, headgear – have received specific Herero names. Herero women who have been initiated into adulthood will still

9 Herero woman dancing, Windhoek

invariably wear the long dress style, even though it is not the most practical of garments for tasks such as gathering firewood, fetching water and cooking, and requires several hours of washing and ironing, usually with a charcoal iron, before it is fit to be seen. It is a serious attire, with ten yards at least of fabric in the dress itself, and several petticoats of thick cotton. Moreover, the various political factions of Herero society, which are organized around the followers of particular nineteenth- and early twentieth-century leaders, are distinguished from each other, at least on formal occasions, by the colour of the dresses worn by the women, which coincides with that of the flags waved by the male adherents. Thus the adherents of Maherero's descendants are known as the Red Flag, and the women wear red dresses, those of the Mbanderu leaders the Green Flag, and so forth.[67]

Whence this conservatism? There can be no doubt that it has come to symbolize Herero womanhood. Such women are supposed to comport themselves in a particular way, which is associated with the specifics of dress. Herero ideas of beauty, too, stress the fullness of the figure, which is accentuated by this clothing.[68] However, such ideas, true though they may be, cannot explain why Herero women in Namibia and in Botswana will wear such clothing while their Tswana fellows, with very much the same bodily aesthetics and the same initial history of mission clothing, do not.[69] The answer to this question therefore lies in the specific twentieth-century history of the Herero, which is dominated by the genocidal war waged against them by the German colonists from 1904 to 1908. This led to the death of four out of every five Hereros, and the exile of most of the survivors into what is now Botswana, whence most slowly trickled back into what was then South West Africa.[70] In these circumstances, the maintenance of an identity which had once been a death sentence was a matter of life. Herero, in both Namibia and Botswana, wear the long dress to affirm their survival, and that of their foremothers. It has become, in a particular way, a method of coping with a collective trauma.

If Herero women assert their identity through a conservative costume, Herero men do it, in part by wearing German-style uniforms and taking up the ranks of the German, and later British, armies.[71] But these are only for special ethno-ritual occasions. More generally, they have taken to displaying such wealth as they have by wearing highly fashionable Western clothes. This is something which goes back to before the genocide, and was resuscitated shortly afterwards, when Nama-speakers (who may of course have been of Herero origin, but who had shifted ethnicity in the course of the war) provoked the German missionaries by wearing top-hats to church.[72] This was a form of defiance and a claim to equality with all who lived in the colony. It has been continued ever since. Otto Mühr, the main fashionable men's outfitters, on Independence Avenue, Windhoek, has long specialized in providing Herero men with the best suits they can afford.[73] More generally, though, the sartorial history of colonial societies, in Asia and Latin American as well as in Africa, was driven by the political need to claim equality with the colonizers. In this, the Herero men have not been alone.

8

Re-forming the Body; Reforming the Mind

Of all the forms of clothing that men and women have put on, uniforms are those whose message is the least ambiguous, and they are also those in which the efforts of those with power to impose their will through the use of dress are most plain. In their great diversity, uniforms do have a number of distinct purposes. The most elementary is to distinguish between "them" and "us". Soldiers need to know who to kill and who to aid. Footballers need to know who is on their side, and can thus be given the ball. Cricketers, given the nature of their game, do not have any difficulty telling their colleagues from their opponents, and all wear the same plain whites (or at least they used to). Equally, and in extension of the same process, uniforms are used to denote a particular status or occupation. In the old days, the retainers of a lord would wear his livery, and in great houses this continued, as servants were given uniform clothing distinct from those of their neighbours. It is part of the same tradition that bus conductors or air hostesses, for instance, wear a company uniform, so that the public can know who they are, and so that a particular image is presented of the firm that employs them. Such liveries may be periodically updated, to ensure that the company seems modern, and not frumpish; in other cases, it may be that the image that has to be presented is of old-fashioned reliability, and employees' dress is similarly behind the times, though rarely to such an extent that it becomes quaint and folkloristic.

There is an exception to this latter rule, though, in some of the most globalized of environments, namely airlines and international hotels, especially those at airports. While the higher management wears the suits of international business and the aircrew has the attire of pilots everywhere – would anyone feel comfortable in a plane knowing that the pilot was wearing a sarong? – the lower staff will usually have some reference to their country's national dress, itself always a construct, in their uniform. It is a way of reassuring those who might otherwise have forgotten in which country they are.

These functions of uniform, however, are relatively trivial in relation to two somewhat contradictory, or at least complementary, attributes of many uniforms. In the armies, in schools, in the nursing profession and in many other institutions, uniforms simultaneously enforce uniformity and demonstrate difference. To begin with the latter, in any hierarchical organisation there are ways to distinguish the officers from the other ranks. The insignia of any European army, since the eighteenth century if not earlier, demonstrate who is a private soldier, who is a lieutenant and who a general. Only the commander, and then not even always him, was allowed a certain eccentricity in the field. For instance, General Bernard Montgomery, during World War II, on occasion wore a beret and jumper. The idiosyncrasy of his dress only served to emphasize his position as the singular leader of the British Eighth Army. Equally, at any British school where uniform was required, there was continual competition to acquire the privileges of exception – in my case, no longer wearing the school cap above a certain class, distinctly striped and coloured ties awarded for athletic distinction or for becoming a school prefect, and a silver fish in the buttonhole of the scholars. The classic case is perhaps Eton, one of the British schools with the oldest tradition of uniform dressing – they are said still to be in mourning for the death of George III in 1820 – where those who are elected to the elite school society "Pop" wear individualized florid waistcoats. Increasingly, too, those in the highest classes of schools no longer have to wear uniforms. They have regained their individuality.

The complementary function of uniform, though, is precisely to suppress that individuality. This was first developed strongly in the European armies from the seventeenth century. The New Model Army, under Cromwell in the English Civil War, was said to have been the first to attempt to dress all its soldiers in identical red coats, but under the exigencies of campaigning too many became tattered for the uniformity to be a satisfactory badge of allegiance on the battlefield.[1] Nevertheless, from the later seventeenth century, the dress of soldiers became a major method of instilling new forms of discipline. This was necessary for a number of reasons. It certainly had to do with the new professionalization of the army, introduced into the army of the States-General of the Netherlands by Maurits of Nassau, though he did not himself apparently introduce uniforms. Once it became accepted that soldiers should be paid on time, and that regiments should be not be raised by what were in effect military subcontractors, then it became reasonable that they should also receive a regular ration of identical clothing. At the same time, Maurice introduced new military tactics, with massed ranks of the infantry firing volleys and countermarching to produce a deadly continuity of fire. The problem was that, once such tactics had been adopted by all European armies, the tactic was not merely deadly but also close to suicidal. The European wars of the seventeenth and eighteenth centuries were among the most murderous in history. In order to be able to maintain the desired rate of fire, and to hold discipline in the face of heavy casualties, armies had to be drilled relentlessly. The psychological process which this involved had the effect of creating a powerful *esprit de corps* among the soldiers of a unit. This was only enhanced by their wearing the same clothing.[2]

For the military monarchs of the later seventeenth century – Louis XIV and the Great Elector of Brandenburg-Prussia above all – those men who had been recruited or conscripted into their armies were dehumanized units, almost literally toy soldiers, who would parade before them with great regularity, both in terms of time and in terms of their deportment and dress. In the French army, from the reign of the Sun King on, there were continual attempts to ensure that the army was properly equipped. A soldier on his recruitment received a waistcoat and coat, to be replaced every three years, two pairs of breeches, replaced every year, and a hat, replaced every two, and in addition

> three shirts, two collars of white dimity ... two pairs of shoes, three pairs of gaiters, two pairs of stockings, two kerchiefs, one collar buckle, one pair of shoe buckles, two pairs of garter buckles, a powder sack and its puff, a hair comb, a toothcomb, a clothes brush, two shoe brushes, a brush for brass ... thread, needles, some old cloth and old linen.[3]

The belief was that the army which sent its troops into the field better clothed and better equipped would, over the course of the campaign, have fewer invalids or deserters and thus in the long term would be more likely to triumph. Whether the quality of the clothing provided was sufficient to stand up to the rigours of a campaign is another matter altogether, certainly in defeat, but on the parade ground they were impressive. In addition, some degree of uniformity across the regiments of an army was encouraged, although obviously in the details some distinction was felt to be necessary, and the elite guards and the cavalry were more flamboyant. Thus there was white for the French, blue for the Prussians, red for the British.[4] They were becoming well-disciplined bodies, again in two senses of that word.

The relationship between clothing and discipline, and between clothing and particular forms of behaviour has frequently led authoritarian rulers into false syllogisms. Many rulers have attempted to expand
the discipline which was imposed in an army to the whole of society,
as part, generally, of authoritarian social engineering, particularly to
bring a "backward" country up to date. If a specific mode of dress is
a sign of modernity, whatever that may mean at any given moment,
then requiring one's subjects to wear that attire may be seen as a way
to modernize them. Conversely, if certain clothing is seen as traditional and against progress, then it is tempting to banish such outfits,
and thus ban backwardness. It should be evident that these are mistaken arguments, which rely in effect on forms of sympathetic magic.
The causal relationship between dress and other forms of behaviour,
social, economic and political, is one-way. People wear the clothes
they do for a number of reasons, one of which is because they accord
with the sort of person they are, or want to be thought of as. Wearing
a particular costume does not in itself turn the wearer into the sort
of individual who would normally wear such clothing, especially not
if the costume is imposed by force of law, or otherwise. The outer may
reflect the inner; it does not seem to effect it.

It is necessary to bring some nuances to this argument. Modernization programmes are never merely sartorial. In so far as the population accepts the broader thrust of government action, to that extent
will they be prepared to wear what is prescribed for them, and they
will also do so with a degree of pride, and as a sign that they are trying
to be modern. But against this the imposition of what is seen as
immoral, irreligious or unpatriotic garb may well have precisely the
opposite effect to that which the rulers desired.

The first ruler to go along this line of drastic modernization was
Tsar Peter the Great of Russia. He was ruler of a country which was
not only, by contemporary standards, backward and poor, but was
also highly diverse. A study of Muscovite inventories has revealed
143 different forms of caftans worn in the seventeenth century, falling
into at least ten basic categories.[5] When he returned from Western
Europe in 1698, Peter set about bringing his empire into line with
what he had seen in the courts of Germany and England and in the
shipyards of the Netherlands. His first actions, more or less, were to
reform the appearance of those around him. He began by requiring
that all the men, barring the Orthodox Patriarch and a few who were
exempted on the grounds of age, were to be shaved. This was an
affront to patriotic and religious sensibilities. A treatise warned:

> Look often at the icon of the Second Coming of Christ, and observe
> the righteous standing at the right side of Christ, all with beards. At the

left stand the Muselmen and heretics, Lutherans and Poles and other shavers of their ilk, with just whiskers, such as cats and dogs have. Take heed whom to imitate and which side you will be on.[6]

At the same time, Peter set about reforming the clothing of his Muscovite subjects. He issued a decree that

all residents of the city of Moscow including those serfs who come to the city to trade, but excluding the clergy and agricultural labourers, must wear German dress. Outerware must consist of French or Saxon coats, and underneath men must wear sleeved vests, breeches, boots, shoes and German hats. . . . Women of all ranks – women of the clergy, wives of officers, musketeers and soldiers – and their children must wear German dress, hats, skirts and shoes. From this day forward no one will be allowed to wear Russian dress, Caucasian caftans, sheepskin coats, pants or boots. . . . Finally, artisans will not be allowed to make or trade [in these goods].[7]

Peter had mannequins stationed at the gates of Moscow to demonstrate to those who were coming in from the country what they should wear, and sent his inspectors through the city imposing fines and chopping the hems off those coats which where too long. Gone, too, were the figure-concealing clothes of the women. At court, décolleté was in order, waists were much more prominent than they had been and headdresses no longer concealed Peter's courtiers' hair.[8] Women so dressed were expected to be sociable with the menfolk, and the old segregation by sex at court disappeared.

For the nobility, increasingly being turned into a service elite, dress was not merely Westernized but was also highly regulated. Not merely in the army but also within the civil service uniforms were worn, primarily in order to distinguish rank. Moving up the official scale entailed the acquisition of insignia. Men moved from white to black trousers, from red to blue ribbons, from silver to gold braid, and celebrated the status this entailed. The successes, and the failures, in the competitive world of the court were continually evident.[9]

These measures made Russia not so much a modern country as rather a schizophrenic one. The nobility and the court tried to be Western, wore Western clothes and increasingly spoke French. In the early days after Peter's decretals, women might revert to their traditional attire when the Tsar was out of town, but even that soon disappeared. The country, in contrast, remained Russian, with the long, and outlawed, caftans much in evidence. The two nations of that most stratified of societies were clearly distinguishable. By destroying the past, Peter had broken the symbolic bonds which held the society together, and retained merely the legal ones.

In time, though, economic growth and increased contact with Western Europe changed the bases of Russian society. As it slowly ceased to be a land of serfs and aristocrats, of old Russia and forced Europe, then the converse of Peter the Great's methods of modernization began to take effect. The new urbanites in an urbanizing and industrializing society, and finally the emancipated serfs and the peasants in general began to take on Western dress, the products of the ready-to-wear industry which was developing in the country, as part of the imitation of the West. Peasant women's dowries contained woollen, silk and cotton dresses, and wool or fur coats and capes. It was not home-made; the women had lost the art of sewing their "traditional" costumes. As a journalist reported from Podol'sk province in 1873,

> All clothes with the exception of undergarments are made from manufactured materials and cloth. Shoes are sewn to fit the foot more closely, and in more attractive styles. Homemade straw hats are worn only in the hot weather; caps . . . are the usual headgear. In inclement weather a few use store-brought felt hats and in the winter sheepskin hats made from local sheep costing one rouble fifty or more. Young men wear wool ribbon in their straw hats. Ribbons are also used as neckties with turn-down collars. Lately the use of vests has spread everywhere. Women wear calico skirts and aprons: traditional dress is only worn by old women. In general, women's clothing is factory-made rather than homemade. This dandyism is particularly noticeable near the cities and sugar factories. Peasants not only wear factory-made clothing, but they even buy linen. Practically every little trading outpost has a shop with these beautiful items.[10]

As usual, this led to reaction. A Novgorod official complained that "Luxury in dress is at scandalous proportions. It is not uncommon for a peasant to lay waste to his household and barn in order to buy his wife a 100 rouble dress and to clothe himself in city clothes."[11] Even before this, the aristocracy were attempting to regain contact with the essence of Russia which was being lost, in their eyes, through the processes of modernization. When off-duty, away in their dachas, they would wear Russian-style clothing "as a conscious statement of one's Russianness", as one memorialist wrote early in the nineteenth century.[12] Both Pushkin and Tolstoy primarily wore Russian dress. The Romantic ideals of Mother Russia were expressed through clothing. Indeed, in the last years of Tsarist rule, virtually the only occupational group which consistently wore peasant costume were the wet-nurses of the aristocracy. It would have been too much to expect the scions of the great families to have literally imbibed Russianness with their mother's milk, but this was clearly the next best thing.[13]

Peter the Great was only the first of a whole series of autocratic rulers who attempted to develop the countries over which they ruled through the imitation of Western Europe, in other words to bring about a forced and accelerated "modernization", and in so doing to impose major changes in the outward appearances of their subjects. From the later nineteenth century there were several such regimes. The first, the most radical and in the long term the most successful was Japan in the aftermath of the Meiji Restoration. In this, the Emperor was of course restored to his position at the head of government, after many centuries, but had as little genuine power as under the Tokugawa shogunate (1603–1868) which the Restoration abolished, and may well have been personally unfavourable to the actions of his government and the costume he was himself required to wear. The new rulers of the country, shocked by the failure of the old ways to repel European and North American influences, began to reform Japan's economy and society along Western lines as quickly as possible, in an attempt to gain equality with the West. Within a remarkably short period of time, posts and currency were reorganized, the first railway opened and compulsory education for children introduced. Part of this administrative reorganization of society was a total reclothing of the population which has been remarkably complete.

The transformation began from the top down. Even before the Restoration, the army and navy of the Shogun were increasingly dressed in European-style woollen clothes, causing a major upheaval in a country which did not run sheep, and which had quickly to train tailors to work in this new material. Indeed, in the 1860s between 20 and 40 per cent of the country's imports were of woollen cloth for the military.[14] After the Restoration in 1868, things moved faster. In November 1872, the Imperial court issued an ordinance that henceforth Western clothing would be compulsory for government officials, and as the official ceremonial dress. The Emperor pronounced that

> The national polity is indomitable, but manners and customs should be adaptable. We greatly regret that the uniform of our court has been established following the Chinese custom, and it has become exceedingly effeminate in style and character ... The Emperor Jimmu [660–585 BCE] who founded Japan and the Empress Jingu [201–69 CE] who conquered Korea were not attired in the present style. We should no longer appear before the people in these effeminate styles and have therefore decided to reform dress regulations entirely.[15]

The last privileges of the Samurai class, including their specified clothing (*kamishimo*) and their caste-designating hair-style, were done away with, and an attempted reactionary coup, in which the armies of new Japan were in woollen uniforms and of the old in traditional cotton and silk, was defeated. The Emperor would appear dressed in the uniform of a Field-Marshal, and shorn as a European male of his time. In 1876, further, a decree was issued instigating frock coats as the standard wear for the conducting of business.[16] At about the same time, regulations were promulgated forbidding from public spaces what the Japanese elite had realized that the Westerners saw as nudity – men wearing only a loincloth.[17] In the 1880s, the Ministry of Education ordered that students in public colleges and universities wear a uniform on Western lines; private universities, colleges and schools took longer to make the change, and indeed girls' schools vacillated between kimonos and Western dresses until well into the twentieth century.[18]

The turn to Western dress was initially a male matter. For a decade or so, in the highest circles of the Empire, the men appeared in frock coats or military uniforms, the women in the traditional robes of the court. Nevertheless, by the late 1880s, the Empress was being seen, and portrayed, in the most up-to-date of Parisian fashions, complete with bustle, embroidered cuffs and accentuated waist.[19] Modernity, in the version then current, had taken over the top of society and was slowly working its way down.

The process by which the jacket, shirt and trousers, or the dress, took over from the kimono as the preferred wear for men and women was slow, and probably delayed by the introduction of new materials, including serge, for the manufacture of "traditional" dress. It was long normal, and indeed it may still be, that on their return from work, or in general from outside, for the Japanese to put off their suits or dresses and replace them with kimonos.[20] Until the 1920s, even in Tokyo, while the majority of men were increasingly dressed in European style on the streets, virtually all the women were in kimonos.[21] As a consequence, it was only as women came in increasing numbers to appear in the streets, and in the places of work, that they began to take on Western clothes. Suits, dresses and so forth were seen as accountrements of the new public world, set aside from the private. From the 1920s, at least, it was expected that those in wage employment would wear European-style attire, of the style appropriate to their station in life. The others wear what amount to uniforms, but they are Western uniforms. So the *sararîman* (salary-man or office worker) will wear a dark suit, white shirt and conservative tie, the "office lady" a "prim company uniform" and even the gangsters will wear what amounts to a regulated dress – flashy suits and loud ties. Children, from the youngest age, go to school dressed in the livery of their establishment.[22] More efficiently than anywhere else, perhaps, clothing has had its effect of disciplining the population, or at the very least of signalling the discipline of a well-organized society.

The sort of dress that was worn during the pre-Meiji period is to be found among those self-consciously being traditional – carpenters, gardeners, those engaged as artists, for instance potters, but also when performing the tea-ceremony, attending calligraphy lessons and so forth.[23] The prime minister, however, wears a frock coat and striped trousers, which has become another form of traditional dress, when performing certain rituals at Japanese temples. It is also something which Japanese will wear for major life-cycle rituals – marriage, funerals, graduations and on similar occasions. Women, too, much more than men, will wear rich kimonos for particular ceremonies at work, for instance the New Year on the Tokyo Stock Exchange. It is thus limited to those moments when it is thought desirable to stress the fact of being Japanese, something which, *pace* the Emperor's proclamation of 1872, is associated with the style of dress worn under the Shogunate. It is, however, something that has to be learnt. While department stores once gave courses in wearing European clothes, they now provide teachers who explain how to put on a kimono, and comport oneself in it.[24]

There were other attempts to impose modernization by modernizing dress, often in direct emulation of Japan. In Thailand, the process of modernization, driven by the Siamese monarchy and known as the Chakri Reformation, entailed the redressing of the Royal Family as one of the clearest statements that the autocratic rulers of the country were driving through a programme of reform. Its major proponent, King Chulalongkorn (Rama V, r. 1868–1910), wore uniform modelled on that of European Field Marshals, and on a visit to Queen Victoria in 1897 a suit. On this occasion, the magazine *Tailor and Cutter* commented that "it can be seen at a glance that his clothes were made by an English tailor. The King, judged by his dress, looks like a typical English gentleman." It did have a few minor criticisms of the silk-facing of his lapels. His Queen was portrayed in a silk dress, acceptable within the canons of European taste, but clearly inspired by the costumes of northern Thailand. His young sons wore sailor suits.[25] Later, in the 1940s, in his own attempts to strengthen Thai society, the Prime Minister (and effectively dictator) Marshal Phibun Songkhram imposed fines for those wearing their shirts outside their trousers and required all men to wear hats in the street – which led to the ridiculous situation that it became possible to hire hats from the local street traders for the duration of a police raid.[26] In the nature of things, subsequent regimes have been concerned to stress the glories of Thai heritage, also in matters sartorial.

More concerted efforts were made in the countries of Western Asia, notably Turkey and Persia. The politics of dress were peculiarly sharp for reasons which go back to two of the *Hadith* (sayings) of the prophet, to the effect that "He who copies others, becomes one of them" and that the turban is the barrier between belief and unbelief. Particularly head-covering, first for men and later for women, has been seen a symbol of, in particular, religious adherence. In Turkish, the phrase "to put on a hat" (*şapka giymek*) came to take on the meaning "to apostatize from Islam", to become a Christian.[27] Women could allegedly demand divorce on the grounds that their husband had worn a hat while in Europe, and had thus abandoned Islam.[28] The result is that there is no area of the world in which the relationship between religion, politics and dress has been as sharp, or as bloody.

Clothing within the Ottoman empire had long been a source of tension and of political conflict. In the mid-sixteenth century, Suleiman the Lawgiver issued specific rules for the headgear of his officials, of the military, of the religious leaders and of the "ordinary classes", who had to wear a simple turban. He appropriated to himself a form of headgear which could henceforth only be worn by the Sultan.[29] Over the centuries that followed, a whole range of further ordinances were issued, which tended to accentuate and to mark difference. They could thus be used by the subject communities of the Empire to claim recognition, and thus protection, from the state, and by the elites within such communities to ensure their own subordinate domination. Such individuals are described by Donald Quataert as prompting the state "to promulgate or enforce" such regulations.[30] More generally, though, successive sultans attempted to curb the display and the luxury of the Istanbul elite, generally without success, in the hope of re-establishing the proper social order. As has been the case ever since Eve, it was the women who got the blame, being accused of bankrupting their husbands in the pursuit of luxury and status. Trying to control such expenditure was a standard practice of Sultans at the beginning of their reigns, at a time when their individual authority was low. At the same time, these were vain attempts to rein in the burgeoning commercial life of Istanbul, which was increasingly providing opportunities for accumulation over which the Sultan had no control, but from which his officials, much closer to the sources of wealth, could profit.

From the last decade of the eighteenth century, two successive Sultans, Selim III and Mahmud II, attempted to reorganize their empires, and in particular their military forces, in part by instituting new forces with new uniforms. Selim was not able to carry through his reforms, and impose his new headgear on the army, which eventually, in 1806, mutinied and deposed him, a death sentence for any sultan. Mahmud, again beginning his reign in weakness, was eventually able to launch what amounted to a government coup, with his new army massacring the Janissaries, who had been the mainstay of Ottoman military might but, as that ebbed away, had become a conservative bulwark. Then, with the support of the Islamic clergy (the *ulema*), he proceeded in 1829 to overhaul completely the dress regulations which had been largely fossilized since the days of Suleiman. In part this entailed the meticulous enumeration of the dress, and even the riding attire, of at least seventeen grades of religious and secular officials, in order to curb extravagance. It did, however, impose on the secular officials Western dress, including a frock coat, white starched and collared shirts, pantaloons, and neckties. Mahmud also trimmed his beard, and required his officials to do the same.[31] Most notably, it imposed a single form of headgear on all men, a flat-topped, slightly tapering cylinder of stiff felt, topped with a red silk tassel, in other words the fez.[32]

The fez, importantly, had no peak or brim, so that wearers could pray in the approved fashion, with their foreheads touching the ground. Nevertheless, it was to be worn by everyone, irrespective of their religion. The only group who refused to don the fez were the *ulema*. It was also initially rejected by those who stood to lose by a relaxation of the privileging of Muslims, notably the Istanbul artisanate, alongside the elite who were the main targets of Mahmud's reforms. In the riots about the introduction of the fez some ten people are said to have been killed. State pressure, and a number of concessions, quickly led to its adoption by these groups. Otherwise, it became a marker, not so much of Islam, as of the subjects of the sultan, and as such was popular with those who were discriminated against as adhering to other faiths or on the basis of class or other forms of status. The rich Christian and Jewish merchants were thus able to compete sartorially with the Muslims, and the subordinate was no longer marked as inferior by his dress. Mahmud's reforms, and the adoption of the fez, and later of the frock coat and pantaloons of the Western European bourgeoisie, came to mark a new Empire, with allegiance no longer merely to the Sultan as Caliph of the Faithful, but as leader of all his subjects.[33]

Mahmud's sartorial reforms were part of an attempt to refashion the Ottoman empire so that it could compete with Western Europe, primarily militarily. This was a concern which continued throughout the rest of the Sultanate's existence, and successive sultans attempted to build up a military and official corps able to cope in the new world. Education and a much greater exposure to the ways of Western Europe created a group, known as the Young Turks, who were at once highly nationalist and eager for what was then modernization. At the same time, the commercial developments and increased contacts with Western Europe led to the strengthening of the commercial bourgeoisie. This was reflected in dress. When they could, the Young Turks would put off the fez, and they would certainly wear Western-style suits. The women who were attached to the movement were also beginning to move to a more secular style of dress. In private, they would wear Western clothes, including waisted corsets – here a sign of liberation – and skirts in place of baggy trousers. In public, they even began to wear "risqué" veils, in effect no more than tailored coats with their faces covered by very transparent silk gauze. Indeed, once the revolutionary Young Turk movement had taken power in 1908, it was forced to send the military into Istanbul in order to control attacks on its women supporters who were appearing in the streets with their arms and legs uncovered, and who were directly addressing the men they came across.[34]

With this history in mind, it is perhaps only to be expected that within a century of its introduction, the fez was outlawed from Turkey as a symbol of backwardness, of the old order which had to be swept away if the country was to modernize. This was primarily the initiative of the founder of the new Turkey, Mustafa Kemal (Atatürk). When he himself had travelled to Europe, with a companion wearing a fez, they had felt humiliated, and their first action on reaching Paris was to buy European-style hats.[35] In the months after the abolition of the Caliphate in March 1924, as he came to power, he began himself to appear in public wearing a panama. As he proclaimed in a speech in August 1925,

> the Turkish people who founded the Turkish Republic are civi
> lized ... but ... the truly civilized people of Turkey must prove in fact
> that they are civilized. ... A civilized, international dress is worthy and
> appropriate for our nation, and we will wear it. Boots or shoes on our
> feet, trousers on our legs, shirt and tie, jacket and waistcoat – and of
> course, to complete these, a cover with a brim on our heads. I want to
> make this clear. This head-covering is called a "hat" (*şapka*).[36]

A cabinet decree was issued on 4 September, requiring all civil servants to wear "the costume common to the civilized nations of the world", the suit and hat. Some months later, on 25 November 1925, Law no. 671 was issued, which was entitled "Law concerning the Wearing of the Hat", which banned the fez and required all men to wear brimmed hats. Atatürk was backed in this by the then head of Religious Affairs, who said that there was nothing in the Koran or the *Hadith* to stipulate what clothes men should wear, so long as they

10 Mustafa Kemal Atatürk

were not donned to imitate the infidel.[37] This was probably actually what Atatürk intended, for the dress reforms were an integral part of his general project, to drag Turkey into what he believed to be the twentieth century, or the modern world. It was thus essential for him to eliminate the symbols of backwardness, as he perceived them.

Atatürk's example was followed by the other main modernizing autocrat of Western Asia, Reza Shah Pahlavi, who had himself raised to the position of Shah of Persia. As in Turkey, as Iranian men began to travel to Europe in the nineteenth century, they would take on European-style clothes, out of a feeling of self-consciousness, and indeed under Mohammad Shah Qajar (r. 1834–48), the Persian army was put in European uniforms – though these were seen as an adaptation of the ancient dress found in the bas-reliefs of the city of Persepolis, a claim to a common ancestry between Europe and pre-Islamic Iran.[38] Iranian society was beginning to bifurcate between those who were accepting what was seen as modernization, and for instance patronized the Parisian dressmakers who had set up in Teheran by the 1920s, and those who believed they stuck to the old ways. Shunning Western dress (both for the men and the women over whom they had influence) was a requirement for those who wished to be considered as potential jurists.[39]

After his accession, Reza Shah set about modernizing the country with all haste. This included major shifts in the dress rules. One of Reza Shah's political associates, and leading intellectuals, Ali Akbar Siassi, explained the reason for the actions. In part a single costume would unify the various ethnicities of the country, and the non-Muslim minorities would cease to be uneasy in their relations with each other and with the Muslims. However,

> the main reason of this policy, and main social problem being the Euro-peanization of the Persian, it was felt that the imitation of [the Euro-peans'] external appearance would not fail to facilitate the adoption of [European] ideas; that the Persian, by abandoning his long robe, his cloak, his bonnet, all of which seemed to serve as a symbol and as refuge for traditionalism, would definitely capitulate to the advance of Western civilization, to which he would thenceforth abandon himself without shame or constraint. And in fact, dressed in a short jacket and a hat with visor, he seems indeed less ill at ease in his march towards modern progress.[40]

Perhaps Siassi was being a bit disingenuous. Even though Reza at least was personally not irreligious, in their policies both Atatürk and Reza Shah were secular, anti-clerical Jacobins, concerned to reduce the power of the *ulema*. In the course of executing this policy, in 1929 Reza Shah issued edicts requiring all male Iranian subjects to wear "uniform dress", defined as a European suit and a Pahlavi hat, a cap closely resembling a French *képi*, which was later to be replaced by a felt fedora. The only ones excepted from this were the clerics, both Muslim and others, and by keeping a very close watch on those granted a "turban licence" Reza hoped to control those he saw as his major opponents.[41]

In both Turkey and Iran, women's dress became and has remained at least as contentious as that of men. Modernization was thought to require a break with the old sartorial order, and in particular the baring of some parts of women's bodies previously covered by layers of cloth. Women had generally been expected to dress so as to conceal the shape of their bodies, their hair and in places their faces from men who were not of their immediate family. In practice this meant that they had to wear some version of what has come to be known as a veil when in public. Even before the ending of the Sultanate, women of the urban middle class in Istanbul were beginning to appear in public wearing European-style clothing.[42] After Atatürk came to power, his vision of modernization entailed the redressing of Turkish womenfolk, although he did not enforce conformity. Ahmet Mumcu explained, long afterwards, what was supposed to have happened:

> When our women gained their rights, they cast off their medieval dress. Clad in modern mode, they took their places beside men. That strange costume ... in which our womenfolk had been unwillingly wrapped, soon disappeared in the course of natural development. The Turkish reforms used no compulsion in this matter. Claiming their own rights, our womenfolk put an end to this *affront* to their self-respect.[43]

Things are never as clear-cut as the ideologues would have it, but there can be no doubt that until the 1960s there was a steady move towards unveiling by Turkish women, in the framework of the expansion and legitimation of the secular state.

In Iran, matters ran differently. Reza Shah, authoritarian as in everything, felt impelled to require the unveiling of Iranian women. There can be no doubt that the reign of Reza Shah did much to improve the position of Iranian women, and to give them the opportunity for education and a degree of emancipation, at least from the power of the *ulema*. The opportunity to go about unveiled formed part of this. It is symbolically appropriate that the first occasion where the royal family appeared unveiled was at the opening ceremony of the teacher training college. The Shah himself found it personally difficult. His daughter once commented that Reza had to "put aside his strong personal feelings in the interest of bringing progress to his country". His wife recounted that he had told her that, for him, death was preferable "to a life in which he had to show his wife bare-headed to strangers, but he had no choice, as otherwise Iranians will be thought to be savage and backward".[44] This was perhaps the reason why he was so vehement in his drive to move Iranian women from head and body covering into European hats, coats and skirts. The shame, if that is what it was, had to be shared.

The point was, of course, that the modernization of Iran was felt to require the sidelining of the religious authorities. This made the policy particularly sharply enunciated. From early 1936, local officials were ordered to ensure that all Iranian women emulated the royal family in their display. Government officials were given grants to allow their wives to buy new clothes. Those who turned up at official receptions without their (unveiled) wives were reprimanded and fired. It was made illegal for women wearing veils to enter shops, bath-houses, cinemas, to ride in cars or horse-drawn carriages, to receive treatment in public clinics or to draw a salary. There was only one exception. In the best tradition of the sumptuary laws, the only group who were not required to remove their veils were the prostitutes. In the words of H. E. Chehabi, "the symbol of virtue was to become a symbol of vice".[45]

Reaction was heavy, and was crushed. The centre of opposition, to both the hat rules and the imminent unveiling, was the Gowharshad mosque at Mashad, under the leadership of Aqa Hoseim Qomi. In July 1935, demonstrators gathered there, and were dispersed by troops, with much loss of life. An enforced change of clothing was seen as an enforced change of faith, and thus something worth dying for, just as modernization was something worth killing for. It was an event that lived on in Iran through the rest of Reza Shah's reign, until he was forced to abdicate in 1941, and through that of his son. Although Mohammed Shah Pahlavi had learned something from his father, and gradually relaxed the ban on veiling, he too was forced into exile, with the revolution begun by the return of the Imam Khomeini in 1979. One of the first acts of the new regime was to enforce what had been banned in 1936. Another was to arrest and execute General Iraj Matbu'i, then in his eighties, who, forty-four years earlier, had led the assault on the Gowharshad mosque. As H. E. Chehabi drily commented, there is "no statute of limitation in revolutionary justice".[46]

9

The Clothing of Colonial Nationalism

In 1930 Monica Hunter was a young anthropologist doing fieldwork in Pondoland in the South African Transkei, and living in a European-owned trading store. She described one of the main ways in which she acquired her information as follows:

> The trader's wife made the cotton skirts which Pondo women wear; customers used to arrive in the morning, order a skirt, and wait until it was finished. The women were in the habit of chatting with my hostess, who was extremely popular, I was accepted as her sister, and shared the goodwill shown to her. Sitting in a corner of the store, I listened to the gossip and joined in the conversation.[1]

She commented further that European trade goods had completely replaced skins as clothing, although the depression of the 1930s had sent a number of people back into skins.

> All through Western Pondoland pagan women wear flared cotton skirts, white or stained with ochre, and trimmed with as many rows of braid as they can afford, up to thirty-six. They are particular about the cut. Women coming to the store would try on a dozen skirts before they were satisfied. Husbands came to inspect the trying one. Men sometimes walked thirty miles to buy a "Paris model". They would get some girl to act as mannequin and study the skirts critically. A breast-cloth and cloak of white sheeting, embroidered in black with geometric designs, completes a Nyandeni woman's costume.

Pagan men would wear "a cotton loin-cloth, a woollen blanket flung over one shoulder, and a felt hat". However, even those who had not adopted full European clothing in the countryside, in part because they rejected Christianity, when they moved to the city of East London, they had to wear "trousers and some body covering", and "the women also adopt European dress". There the once-married women rivalled each other in their dress, and "parade the streets in great finery. One Sunday there was a fight between two who had quarrelled as to which was better dressed."[2]

At the end of the 1930s, Monica Hunter had married Godfrey Wilson, and the two of them did fieldwork in the zinc-mining town of Broken Hill, now renamed Kabwe, in what was to become Zambia. In his report on the lives of the miners Godfrey noted that over half of their cash income went on clothes. (Food and lodging were provided by their employers.) Their usual answer to his question "What made you leave the country?" was "nakedness". In a wonderful passage he wrote:

> Every African man of whatever social group tries to dress smartly for strolling round the town, or for visiting in his spare time, and loves to astonish the world with a new jacket, or a new pair of trousers of distinguished appearance. Women behave in the same way; and they judge husbands and lovers largely according to the amounts of money they are given by them to spend on clothes. Clothes are discussed unceasingly, in much the same way that I have heard primitive villagers discuss their cattle; they are tended lovingly and carefully housed in boxes at night. It is largely by accumulating clothes that men save. Clothes . . . are the chief medium in which obligations to country relatives are fulfilled. The Africans of Broken Hill are not a cattle people, nor a goat people, nor a fishing people, nor a tree cutting people, they are a dressed people.

These clothes were purchased in European- and Indian-owned stores, which in turn bought in clothes from Japan (at least before the war), America and Europe. There were also English firms who sold clothes by mail order, "cash on delivery", to the Africans of Kabwe. They were displayed in many places, but above all while ballroom dancing in the clubs.[3] The indications are that European clothes were already to be found deep in the Zambian countryside, despite the problems of the depression which hit the mining industry during the 1930s. Missionaries were writing cautionary tales in which the villain was the young man who went to town and returned wearing what was seen as uncoordinated and garish clothing, instead of diligently attending their school. In the early 1930s when J. Merle Davis travelled through the country he noted that

> the former nakedness or bark cloth garments have given place to a medley of gaudy trade cotton garments covering the body indifferently

from shoulder to knee, and the blankets when the nights are cold. This has been slightly supplemented in recent years by nondescript cast-off apparel and cheap factory-made clothing brought in by returning mine and domestic workers.

Certainly the accounts given by these migrant workers of what they purchased always stressed the importance of clothing.[4]

What the Wilsons, two of the most acute ethnographers of the early twentieth century, were describing was part of a major shift in the material culture of southern and eastern Africa which was effected between the 1880s – earlier in some parts of South Africa – and the 1950s, though in most parts of the continent it had been completed before then. This entailed the virtually complete reclothing of half a continent, and also the remaking of a whole variety of other articles of consumption, particularly in housing and the domestic interior, and of care for the body. Surprisingly this change has been remarkably little addressed by historians.[5]

To stay with dress, or rather cloth, there had been a tradition of producing and wearing bark cloth, at least in the damper areas of Africa.[6] There was also a degree of cotton cloth production in a variety of coastal areas of eastern Africa. Fine raffia cloth was woven in the Comoro Islands, and in Pate, in northern Kenya, silk clothing was unravelled and rewoven.[7] In the coastal towns of the Swahili, these cloths were worn together with imported stuffs in ways which befitted an Islamic society, with the aristocratic women and men well covered, and able to display the latest fashions and their wealth through their clothes, including, for the men, their silken turbans. The slaves, both men and women, were draped in a single piece of cloth around the waist.[8]

From the nineteenth century, the commercial wealth of East Africa began to increase, primarily as a result of the ivory trade, although exports of gum copal (for varnish) and hides were also of importance. The result was a sharp increase in the import of cloth into the region, particularly merikani, unbleached cotton produced in Salem (Massachussetts), where the East African market encouraged the building of the largest cotton mill, and the first to be powered by steam, in the United States. After the American Civil War, however, the New England merchants lost their prime position on the East African coast, and were replaced by Indians, working out of Mumbai (Bombay). Initially they mainly re-exported English unbleached sheeting, in the nearest equivalent of merikani, but increasingly mills in Mumbai and elsewhere on the subcontinent were producing the cloth in question. By 1888, some 15 million yards of cloth, English-made and locally produced, was being exported from Mumbai to

Zanzibar. East Africa had become the major overseas destination for the products of Indian industry.[9]

From at least the 1890s onwards, merikani cloths were block-printed in black and red – and later in all imaginable colours – to create what are known as kangas, highly coloured cloths sold by the pair and used mainly by women and girls as body wraps, and also for carrying babies, as sleeping sheets and so forth. Many of them are printed with various sayings in Swahili, to allow a degree of silent, but not wordless, communication between the women who wear them and their husbands, lovers or more generally. It is one of those occasions where communication through clothing is more specific than usual, and, with the T-shirts of the modern West, is one of the few major traditions where language in the restricted sense has been incorporated into the wider language of dress.[10]

Outside the coastal regions of East Africa, there were many areas which had not been reached by either the materials or the principles of Islamic, or for that matter Christian, dress before the beginning of the twentieth century. The best worked out case concerns the Luo, whose home territory was, and is, the lands in western Kenya running down to Victoria Nyanza. When European colonization reached this area, in particular with the coming of the railway to Kisumu in 1906, the Luo had an elaborated code of dress and body decoration. Married men wore a "small piece of goat skin" and married women a loincloth and a tail of strings, and in both cases it would have been considered very bad manners to appear before one's husband or mother-in-law (for the men, and perhaps also for the women) without them. For the rest, bodily ornamentation consisted of cicatrization, flashy ostrich-feather headdresses, body paint and wire armlets. As the Kenyan climate did not require further protection, this was considered to be decoration and modesty enough.[11]

As colonization took hold, there was pressure from both officials and from the missionaries for the men and women under their influence to cover their nudity. This did not, however, mean the adoption of European clothing, certainly not for men. Rather, Luo chiefs were expected to take on a dress style which found its basis in the Zanzibari court, not in that of the King-Emperor in London. They were issued with the kanzu, a nightshirt-like cotton garment reaching down to the knees, an embroidered jacket and a fez, and they took to boots. The idea, clearly, was to ensure that Africans remained exotic, if no longer offensive to Western eyes, and did not seem to be black Europeans. Women at the mission stations were attracted by a piece of cloth round the waist, and were soon taught to sew simple dresses, but they were more often encouraged to wrap what amounted to a kanga around their bodies. Above all they were expected not to acquire any new scarification or other such bodily enhancement.[12]

The European distrust of Africans in Western clothes was complemented by that of "traditionalist" Africans for their fellows in any clothes whatsoever. Bodies washed with soap were thought of as stinking. The real purpose of hiding the body could only be to hide the marks of a terrible disease, or of witchcraft. Moreover, clothes subverted the proper order of society. Dressed women were evidently not accepting the authority of their husbands and fathers. Many husbands indeed refused to buy clothes for their wives and even destroyed such dresses as the latter might have acquired. According to one observer, a European woman, "it is generally accepted that once a native woman adopts European dress, she sheds her morals".[13] The Government began to favour young men in kanzus, with a modicum of education, over the old and naked. This led for a while to a reaction from the Jokoyo, the "real men of culture", and from those of the young who felt that the Christians had no fun. But it was the Jonanga, the people with clothes, who were acknowledged as the modernizers, the men and women with the future. In the first instance they were likely to be migrant labourers, returning with khaki shorts and shirts, and equally "readers" at the missions. The result was that within a generation western Kenyan men and women were almost all dressed in European-style attire. By 1927, there were said to be seventy-two tailors with sewing machines, producing mainly for women, as men tended to buy ready-to-wear. A decade later, according to a survey made by the district commissioner for Central Kavirondo district, just under 60 per cent of all consumer purchases in his district, the Luo heartland, went on clothing, a figure which rises to over 70 per cent if expenditure on production goods such as ploughs, agricultural equipment and fishing nets are excluded.[14] The Luo had become a dressed people, to the extent that by the 1980s a well-educated young man of Luo extraction was shocked to discover that a collection of photographs in a museum "show us naked as the day we were born, naked, without any clothes. I can't believe that we Luo went about naked and without shame."[15]

One question raised by this story is: why were both the missionaries and the colonial officials so concerned that the Luo notables and converts should not dress in standard European clothing? It is easiest to approach this by way of the answer to the converse question. The Luo took on shirts, shoes, socks and trousers because they were seen as signs of modernity. The converse was that the British, whether missionaries or colonial officials, did not want Africans to be modern. They were much more comfortable, at the beginning of the twentieth century, with "traditional" African societies and individuals. In the run-up to the formulation of ideas of indirect rule, by which the British attempted to rule Africa by maintaining what they believed to be the indigenous institutions of pre-colonial society,[16] this was in general a more suitable way to operate.

The attempt to establish "indirect rule", and thus to favour various forms of indigeneity, or at least of non-Britishness, was in part a consequence of the rise of African elite groups, in both South and West Africa, who claimed full acceptance into the system of the British Empire. These were the groups who had taken on board fully the messages of earlier generations of British colonists, acquiring education and generally becoming Christian, although the category did include Muslims in Cape Town and adherents of Yoruba religion in Lagos, among others. Often they were of slave descent, both in the Cape and among the Saro, who had descended from those who had been recaptured from slave ships and put on shore in Sierra Leone. Others were simply those who had converted to Christianity, or their second generation descendants, both in West Africa and in the Eastern Cape. On the Gold Coast they were frequently the descendants of the mulatto children of English and Dutch traders and administrators, and many had European surnames. They were the first black doctors, lawyers and journalists in the various colonies, and they formed the core of a nationalist elite, from at least the 1880s onwards.

The political claims, to equality within the British Empire, of these elites were backed by sartorial claims. The photographs which were taken of these groups in the course of the later nineteenth century invariably show them dressed as English ladies and gentlemen. As good an example as any other can be seen in the section of photographs in André Odendaal's *Vukani Bantu! The Beginnings of Black Protest Politics in South Africa to 1912*.[17] As could be expected, this includes portraits of all the most important black political leaders in South Africa around the beginning of the twentieth century, at least those who acted within the idiom of colonial society.[18] Without exception the men had themselves photographed in dark suits, white shirts and ties and shiny black shoes with socks. These men were projecting an image of absolute respectability, and almost of innocence. This, of course, was precisely the point. They were mainly from the Cape Colony, and therefore had the vote. The essence of their campaigning was for equality with the whites, both within the Cape and in the other states that were to make up the Union of South Africa in 1910. They were thus demonstrating their level of civilization, according to the concepts of the wider colonial society in which they were active, and at the same time their distance from the "raw blanket" Africans, who had not put on the benefits of European civilization. What appears to be innocence was thus a thoroughly calculated piece of political rhetoric. It was seen as such by their opponents, and thus rejected.

One of Odendaal's photographs is of Dinizulu ka Cetshwayo, the Zulu King, dressed in hat, shirt and collar, and what looks like a three-piece suit. In this case, it was part of a clear strategy by which successive Zulu monarchs had themselves presented, to European audiences, as modernizing and powerful figures. They had learnt to manipulate the image, not merely in the metaphorical way that all successful politicians do, but also that presented by the camera and the literal image on paper.[19]

In West Africa, as elites began to emerge in the cities of Freetown, Lagos and Accra, the same process developed. In Freetown, from the 1860s if not earlier, women were wearing crinolines and high-heeled boots and men were ordering their suits from the London tailors who were advertising in the *African Times*. Others no doubt had to make do with the products of the local tailors, but these men produced dark broadcloth suits, however unsuitable for the tropical climate.[20] In Accra, by the 1880s there was what was known as the "frock coat class" of Western-educated elite lawyers, setting them off from the traditionalist "cloth portion" of the Gold Coast's capital.[21] In Lagos, too, it was claimed that the Bible and the tie appeared simultaneously. Missionaries were even claiming that the dress of the Christians was a "badge of distinction" setting them off from the rest of African society, and thereby raising a barrier against conversion – this in contrast to the openness of Islam.[22] In a study of what seems to have been an elite, educated, Christian Lagos family, with jobs in the colonial service or elsewhere in the formal sector, Betty M. Wass has shown that by 1900 European dress was very general, and was kept through at least until World War II. Indeed, one of the ways by which the elite set themselves apart from the rest of the African population was through their "consumption of ideal and material goods such as European clothing and furniture".[23] The display of clothing at fashionable weddings was particularly extravagant.[24] The social argument was that, because English culture was seen to be superior, it was necessary for "easy and free native cloth, toga and sandals" to give way to "costly and inconvenient dress, boots, shoes and hats".[25]

In the end, this tactic did not succeed as was to have been hoped, at least within the British Empire. Colonial African elites saw themselves as, and hoped to be seen as, British. They worshipped as such, wrote as such, and dressed as such. British colonialism from the later nineteenth century did not accept the Africans as British. In the increasingly illiberal world of the Cape Colony, let alone in the rest of South Africa, white society was certainly blocking the advancement of the Christian amaXhosa of the Eastern Cape, or of the Christian and Muslim educated Coloureds of Cape Town. When the South African War (1899–1902) led to the incorporation of all South Africa into the British Empire, the hopes of these groups for British Imperial recognition were never taken seriously, compared with the necessity, as the imperialists saw it, of bringing the Afrikaners back into the fold, and imposing the political and social segregation which both Dutch- and English-speaking whites desired. In West Africa, too, as quinine made it more possible for Europeans to survive on the coast, colonial society became more segregated. Creoles were driven out of government service. The idea of Indirect Rule, which was being developed from around 1900, had no place for Africans who seemed to have rejected the "tribal" societies through which the British now wanted to rule their Empire, particularly not when those Africans might be trained lawyers well capable of challenging the rule of those who thought themselves to be inviolate,[26] and who attempted to demonstrate that inviolability through their own dress and through the rituals surrounding it.[27] The main architect of Indirect Rule, Frederick, Lord Lugard, specifically complained about those missionaries who encouraged their converts to wear European clothes, and was no doubt happy with the solution found among the Luo.[28]

African elites in both southern and western Africa reacted to this betrayal politically in much the same ways, with the establishment of nationalist politics. Sartorially, though, two different strategies were employed. In the South, where there was no indigenous tradition of dress which could be adapted to the decencies of twentieth-century life, African nationalists have generally remained true to the claims for equality which were made at the beginning of the century. This was as true for the Zimbabweans in mid-century as it was for the South Africans, although on occasion their clothing has, together with world trends, become substantially less formal.[29] This lasted up till the Great Transformation of South African politics in the 1990s. "The story is told of the 1991 gaffe when Mayor David. N. Dinkins of New York and his entourage arrived for cocktails at Winnie Mandela's house in long, colourful caftans. The (African National Congress) elite met them in their uniform: dark business suits." The New Yorkers are said to have been asked if they thought they were visiting Cameroon.[30] In post-apartheid South Africa, there have been attempts to Africanize clothing, particularly that worn by women, which is in general more mutable anyway. Nelson Mandela, whose semi-saintly status has given him freedoms beyond those of even normal politicians, regularly wore colourful silk shirts, but even he would revert to a business suit on particular ritual occasions.[31] His successor, as we have seen, has rarely been seen in anything else, and the new young black elite are not for nothing known as "Armani socialists".

In Anglophone West Africa, matters were very different. Nationalism took pride, at least in part, in African forms of dress. As early as 1887, a Dress Reform Society was founded among the creoles of Freetown, under the patronage of the most distinguished West African cultural nationalist of the time, Edward Blyden, to propagate the wearing of loose cotton robes instead of British-style suits. It did not take hold, however, it is said because the womenfolk of Freetown did not want to be associated with such unfashionable, and backward, clothing.[32] In Lagos and Accra, in contrast, a measure of sartorial nationalism took deeper root.

Obviously the first condition for such nationalism was a deeper tradition of weaving and clothing with which the potential cultural nationalists could identify. In both Ghana and Nigeria, cloth was woven, mainly from cotton, in substantial quantities. In Nigeria, it was often dyed in indigo, with complicated forms of resist dying to produce intricate patterns. When in 1861 the traveller and British consul Richard Burton visited Abeokuta, to the north of Lagos, he noted that "people are tolerably well clothed. Dressy men wore *shogoto*, or loose cotton drawers fastened above the hips ... and extending to the knee. The body was covered with a cloth gracefully thrown like a plaid over the shoulder."[33]

The great Yoruba historian Samuel Johnson devoted several pages of his *History of the Yorubas* to describing the variations in costume among the Yoruba, both men and women, which were, of course, heavily dependent on the owner's income. It was a fashion-conscious society, both in the details and in larger matters, as for instance, in the adoption of *agbada* gowns from Hausaland to the north, in the course of the nineteenth century.[34] In Ghana, large cloths were also painted or stamped, but the major form of artistic production was of *kente*, whereby narrow strips were woven from coloured yarn, in complicated patterns, and then sewn together to produce highly decorative – and highly expensive – cloths, which were then draped round the body. It was said to be one of the demonstrations of the power and wealth of the Asantehene, the ruler of Ghana's major kingdom, that he never appeared in public in the same cloth twice.[35] Moreover, in both places, cloth had been long imported from Europe, and from the early part of the nineteenth century European manufacturers began to produce dyed cloths specifically for the African market. These were usually produced as wax prints, and were highly specific. The designs were often influenced by West African designs. Thus, the Nigerian market would be supplied with material dyed as if by indigo; the Ghanaian with more orange and black in the colouring. These

became a cheaper, but not very cheap, alternative to the local manufactures, and again could form the basis of an indigenizing clothing
style.[36]

In Lagos, there developed a major move towards a rejection of
European clothing, from the 1880s onwards. There were a number of
men, including clergymen who had rejected, or been rejected by, the
Anglican church, and the association of teachers, who began to adopt
"full native dress".[37] Certain others of unimpeachable elite status,
both men and women, took to wearing various versions of Yoruba
dress. The argument was clear, in its way. As the main paper of the
city editorialized, millions of "genuine Africans on the continent have
not found it necessary to adopt the [European] attire. . . . The Euro-
peanised African is a nondescript, a libel on his country, and a blot
on civilisation. . . . In the world around and above us every beast has
its skin and every foul its feathers."[38] It was not always straightfor-
ward. One lawyer wrote that health in West Africa "was impaired and
lives shortened by the adoption of European tastes, customs and
habits, materials and forms of dress", but did not himself change his
regular costume.[39] Another man, Adegboyega Edun, who had changed
his name from Jacob Henryson Samuel, only wore Yoruba dress when
in England, and remained in European suits while in Nigeria.[40] But
slowly, even the most Westernized of the Nigerian elite came to take
on various forms of West African dress.[41] Equally, in the Gold Coast,
Kobena Sekyi, a coastal lawyer, is said, in the family tradition, to have
been subjected to racist insults when wearing a suit while being
trained in London during World War I. In consequence, he vowed
never to wear European clothing again, and became the first lawyer
in the colony to appear in court in a cloth.[42] Later nationalists were
not as consequent. Kwame Nkrumah wore both cloth and European
dress as occasion suited him, but on the most important moments he
would be clad in *kente*, and for the formal photographs, his first cabi-
nets all wore *kente*.[43]

What was happening throughout the British West African colonies
was of course the assumption of African styles of clothing as ceremonial, formal wear – and later the incorporation of African cloth and
dress styles into the repertoire of fashion designers.[44] For daily dress
the productions of the artisanate could not compete with industrially
manufactured cottons. In 1937 a missionary lamented how in Gover-
ment-aided schools in Nigeria, students were increasingly having to
wear a school uniform. European dress was "practically compulsory"
for teachers, and in effect for government clerks. And at leisure,
"When young Africans take up English sports . . . and get up dances
in European style – where men and women wear evening dress – they

11 Kwame Nkrumah (left) with a member of his cabinet

receive an amount of attention from Europeans that they would never arouse by doing something purely 'African'."[45]

The pulls of modernity and of political statement could run in opposite directions. Indeed, tellingly, Judith Byfield noted that the "women's pages" of even the most nationalist of Nigerian newspapers, the *West African Pilot*, were entirely concerned with European dress.[46] The editors had no difficulty, apparently, in providing what they thought was wanted.

Similar processes of the sartorial politics becoming intertwined with anti-colonial nationalism were to be found widely, most notably perhaps in the Indian subcontinent. Nationalist politics in general, and its sartorial aspects in particular, were transformed by the return from South Africa of Mohendas Gandhi in 1915. Gandhi had originally been a dapperly dressed lawyer, very concerned about making the right impression when he arrived in London for his studies, but while in South Africa he had begun to develop a style of political agitation based on self-denial and various forms of non-violent civil disobedience which did not accord with well-cut English suits. Already while in South Africa he had begun to wear various forms of white cotton attire for his political actions. Once back in India, he experimented with the peasant dress of his home region, with which he had little affinity as a scion of a prosperous merchant family, before adopting the loincloth, if necessary accompanied by a shawl, in and for which he became famous.

Gandhi's particular attire was not widely followed, even as his power within the Indian nationalist movement increased. In the end it had too many connotations of social egalitarianism to be acceptable, and moreover it suggested a claim to sainthood – which Gandhi himself hotly denied. What did spread, and become the symbol of the nationalist movement, was the stuff from which it was made. This was *khadi*, homespun, undyed cotton woven on a hand loom and in India. Each nationalist was enjoined to spin cotton for at least half an hour a day, in part as meditation and in part in order to provide competition for the English machine-made cloth which by this time had penetrated most of the subcontinent, driving the local weavers into poverty. Gandhi hoped that the general wearing of *khadi* would unite Indians of all backgrounds. In the event, it could not, as the distinctions between Muslim, Hindu and Sikh, let alone all the various divisions in any given district, were far too great. Rather the wearing of *khadi* became the badge of the Indian National Congress, though each nationalist found a personal way in which to interpret it. Thus the Nehru family, over the generations the most prominent Indian nationalist family, wore *khadi* cut and tailored in the style of their forebears, the Hindu service elite (of Kashmiri origin) in the Muslim courts of the north Indian plains.[47] This is what has since become known as the Nehru jacket.

With the attainment of independence, the message which had to be conveyed by the clothing of the ruling elite of the new nation was different, and moreover the Gandhian ideal of creating uniformity

12 Jawaharlal Nehru and Mahatma Gandhi

through dress was evidently doomed. The alternative, as propagated
by Jawaharlal Nehru, the first prime minister, was to develop a sartorial equivalent to the motto "Unity in Diversity". Although at times
he and other members of his family would wear a Gandhi cap (which
the Mahatma himself had only very temporarily worn), the main
stress, as he wrote in an official note to his higher officials, was to
avoid European clothes "which marked them out as a privileged,
denationalised, and out-of-date class, and to adopt such clothes as
would take them closer to the people".[48] In the long term, though,
Indian elite males have tended increasingly to wear versions of European clothing styles, except for high formal moments when, as Nehru
himself did, they put on those clothes appropriate to the region and
social status from which their family originated – at least if in so doing
they are not revealing a background of which they might not be
proud. But of course some markers are not to be avoided. Manmohan
Singh, Prime Minister of India since 2004, a Sikh, would never be seen
without the turban which is in fact one of the markers (though not
strictly one of the duties) of his faith.

For women, as ever, matters ran differently. Colonial society had been heavily segregated by sex. For virtually all Indian women there was no incentive to put on European dress, and only the danger that by doing so they would cause aspersions to be cast on their virtue. Equally, there were relatively few who took sufficient part in the nationalist struggle for it to be incumbent upon them to wear *khadi*, although some members of the major families did so. Indeed there were women whose prominence within the nationalist movement gave them, as it were, the licence to continue to wear silk saris dyed into rich colours. After independence, most Indian women have continued to wear saris as a matter of course, although the young and unmarried, certainly in towns, will increasingly wear European-style tops and often jeans. What is most significant in this regard has been the spread of the *shalwar kamiz*, a top and trousers originally from the Punjab which is the national (female) dress of Pakistan. This has the advantage that it does not suggest marriage and fertility in the way the sari does, and is thus more appropriate in a society where the age at marriage for women is increasing significantly. Remarkably, the Islamic connotations which this outfit once had are dissipating, and it has become perhaps a prime symbol for the new India in the process of creation, modern but not forgetful of its roots – but of course like all such nations forgetful of some of its roots, and of the sectarian conflicts which still rend the country.[49]

Two other Asian countries showed significant contrasts with the pattern in both Africa and India. In Sri Lanka,[50] driven by similar impulses as in much of Africa, the elite from the later nineteenth century took to demonstrating their modernization by wearing the same sorts of suits, ties and hats as their British colonial masters. This was a reaction against the British attempts to hold the Sinhalese in a state of sartorial fossilization, as a way to contain nationalism. As late as 1935, the *Ceylon Government Gazette* issued extensive sumptuary regulations for the various ranks of Kandyan court officials.[51] Eventually there emerged a movement for the creation of a national dress, articulated for instance by the British philosopher (of partial Sinhalese descent), A. K. Coomaraswamy, for whom the rejection of British-style clothing was primarily an aesthetic matter, not one driven by ideas of national political economy.[52] By the 1920s a form of national dress was being created, for both men and women. Women were increasingly expected to wear saris according to the style developed by the kingdom of Kandy, although it was thought not correct for women of the higher classes to wear a blouse of any colour except white. For men a version of the sarong, preferably white, should cover the lower body, while for the torso a long banian[53] was enjoined. It was a costume which was based on that of the Buddhist farmers, and would not have entailed a major shift for it to be adopted. Wearing trousers was thought to be Portuguese, wearing combs in the hair (a privilege of some high Sinhalese castes) to be Indonesian, and "a hat wrapped in cloth, comb, collar tie, banian, shirt, vestcoat, coat, trousers, cloth socks, shoes all at the same time" was "a ludicrous dress", but evidently not impossible.[54] There were politicians who did wear such clothing on ceremonial occasions and in public before Independence. There were also those who, for instance, appeared at school in such attire, instead of the prescribed uniform, and, as they hoped, were severely dealt with. However, national dress was by no means universal. Indeed, at the moment of the Independence ceremonies, the new Prime Minister, D. S. Senanayake, was resplendent in his black top hat and tailcoat, pin-stripe trousers and, no doubt, highly polished black shoes.

The post-Independence vicissitudes of Sinhalese national dress are instructive. The more leftist, or at least populist, regime of S. W. R. D. Bandaranaike, coming into office in 1956, distinguished itself from its more elitist and Westernized predecessors by systematically wearing cloth and banian. However, national dress came to be seen as the preserve of one particular group, the Sinhalese Buddhists. The grip which they had on power was too great for the expression of local origin through dress to be unchallenging, as, to some extent it has become in India. As Nira Wickramasinghe comments, ethnic "minority leaders often preferred wearing the western coat and trousers at formal occasions".[55] And even there it has been declining. Some politicians have used national dress either to hide their elitist origins, or to stress their popular credentials. The national dress has been downplayed, and the cloth generally replaced by a pair of – admittedly white – trousers. The rebel Tamil leaders have rigourously refused any form of ethnic dress, and demonstrated their revolutionary intentions by donning a variation of the combat fatigues and beret made famous by Che Guevara. And outside politics, and some major life-cycle ceremonies such as weddings, the basis of male national dress has almost disappeared. No longer do men in the rural areas of Sri Lanka wear sarongs, though women of all classes wear saris. Social mobility and the desire to emulate the rich has led to almost all men donning trousers. National dress has become folklore, with the not impossible connotation that it can be revived as "ethnic chic".[56]

In the Philippines, too, the dialectic between the adoption of Western dress and the creation of various forms of national costume has been complicated, and highly gendered. In the first half of the twentieth century, under American rule, Filipino men who wished to appear modern would wear what was then known as an *Americana*

– a suit of jacket and trousers. This was the classic colonial statement of equality with the colonial masters. As against this, women in prominent positions wore the *terno*, a long dress with characteristic butterfly sleeves, which had developed out of Hispanicized clothing from the eighteenth century on. At times it was made of *piña*, a light, near enough transparent cloth made of pineapple fibres, generally heavily embroidered. It was accompanied by a *pañuela*, a cloth draped to veil the breasts. As time went on, though, the *pañuela* disappeared, and the *terno* became essentially a specific national form of dress, one of a number of possible styles including local versions of Islamic dress. But the specifically Filipino forms of female attire are held to have symbolized women's absence from the public sphere, and their modest status as wife and mother. Even the Filipino suffragists wore such dress, to avoid exposing themselves to unnecessary ridicule and opposition.[57]

After independence, achieved in the immediate wake of World War II, a remarkable cross-over occurred. First, leading men came to wear the *Barong Tagalog*, a loose shirt with long sleeves, often highly embroidered, which is worn outside the trousers and buttoned up to the throat. In 1953, Ramon Magsaysay became president after a campaign claiming to be "the man of the masses" and wore *Barong Tagalog* to his inauguration ceremony, to stress his distance from the old elite and his populist credentials. Since then, the *Barong Tagalog* has become the standard dress for Filipino men – at least when they are not just wearing T-shirt and jeans. It has become a way to express pride in Filipino identity, and as such has become essential for political display.

For women, in contrast, the *terno* has become problematic. In part this is a consequence of its having become the sartorial symbol of Imelda Marcos (in addition of course to her shoe collection, but her opponents could not be expected to go about barefoot in protest). More significantly, as women in the Philippines came to assert themselves in the public arena, they put aside those elements of dress which had come to represent their female subservience, and thus the specifically Filipino clothes of their mothers. For the new generation of women, American-style suits came to be what they had been for pre-war Filipino men, a way of claiming their right to operate as independent individuals. Thus Gloria Macapagal Arroyo was first inaugurated as President in a Western suit, expressing her desire to be considered an efficient professional economist. There remained, though, the necessity, in some contexts, of demonstrating Filipino identity. Eventually, on high ceremonial occasions, such as her second inauguration, President Arroyo has been prepared to wear a *terno*, perhaps because no one would any longer think of her as anything but a powerful individual. Others, including Filipino diplomats, have found the elegant solution of donning a somewhat feminized version of the *Barong Tagalog*, worn over black trousers.

It is necessary in this context to make two further points. The first is that the conceptual distinction between nationalism and ethnicity is hard to make. Outside Europe, in general, nationalism was the agitation against colonial rule and, later, the feeling towards the (postcolonial) state. Since these states are the building blocks of the world order, so nationalism is generally seen as legitimate. Ethnicity, in contrast, is an expression of attachment to some group, generally linguistically defined, which is not congruent with a modern nation-state, and thus in danger of being illegitimate, and a threat to those states. However, both nation and ethnicity – "tribe" in some contexts – are inventions, or intellectual creations, driven by much the same impulses, and ethnicity has often been a more powerful force.[58] It is thus not at all surprising that many of the processes which are discernible within the creation of nationalism are equally to be found in the sartorial histories of ethnicities. Certainly the use of dress to mark a particular ethnic identity has been very common. It is, after all, one of the clearest ways in which a group of people can establish themselves as different from some other group.[59] What is seen as ethnic dress is thus, almost by definition, distinct from the general pattern which has increasingly spread across the globe. The message it is meant to send out is of local affinity, not of universalism, or for that matter of adherence to the nation-state.

Nevertheless, since the process of incorporation into the nation-states of the world has been anything but smooth and unidirectional, and since so many of the world's states have had to recognize their multicultural foundation, and the politics of identity which this entails, ethnicity and ethnic dress have flourished. Perhaps as clear a case as any has been in the Andean nations of Latin America. It is an area in which the various forms of "traditional" dress, as they developed since the Spanish conquest, are very diverse, although often it is, as Carola Lentz commented, "a fossilised form of city dress".[60] It has been possible for folklorists to go from valley to valley and everywhere discover a distinct local costume.[61] In general, though, as people moved out of the highland villages they put off the clothes they had worn. Migrant labourers in the coastal plantations did not want to parade their Amerindian ethnicity – which was a sign of inferiority. Admittedly the clothes they chose, which they had falsely thought to be correct, marked them as country bumpkins. However, on returning to their natal villages, they would continue to wear the clothes they had worn on the coast, which marked them as sophisticated men and

– to a lesser extent – women of the world.[62] There were also whites who viewed those whom they knew to be Indians, but who wore European garb with disdain, as a sign that what they believed to be the proper order of society was breaking down. But equally, women from the highland villages, as they become politically aware and able to organize, will disparage those who do not know how to wear the *polleras*, the highly embroidered skirts of southern Peru, properly.[63] And presidential candidates, in both Peru and Bolivia, have been successful by parading their indigenous ancestry in their attire.

Secondly, there is a considerable and surprising degree of coincidence between the forms of colonial policy and the politics of dress. In the French African colonies, the rejection of creole elites never happened. From the mid-nineteenth century onwards, Africans living in the four communes of Senegal[64] could become French citizens and send a representative to the parliament in Paris. Of course, in order to do this, they had to meet certain criteria of Frenchness, and in the terms of colonial society become an *évolué*. As time went on, this right was extended to the inhabitants of all France's colonies. There were clear benefits from behaving like a Frenchman, or a Frenchwoman. The French colonial authorities never rejected the *évolués* in the way that the British did, and the orientation of the Francophone African elites remained on Paris. The political elite, and wider sections of society, were prepared to take on French attire, just as they took on French language.

In Senegal and Ivory Coast this tendency was clear. The first presidents, for instance, were in a many ways assimilated to French culture. Thus Felix Houphouët-Boigny of the Ivory Coast, who had been a minister of colonies in a French government before becoming president of an independent state, would never have been seen out of a well-cut French suit. Leopold Senghor of Senegal was even more clearly an *évolué*. He ended his life in Normandy with a French wife as a member of the *Académie française*. During his time as president he had banned *tenue traditonnelle* (traditional dress) from official audiences. Only with his retirement was there an explosion of Senegalese fashion, based on the *boubou*, or wide, straight-seamed and often highly embroidered long shirt, which was worn by both men and women and derived in part from the Islamic traditions of the area.[65]

In the western parts of central Africa, particularly in the two Congoes, matters have taken a different turn. In this region, there was a tradition of raffia cloth wrappers providing the essentials of modesty and forming the basis of a system of prestige, whereby slaves might wear two or three wrappers and a chief a robe containing up to forty-two pieces of fine cloth. However, the real contests of dress came from the elaborate coiffures and body painting.[66] As the slave trade developed from the sixteenth century, moreover, European cloth was brought into the processes of competition, creating a system of distinction based on dress. The poor and the slaves had to be content with unbleached cotton cloth, while the rich princes might be wearing "cloaks, capes, scarlet tabards, and silk robes, every one according to his means". Sartorial inflation reached such a point that the truly rich wore so much cloth that they could scarcely move.[67]

With the advent of colonialism, this tradition was continued, particularly in Léopoldville (subsequently Kinshasa) and Brazzaville, twin cities divided by the River Congo and colonial rule. From the early twentieth century, European observers commented on, and sometimes mocked, African sartorial competition. In 1913, Baron Jehan de Witte wrote that

> Today, the locals in the region of Brazzaville dress up too much, and, on Sunday, those that have several pairs of pants, several cardigans, put these clothes on one layer over the other, to flaunt their wealth. Many pride themselves on following Parisian fashion and, having known that not long ago Europeans joked about the blacks' passion for the top hat, so inappropriate for the tropical climate and completing in a sometimes comic manner an outfit which was more than scanty, most of them have given up and now sport elegant panama hats.[68]

What the baron was witnessing was a shift from an emphasis on sartorial quantity to one on quality. Soon, no Congolese would make the mistake of wearing pairs of trousers on top of each other. A young clerk, Camille Diata, wrote a letter commenting

> Do you know that in Brazzaville and Kinshasa all the gentlemen or young men are dressing in Popo? That is to say, owning a helmet from Ollivant's worth 150 francs, a silk shirt, a suit of poplin, or other fabric that is worth 250 to 300 francs at least and trousers which must reach down to touch the heels of one's shoes. Well-dressed women are wearing silk head scarves that cost 50 francs each and their cloths, costing 150 francs, must be well-cut by a skilled tailor.... The town of Brazzaville is developing and so are its inhabitants.[69]

The salary of an interpreter-typist, at the head of the colonial hierarchy, was 12 francs a day. In this way, as in so many colonial contexts, claims were made for equality with the colonial rulers, in concert with the possibilities for competition for prestige among the townspeople themselves.

From the 1960s onwards, this concern among the young men about the towns of Brazzaville and Kinshasa was to a degree formalized in the *Sape* (*La société des ambianceurs et des personnes élégantes* – itself an acronym created from the French slang word *se saper*, to dress up). The *Sape* revolves around two concerns. The first is to display oneself in the most exquisite, and expensive, labelled clothing, in other words the right *griffes*. Shoes should be English, Lobb's or Weston's, or Italian, Capo Bianco; suits by Yves Saint-Laurent, Dior, Armani or Gaultier, watches by Cartier, socks by Burlington and so forth.[70] Secondly, it thrived on the connection between the Congoes and Paris. Only the very well-connected civil servants could afford the stores in Brazzaville where the highest forms of European fashion could be purchased. To succeed in the *Sape* thus required visiting Europe, and the movement increasingly became a transcontinental community, located on the banks of both the Congo and the Seine. Those in Paris were often there illegally, and may well have had menial jobs, but increasingly they became active in various forms of possibly legal trade. It has been treated as a movement in opposition to the powers that be, although this is an argument which is difficult to sustain for a number of reasons – how could something so individualistic be a movement, were there powers that be in place, and so forth? What is clear is that it offered a route to prestige outside the control of the rulers of both Congoes, and that it was in some sense a reaction to the chaos which engulfed both countries from the 1960s onwards. It was also a defiant snub to Mobuto Sese Seko, the president of Zaire, as he renamed Congo-Kinshasa. In an attempt to produce a Congolese nationalism, and in fact to glorify himself, Mobuto had introduced a programme of "authenticity". Part of this attempted invention of tradition was the rejection of Western suits and the introduction of a jacket, based on the Nehru jacket, which Mobuto named the "abacost" – *à bas la costume*. To wear Yves Saint-Laurent in Kinshasa, or indeed in Brazzaville or Paris, was to signal a different political orientation.[71]

10

The Emancipation of Dress

In 1960 the social psychologists George Bush and Perry London proposed the hypothesis that "The greater the variability of clothing styles in a society, the less well-defined and conflict-free are social rôles in that society." Conversely, "the smaller the variability of clothing styles in a society, the more enduring, clearly defined and conflict-free are the social rôles of individuals in that society." They proceeded to test this hypothesis with regard to the ending of the practice whereby American boys (of a certain class and ethnicity) used to wear knickerbockers until they had reached puberty.[1] This is the sort of hypothesis which indeed seems closer to a platitude. Nevertheless, when historicized and applied to North-West Europe and America north of the Rio Grande in the twentieth century, some use can be made of it. It is clear that as the twentieth century progressed the clothing of women, and later of men, became freer. This formed part of the slow and incomplete social, political, sexual and economic emancipation of women within what is conventionally known as Western society – although, to continue the metaphor, it is not necessarily self-evident which was object and which reflection.

I will only briefly sketch the social shifts which have taken place in regard in particular to gender. Women are no longer limited to the position of wife and mother, in the ideology of the West – how far they ever actually were in practice is another matter. From the later nineteenth century through into the early twentieth, women acquired the right to vote. The likelihood that women would work outside the house increased. It was no longer seen as a stigma for married women to do so, and the restrictions against them doing so were finally lifted in the 1950s and 1960s. Rather, education and almost all occupations have opened to them, although there remain difficulties in pushing through to the highest positions in firms or in government, levels of pay and so forth are by no means always suitably equal and there are further informal restrictions. Part of this process is also an acceptance of female sexual activity before marriage, to a sharp decline in the number of children a woman will have (and a rise in the age at which she has them), and a very considerable increase in the likelihood of divorce.

How these improvements in the social status of women have been played out in their clothes is not something to which there is a simple, functionalist answer, but the compatibility of the social and the sartorial is beyond question. It was, of course, long accepted that women would wear clothes reasonably appropriate to the occupation in which they were engaged, although having to wear appropriate clothing might be a reason to prevent women from engaging in particular occupations. The sight of women who were working as miners and thus wore sturdy trousers caused a scandal in later nineteenth-century England, primarily because they were seen as taking on male apparel, and thus behaving immorally.[2] In the main, though, women outside of agriculture were employed in the tertiary sector, or in relatively light industry, such as the sweatshops and other establishments which made clothes, so that, within limits, clothing was not limited by the nature of the work undertaken. When, as during the two world wars, many women were employed in munitions factories, on the land and so forth, at least on the job they wore overalls, usually with trousers rather than a skirt. However, whatever the long-term effects of these forms of economic costume change may have been, in the short term at least the effects of women's fashions were to increase what was conventionally seen as femininity. In 1916, in the middle of World War I in Britain, the fashion commentators announced that "women are to present a more fluffy, feminine appearance than has been the case for some long while. The trend in favour of a less masculine style of dress is unmistakable." There were even skirts which used large quantities of material, up to "six yards around the hem". These descriptions occurred alongside descriptions of the "sensible" dress of the working women, suggesting that the two trends were part of a highly bipolar practice. The only cross-over seems to have been that the leisure clothes were much looser and less corseted than had usually been the case.[3]

The same levels of what was then seen as frivolity would not have been possible in World War II. Clothing rationing and a much more heavily planned economy meant that the consumption of material on such a scale was impossible. Even those who had hoarded stuff and could use it for their dresses would have been heavily stigmatized.[4]

13 The New Look

Women were employed increasingly in industries and other forms of war-work for which overalls, however "unfeminine" they may have been, were the only acceptable attire.[5] The post-war reaction, though, was sharp. The New Look, which Christian Dior launched in Paris in 1947, was a reclamation of frivolity, with a heavily accentuated waist, much nakedness around the shoulders and wide, cloth-intensive skirts buoyed out by a mass of petticoats.[6] Protests abounded, particularly from the Labour government. Bessie Braddock, a Liverpudlian battle-axe of a Labour politician who was perhaps the woman in England least likely to take on the New Look, described it as "the ridiculous whim of idle people". The Chancellor of the Exchequer,

Sir Stafford Cripps, wished to have it outlawed.[7] But, at least in Western democracies, political puritanism can rarely trump the desire for pleasure and display.

In addition, there are a number of complicated issues of historical causation involved in attributing too much of the undoubted shift in Western women's dress to the effects of the world wars. The most notable difficulty is chronological. Many of the most important whiffs were already under way before 1914. Skirt lengths were already rising, not to the heights they would reach in the 1920s, let alone the 1960s, but certainly sufficient to reveal a substantial proportion of women's calves. Or take cosmetics. During the nineteenth century, make-up had come to be associated with immorality. It was normal, for instance, for a New York society woman to describe one of her fellows who had overstepped the mark of propriety, in her eyes as "painted like a wanton". This began to change in the first decade of the twentieth century, as Helena Rubinstein, Elizabeth Arden, Estée Lauder and their fellows began to establish what would become one of the world's major industries.[8] The basis was laid well before World War I, and continued through after the war. If a cause has to be found, it is more likely to lie in the political campaigns which strove for and achieved women's suffrage than in the social upheavals of the war. These went together with the trends which allowed women a degree of physical independence and mobility, and which had their sartorial consequences, for instance in the adoption of a costume in which cycling was reasonably feasible.[9]

Nevertheless, there is often a danger of reading too much into the origins of a phenomenon, and not enough into the circumstances by which that phenomenon became popular. Shortened skirts and the use of lipstick, rouge and mascara by the putatively respectable both predated World War I, but it was only after 1914, and particularly in the 1920s, that they became widespread. The idea of the New Women, emancipated and self-assured, according to the criteria of the time, may have brought about the basic change in fashion, but its general acceptance was dependent on the changes in the socio-economic status of at least some women which came through rather later. In other words, ontogeny and evolutionary success have to be kept analytically distinct.

The main reason why this became possible was undoubtedly, at bottom, the increase in the disposable income of at least some Western women, allied to some decrease in the level of male control over women. But an increase in income inevitably brings forth new opportunities for expenditure. From the later nineteenth century onwards, shopping became an acceptable form of recreation for respectable women. Large department stores began to provide the opportunity for their customers to take tea, and so forth, and, equally importantly, to provide lavatories. A day out in the city became increasingly acceptable. One result, among many, was that more and more of a woman's wardrobe was purchased "off the shelf", rather than being manufactured by the local seamstress, or by the lady herself.

Another consequence of the changing social order was that the reference group for fashion shifted from the old aristocracy to a new one, revolving above all around the stars of the film industry. Certain of the trends which became important in the 1920s and 1930s clearly had their origin in what is conventionally known as Hollywood. It was above all through the movies that cosmetics became generally acceptable, as what had been necessary on stage now became the norm in society. Helena Rubinstein, for instance, recalled at the end of her life how in 1917 she had been approached by one of the current stars, Theda Bara, with the request to provide make-up which would be more flattering to the star's eyes than that which was presently available.[10] The result was the development of mascara and eye-shadow, first individually and then commercially. Since then, women's faces without eye make-up are seen by some people to be in some sense underprepared. Equally, it is said that the wide dissemination of pyjamas as women's nightwear derives from the great romantic comedy *It Happened One Night* (1934), in which Claudette Colbert appears so clad. Miss Colbert and her studio were in this reflecting a trend, not setting it,[11] but were nevertheless spreading it across the United States and Great Britain (and no doubt elsewhere) at a pace which would otherwise have been impossible.

At the same time there was a steady move throughout the West towards the simplification and increased informality of men's attire. Around 1900 there was still a wide variety of prescribed clothing, for every conceivable occasion. King Edward VII famously commented: "I thought everyone must know that a *short* jacket is always worn with a silk hat at a private view in the morning."[12] An advertisement for a Savile Row tailor in 1908, not perhaps the least suspect of sources, suggests that a true gentleman would need sixteen outfits in order to be properly dressed for all elite activities.[13] Hats – both ladies and gentlemen would always have their heads covered out of doors – varied from the silk topper to the cloth cap or straw boater; coats and jackets varied in length, material and coverage. Slowly the requirements for formal wear decreased. There remained occasions for which men might require a dinner jacket, or tuxedo, but for anything else recourse could be had to clothes rental businesses, so rare was the need for them. Eventually, the moment was reached when there were hardly any situations for which men had to wear anything more serious than a lounge suit and tie, albeit with a stiff, and detachable, collar. As early as the 1890s, lounge suits could even be seen in the dress circle (the name for the best seats is indicative) of the theatre in Britain,[14] though not, of course, the much more formal opera, especially in Germanic countries.

By the early twentieth century, the suit of clothes had become one of the prime markers of masculinity, at least of adult masculinity, at least in Britain. Until after World War I, the old combination of the frock coat and striped trousers held on among the more elderly and conservative, but was increasingly replaced by the lounge or business suit, known by many as the "ditto" because the jacket and trousers (and indeed the waistcoat) were made of the same stuff. This has been seen as a triumph of the middle-class, and perhaps American, values and habits over those of the old aristocracy. What had to be decided was the relation between the bespoke, made to measure suit and that bought ready-made. For a long time, the suit was for most male customers the only part of his outfit which had been made to measure, even if there were a number of chain stores, notably Montague Burton, which offered a half-way house, with the measuring, fitting and adjusting being done where the client was met, but the full range of cutting and most of the sewing being done in a central factory, in this case in Leeds. By World War II, indeed, the provision of choice in stuff, size and fit was becoming sufficient for the bespoke suit to be slowly relegated to the circles of the very rich and the very fastidious.[15]

At the same time, it was from the later nineteenth century that the necktie began its rise to its later position as a signifier of belonging, to a club, a regiment, a school, and so forth, and also as a metonym for masculinity. It is said that the fashion derived from the decision of the members of a Cambridge boat club, that of Corpus Christi College, to remove the maroon bands round their boaters and tie them round their necks instead. It is somewhat less mythical that the blazer, or at least the name for it, came from nearly the same source. Initially, only the scarlet boating jackets of the Lady Margaret Boat Club of St John's College were called blazers, in recognition of their flaming colour. Origins and etymologies, though, do not really matter. What is important is that what began as leisure wear came to be accepted in more formal contexts. The blazer, often navy blue, in defiance of all etymology, could be combined with flannel trousers and later other models of slacks in many circumstances, by 1900 even at posh race meetings; the necktie in almost any, up to and including the inauguration of the President of the United States.

Nevertheless, the progression towards a looser and less formal general attire did not go fast enough for some men. In Great Britain, the Men's Dress Reform Party was founded in 1927. In its early literature it complained that

> Men's dress has sunk into a rut of ugliness and unhealthiness from which – by common consent – it should be rescued ... Men's dress is ugly, uncomfortable, dirty (because unwashable), unhealthy (because heavy, tight and unventilated). ... Only through wider individual choice and variation will men's clothes be capable of healthy evolution and reasonable adaptation to progressive social, hygienic and aesthetic ideals. At the same time, it is desirable to guard against the danger of mere change for change's sake, such as has often occurred in women's fashion. All change should aim at improvement in appearance, hygiene, comfort and convenience.[16]

The prescription was that men should wear jackets and shorts, with matching socks, much on the lines of what was stereotyped for colonial officers. If a tie was to be worn, it should be hanging a few inches below the chin, and not constricting as collars and ties then were. This was seen to be healthier than what was currently worn (which given the difficulties of laundering at that time it probably was). There was a reaction, as might be expected, from the conservative, and from the tailors. Traditional – though of course not very old – male dress kept "the social fabric together", it was claimed in the pages of the *Tailor and Cutter*, while another article in the same journal announced: "A loosening of the bonds will gradually impel mankind to sag and droop bodily and spiritually. If laces are unfastened, ties loosened and buttons banished, the whole structure of modern dress will come undone; it is not so wild as it sounds to say that society will also fall to pieces."[17] These were metaphors which were taken seriously, perhaps even literally. Correct and formal dress, often uncomfortable to wear, was certainly seen as a way of maintaining personal discipline, which in its way was also the foundation of bourgeois society. This was the main psychological motive behind the famous custom of British colonial officers and their wives always dressing for dinner even in the depth of the bush.[18]

The Men's Dress Reform Party was a minor aberration, but in its slightly quirky way it attempted to propagate what became, without its help, the two major trends in Western dress in the latter two-thirds of the twentieth century, if not earlier. These were a decreasing emphasis on sexual dimorphism and a steady cross-over from leisure wear to more formal attire. To begin with the former, the main ideologue of the MDRP was J. C. Flügel, a Freudian psychologist and coiner of the concept of "the great masculine renunciation". He saw dress reform as one way of reducing what he saw as the harmful overemphasis on the male superego, by bringing colour and softness to men's attire.[19] To a degree this has happened, though not in the way that Flügel would have envisaged, and seldom in formal contexts. There was, of course, another way to achieve the same rapprochement, namely by allowing women to take on what were conventionally male clothes.

Within the Western Christian tradition, the sartorial distinction between the sexes, thought to be ordained of God,[20] was primarily signified by the prohibition to women of wearing bifurcated garments to cover their legs or, in other words, trousers. Indeed, the expression "She wears the trousers" was a metaphor for the dominance of a woman within a marriage, something which was seen as against the true order of society. As we have seen, women wearing trousers were thought to be usurping the place of men, and thus sexually loose – the assumption may have been that men were inherently immoral. Thus, the move towards women wearing trousers signalled a major shift in the ways in which the relationships between the sexes was expressed.

Until World War II, women were only seen in trousers in contexts of leisure. It was long considered appropriate for women to wear slacks on a yacht or to cycle. It is not for nothing that they were generally known in English as "slacks". There was a clear semantic association between the wearing of trousers and idleness, or at least the absence of tension. The main exceptions to this were among women of uncertain sexuality, including the film-stars Marlene Dietrich and Katherine Hepburn,[21] or of certain, but unacceptable, sexuality, such as the Paris lesbians around Radclyffe Hall.[22] Only from the early 1960s were trouser suits introduced as haute couture, above all by André Courrèges in Paris.[23] It is perhaps surprising how quickly trousers for women came to be accepted on all but the most formal of occasions, and by all but the most formal of ladies. The Queens of Great Britain and the Netherlands, for instance, have almost never been seen wearing trousers while on duty,[24] nor was Margaret Thatcher while Prime Minister. However, by the 1970s, it was acceptable for women to dress in a trouser suit even in the Royal Enclosure at Ascot race meeting, and by the early twenty-first century, Angela Merkel, as Chancellor of Germany, invariably appears in trousers, at least when her male colleagues are in suits, though she may wear full evening dress to the opera, for instance. At the same time, those whose work required physical activity were allowed to wear trousers, and such garments could even become part of ordinary uniform, as for instance in the police force. Symbolically, the New York City police department put its female officers into trousers in 1973.[25] Those in less physically demanding professions slowly followed suit. By

1987, to take one example out of many, even the South Carolina House of Representatives was prepared, overwhelmingly, to adopt the resolution that "pages and guests of the House shall observe appropriate and dignified attire which means shirt and tie (with coats optional) for males and dignified dress (meaning dress, skirt or slacks and blouse, or pants suits) for females". It was taken for granted that men would be wearing long trousers.[26]

That women might wear trousers does not necessarily imply that this was always appreciated. There was, and remains, a complicated balance that has to be found between women over-emphasizing their sexuality, so that they are not taken seriously, on the one hand, and women dressing in such a masculine fashion as to present a threat to male egos. This is of course primarily a matter for the office. From the early part of the twentieth century, female secretaries had replaced male clerks as the essential administrative link within companies and other workplaces. It was a role which accorded with accepted gender norms, and the secretaries were expected to dress the part, to present an image which combined efficiency and sexuality, thereby boosting the ego and the prestige of their (almost inevitably) male superiors.[27] Those women who did achieve executive positions had the further problem of distinguishing themselves from the secretaries (from whose ranks, of course, they might have risen). The solution was the female version of the business suit, dark in colour, with matching jacket and skirt. The skirt would be to just below the knees. The blouse was light in colour, or perhaps there would be a woollen jumper, with a brooch at the throat; otherwise a floppy bow-tie[28] or a scarf would mark the neck. Stockings were undemonstrative and flesh-coloured. Shoes were sober, and relatively low-heeled, dark pumps. The line, however, was generally softer than that of a man's suit. The wearer's gender, though understated, was unmistakable.[29]

This professional uniform for women both preceded and mirrored in a slightly distorted fashion that of the men. For a time, in the 1960s and 1970s, men began to be allowed to loosen up at work and in public. The most conspicuous and (so far) lasting element in this was the general abandonment by both men and women of hats in public. In January 1961, for instance, John F. Kennedy became the first American president to be formally inaugurated in Washington bareheaded – inaugurations of course take place in the open air. At the same time, the fashion houses which had long showed women's dress began to attempt to dictate to men, too, what they should wear, though of course the informal college of high-class and expensive London tailors had long done so. The result was what is known as the "Peacock Revolution", an attempted reversal of the Great Masculine Renunciation.[30] As revolutions go, this one was bloodless, ineffective and short-lived. From the 1970s, as the global economy turned down, the business suit came to be even more than before the dress of those men who wished to be taken seriously. The corporate world, and everyone else who wished to be associated with it, quickly reinforced its dress codes.[31] Only perhaps in universities, where students and younger members of the faculty are uncertain whether they ought to be taken seriously, and in such institutions as advertising agencies, publishing houses and some computer firms, was informality of dress allowable. Even there, men who did not want to be in suits were long likely to be wearing a sports jacket and a tie.

What was happening in the later twentieth century was, on the one hand, the embedding of the lounge suit as the formal respectable dress for men in most circumstances and, on the other, the general acceptance of forms of informal attire as appropriate in ever more situations. In a major reversal of the established norms, the "street" came to set the tone, above the dictates of fashion, and leading fashion designers took their inspiration from what was being worn by the youth of major cities. This can be easily seen in the history of two of the late twentieth century's most characteristic garments, the mini-skirt and jeans.

In terms of high fashion, the miniskirt – a women's skirt with the hem way above the knee – was introduced by Mary Quant in 1960. Quant was a British designer, at that stage about twenty-five years old. Her designs contributed to and reflected the broader shift in clothing codes which for the first time celebrated – indeed almost demanded – young female sexuality and sexual availability, aided by the introduction of contraceptive pills, in what was then known as the "Swinging Sixties" and was centred both around London and in various parts of the United States, especially California. Admittedly, the effect was somewhat mitigated by the wearing of elasticated panty-hose under the miniskirt. Nevertheless, the general effect was to celebrate what was seen as freedom, and certainly entailed the liberation from the stuffier aspects of Western middle-class life. It was only slowly that it came to be realized that women's liberation also entailed women's control over their own sexuality, with consequences for the way in which they decided to present themselves. Many women were concerned not to present themselves as asking for "it" by the way in which they dressed, even though the way in which they dressed was in fact little protection against male assault. Conversely, a woman's dress at the time of the event was often used as a defence in cases of rape, although there is no evidence that revealingly clothed young women were more likely than others to be raped. Indeed rape victims tended to reject the social scientific assumption (which this book acknowledges as much as any other) that clothes can send messages.

Their experiences had led to them to confuse the legibility of clothing with the danger that clothes could be misread. The problem was that the clarity of sartorial utterances was not sufficient.[32]

Throughout the later twentieth century there was thus a general extension of the decisions as to effective control over what was considered a fashionable look away from established designers, and a greater pluriformity of outfits, not just for women but also for men, at least in informal circumstances. Within this context the possibilities for alternative cultural expressions were increased. A whole variety of counter-cultural statements came to be allowable, and in various ways celebrated by commentators.

Within this, probably the most salient shift has been in the status of jeans. A particular variant of tough working man's trousers – the name of the style derives from the city of Genoa in Italy and of its constituent cloth from Nîmes in France – this garment was first produced in America in the mid-nineteenth century. Its main characteristics were the tough cotton cloth – denim – died blue with indigo, with which they were made, the up-standing seams and the rivets which were believed to strengthen the seams and which were introduced, more or less as a trademark, by the Levi Strauss Company, the first major group producer of such clothing. The original model, the 501 with button flies, remains in production, although no longer made in California. Jeans were almost exclusively worn in the United States, and almost entirely as working clothes, until after World War II, during which they had been declared a "vital commodity" by the US army and restricted in their sales to those forces. Thereafter, jeans came to be associated with rock-and-roll music. Rock-and-roll was a genre which took its force and popularity from being a black American style played by white men, above all those from the Southern countryside who had been brought up listening to black radio stations. These were the main group in American society who wore jeans, and they continued to do on stage. Elvis Presley was the most famous star to do so. At the same time, a pair of films, *The Wild Ones* starring Marlon Brando and above all *Rebel Without a Cause* with James Dean, had their heroes in such clothes. Thus jeans became perhaps the first garment to become fashionable from below, progressing upwards in social status from the working class to at least the bourgeoisie.

For a while, then, jeans were a major symbol of the Western youth culture of rebellion. They demonstrated a degree of independence from the dominant norms of bourgeois life, although one which was particularly expressed by the sons and daughters (and future members) of the bourgeoisie. However, the charisma of rebellion which they had once evinced eventually became routinized. Jeans

14 James Dean in *Rebel Without a Cause*

ceased to be more than a regular item in everyone's wardrobe. By the early twenty-first century, they had become so regular that, for instance, an informal and totally unscientific survey at my local supermarket in the Netherlands on a weekday afternoon showed that about half of adults, of both sexes, and all ages, were wearing them. Jeans had become the off-duty apparel of choice.[33] And they could appear at places of work. At my university everyone, from cleaner to student to professor, is likely to wear jeans.

Long before this, jeans had become a longed-for article in those areas of Europe under Communist rule, as they could be, and were, interpreted as part of a culture in opposition to the state-directed norms of Eastern Europe, and as a claim for individual freedom, albeit one in which most of those concerned expressed congruent individualities. In a remarkable reversal of what fitted with the ideology, the official line of the proletarian revolution rejected the most proletarian of internationalizing garments, and those who rejected the straitjacket of communism (indeed so cut as to minimize the consumption of cloth) did so by adopting the uniform of the American working class. If such ironies were not so common in the history of clothing, it would be remarkable.[34]

Nevertheless, rebellion and individuality did come to be incorporated in one of the competing ideological and governmental systems. It is at least arguable that the eventual demise of communism was brought about by the relative failure of supply-driven economic planning to satisfy the demands for innovation and fashion. In contrast, whatever its other failings, consumer capitalism of the later twentieth century was above all able to supply customers with what they desired, and admittedly also to create and steer those desires – though this is not the same as commanding those desires. Within the system, then, individuality is a good. An extensive retail network grew up to supply customers with their wants, and to provide a very wide range of choice. The high streets and shopping malls of the world became crammed with shops selling clothing, among many other commodities. With immense skill in marketing and distribution they managed to break the contradiction which the Communist regimes had failed even to address, namely how efficiency of production could be combined with the provision of the wherewithal for individuals to use dress to demonstrate their own individuality. The ways in which the changing style of ready-to-wear clothing is determined by the industry are, of course, subtle, and not always successful. The leaders of the profession will often say that they follow the "street", rather than determining it. Be that as it may, the trick is surely to follow fashion at a very close interval.

The ability to do this has had a lot to do with the wide, nearly global reach of clothing chains. A major part of the strategy of such firms has been to be represented in as wide a spread of markets as possible, both within individual countries and internationally. For example, the Italian-based United Colors of Benetton claims to be represented in 120 countries and to have some 5,000 individual outlets. This means that it, and many other such firms, can provide a slightly diluted and slightly belated version of what is fashionable to almost anywhere in the world within a very short period of time.[35] The result has been that the consumer in most major cities of the world, and a lot of smaller ones, has at least the opportunity to dress in something approaching the current global dress.[36]

In order to achieve this, it is not only necessary for companies to have an efficiently working system of distribution across the world. They also require a production system which is fast, flexible and cheap. The result has been the growth of garment factories in low-wage countries, particularly in South East and East Asia. Much of China's phenomenal economic growth over the last decade has been fuelled by the export of clothing. There has thus been a steady shift of both textile and garment manufacture away from Europe and North America to new areas. As has been the case throughout recent history, such work has been primarily done by women, and under conditions of considerable exploitation. Sweatshops, once a phenomenon of garrets in London or New York, have moved to the cities of China, of Indonesia or of Malaysia. Indeed, clothing designers have been prepared to alter their products to take advantage of the new possibilities for labour. To give one example, the layered skirts which became fashionable in the middle of the first decade of the twenty-first century, and which require more sewing than most garments, are a clear exploitation of the opportunities, and the labour, that are now available.

Even though Benetton and its confreres are not present everywhere and even though by no means everyone can afford their products, the desire to dress fashionably and well is exceedingly widespread. Obviously the trade in pirated copies and fake labels panders to these demands. So does the widespread export of second-hand clothing, in particular to parts of Africa. The best studied and probably largest recipient of used clothing is Zambia.[37] The business feeds on European and American garments which have been cast off, for whatever reason, but are still in reasonable condition. They are then often donated to various charitable institutions, often under the assumption that the clothing itself is going to be distributed to the needy. On the contrary, from this moment on the garments are treated totally commercially (though the profits from the first sale are of course used for the stated purpose). Clothing is sorted and baled and shipped to Zambia, where it is bought by the market traders, men and women in approximately equal numbers. It is always a gamble what precisely is in the bale, although the traders know whether they are getting shirts, pants, jackets or whatever. The clothes are then prepared and exhibited for sale on one of the many open-air markets, particularly in Lusaka. It is known as *salaula*, a word deriving from a Bemba verb meaning "to pick from a pile".

The trade in *salaula* developed in the 1980s, a period when the economy of Zambia was going particularly badly, after a time of relative prosperity. Those Zambians who had been used to dressing elegantly were thus forced to use the *salaula* markets in order to maintain the standards to which they had become accustomed, and thus to present themselves to the world as modern and sophisticated people. This was in essence the same operation as that of the customer in a European or American shopping centre, though the means which the Zambian has at his or her disposal are more meagre; the results, on the other hand, certainly need not be.

11

Engendered Acceptance and Rejection

In all parts of the world, the ways in which new sartorial regimes were accepted was highly determined by gender, not merely because there has hardly been any dress, anywhere or at any time, which is not in important ways highly gendered. Rather, women are so often seen as the carriers of the virtue of a nation, and thus as people who need to be controlled. An Indian woman may be admonished to wear Indian clothes, rather than, say, jeans and a T-shirt by a male official in shorts and a shirt, who sees no contradiction in this. On Indian television, there is a clear distinction between the government channels, whose announcers wear saris or *shalwar kamiz*, and the commercial stations, which put their announcers in Western dress.[1] This is not an unusual type of contrast.

In this chapter I will discuss the issues which this raises on the basis of three case studies: China through the twentieth century; post-independence Anglophone Africa; and the world-wide set of tensions which have arisen with regard to Islamic dress for women, in particular their head covering. To begin in China, it was long a trope that the Middle Kingdom had not the cycles of fashion which the west of the Eurasian continent had known. As Fernand Braudel wrote, the mandarin's robes "scarcely changed in the course of centuries, but then Chinese society itself scarcely moved at all".[2] Neither part of this statement is accurate. As early as the Tang, trends in fashion are easily discernible in the demand for exotic Western goods and clothing.[3] By at least the later Ming dynasty the rich in China were concerned to follow the latest sartorial trends. In the 1590s a moralist was complaining, as moralists tend to do all over the world, that

People from all over favour Suzhou clothing, and so Suzhou artisans work even harder at making them.... This drives the extravagance of Suzhou style to even greater extravagance, so how is it possible to lead those who follow the Suzhou fashion back to sensible economy? ... The present having become so decadent, how could we now return to a simpler beginning even if we wanted to?[4]

The cities of Yangzhou and Suzhou, both in the lower Yangtse region that is now the hinterland of Shanghai and both among the richest places in the kingdom, emerged as the centres of extravagant forms of dress, in competition with each other. The clothes worn in Yangzhou, it was written in the later eighteenth century, "are always in the newest style". From here out, the fashions spread to other centres.[5] Styles, fabrics and colours were continually changing, and it is only the inability of Western observers to read the sartorial languages within which the changes were written which has lead to the image of immutable China. The "cycles of Cathay" were shorter than is often believed.[6]

Nevertheless, from the second half of the nineteenth century, the enforced opening of China's markets to Western merchants, through the treaty ports, above all Shanghai, meant that the old arrogances of the Middle Kingdom were challenged. The confrontation with the "west' – this time in its conventional manifestation as Europe and North Americas – led to major changes in China's sartorial regimes, as in the political. The same ideas of the sympathetic magic of Western clothing began to permeate at least some portions of Chinese society, though not the imperial court and the centres of power. The influences coming in through the treaty ports, where Western power and prowess were evident, began to set a number of difficult questions. European clothing began to spread among the small group of those who saw themselves as Westernized. In the formulation of Steele and Major, "if the sources of European power were to be found obviously in steamships and power looms, were they to be sought in bustles and tailored suits as well?"[7] The answer to such a question in China was rarely as unequivocally affirmative as in Turkey under Atatürk, for instance, as the Chinese began to develop new ways of being simultaneously Chinese and modern. It did, however, force a whole variety of new ways of dress onto Chinese bodies.

Part of the problem lay in the fact that the grammar of Chinese dress was almost diametrically opposed to that of Europe and its extensions. At levels above that of the peasant, the distinction between the dress of men and of women was that the former ideally consisted of a one-piece robe, with an open skirt, while the latter would wear a jacket and trousers, preferably with an over-skirt covering the trousers. Modernity seemed to require that women wear skirts and men trousers – admittedly just as arbitrary an order for society as the reverse.

Through the end of the Empire and the period of the Chinese Republic, a variety of attempts were made to produce sartorial answers to these conundrums. Some parts were relatively easy. The early twentieth century saw not only the banning but also, more remarkably, the virtual abandonment of the binding of girls' feet to produce what were seen as acceptable and desirable lower limbs.[8] The abandonment of the pigtail was not problematic, since this had always been imposed as symbol of loyalty to the Qing regime.[9] However, the coming of the Republic in 1912 meant that the basic problems became acute. One satirical writer wrote in that year that:

> We now suddenly find ourselves to be Republicans and want everything to be improved and made better, with the clothes on our backs being the most pressing concern of all. Let's mention the things that a lady can't do without: a pair of sharp-toed, high-heeled, premium leather shoes; a pair of "violet mink" gloves; two or three plain or jewel-encrusted gold pins; a white lace . . . handkerchief; a pair of gold-rimmed, new style eyeglasses; a curved ivory comb; and a silk kerchief. Now let's address the things a man can't do without: a Western suit, greatcoat, Western hat, and handkerchief, with the addition of a boutonniere, a pince-nez and a few words of pidgin English.[10]

Fashion – *shimao* – had become central to the creation of a new China. The pigtails which had been the symbol of loyalty to the Qing were cut off. In the prosperous city of Suzhou, the sale of "traditional styled silks" fell to half their previous level, and its citizens, when they could, took on foreign dress, in style if not always in manufacture.[11] *Shimao* was nevertheless dangerous. The Nationalist Revolution in China was nationalist as much as it was revolutionary. The Nationalist government thus proceeded both to promote the use of Chinese fabrics and to legislate the requirements of formal dress. In both August and October 1912, in the first year of the Republic, the government indeed issued ordinances detailing appropriate wear for both men and women. That for women, known as "regular formal dress, type B", consisted of a long jacket and a long skirt covering the feet. Within a short time, in Suzhou at least, the sales of Chinese silk began to rise again. By the 1920s, observers in Shanghai were either pleased that the Chinese were no longer "infected with Yankee customs" or denigrated the city as still backward and feudal for not rejecting the old apparel.[12]

How true this was depended to some extent on what was meant by Chinese. Fashionable women's clothing began again to be

modelled on that of the West, but in specific Chinese ways, just as the
novelty of the "New Woman", a phenomenon which dominated much
of Chinese socio-political thought in the first part of the twentieth
century. The most notable of such attire was, for women, the *qipao*
or *cheongsam*.[13] This was a long skirt, fastened across the shoulder
and down the side, and with a notably high, fairly stiff, collar. Originally it was seen as a way of women dressing like, and thus in some
way claiming equality with, men. Within Chinese sartorial semiotics,
this is not so unreasonable as it may seem to Westerners and to later
generations. It is after all a one-piece dress. For this reason, one
Chinese commentator in 1928 remarked that

> Women's clothing in recent times has been modeled on men's. To the
> eye they look just like males, their womanly loveliness submerged. The
> style is especially unsuited to their physique. The woman's robe (com-
> monly known as the qipao) seems the same as the man's, but actually
> there is a difference between the two. It should not be large in style –
> long and wide at the waist – but cut to the shape of the body, showing
> the curvaceous beauty of the female and in this way displaying the
> woman's sex, what it is about a woman that makes her a woman.[14]

This was the essential change. What Li Yuyi, the writer of this passage,
was noting was a significant change in the forming of the ideal female
body in China. Just as tiny feet were no longer appreciated, so women
were encouraged to display their curvaceousness. Where once breasts
had been bound flat, now they were thrust up by the brassiere.[15]
Where once clothing had tended to conceal form, now the *qipao* was
figure-hugging and revealing. In its developed style, from the mid-
1920s onwards, it was notable for a pronounced waist and a tight skirt,
which came down to below the knee, even to mid-calf, but which was
slit to well up the thigh, supposedly to allow the wearer to walk with
some ease. At the same time, the high collar had the effect of giving
women a desirable, almond-shaped face. To Western eyes, at least, the
qipao is generally seen as a sexually explicit garment, and there were
those Chinese who wanted it banned as such. Nevertheless, with the
endorsement of Song Qingling, the widow of Sun Yat-sen, the *qipao*
became in effect the official attire of the Guomindang. It was, through
the 1930s, the symbol of urban China.[16]

The closest equivalent of the *qipao* for men was what became
known as the Sun Yat-sen jacket, or *Zhongshan zhuang*.[17] Sun himself
was briefly the first president of the Chinese Republic and later, particularly after his death in 1925, the symbol of that state. Sartorially
he was far from consistent, although his attire was always appropriate to the situation in which he found himself. In exile before the

15 Woman in a *qipao*

revolution of 1912, he had often worn a Western suit with collar, tie and Western shoes. He had already cut off his pigtail. When the members of his short-lived government of 1912 had themselves photographed they were all similarly dressed.[18] Out of office, there were moments when Sun sported a scholar's gown, and others, particularly as leader of the military government he attempted to form in Canton, when official portraits show him in the regalia beloved of military leaders who had been in touch with Western models of pomp, with a uniform festooned with gold braid and accessoried with epaulettes, plumed hat and white gloves. The costume which came to bear his name was much simpler, a jacket buttoning in the centre up to the throat, with a stand-up collar and patch pockets. It was accompanied by trousers.

The Sun Yat-sen jacket has a complicated provenance. Superficially, it may bear some resemblance to the padded jackets of the Chinese peasantry, but it was explicitly modelled on what was at that time often worn by the Chinese in South East Asia, and, perhaps more distantly, on the uniforms of Japanese students, themselves deriving from Prussian prototypes of the later nineteenth century. It was semiotically overloaded. According to Peter Carroll, "the five front buttons symboliz[ed] five branches of the Republican state, the three sleeve buttons represent[ed] the Three Principles of the People, and the four front pockets [stood] for the basic tenets of national ethics (propriety, righteousness, honesty, and shame)". However, it was generally made of woollen cloth, in khaki, green or blue, and at least for the tailors' guild of Suzhou was counted as Western dress.[19] It was a clear attempt to provide a fashion which was at once Chinese and conformed to the new vision of masculinity, which enjoined, in particular, figure-hugging trousers and a determined, long-striding gait, something which was both previously undesirable and physically very difficult in a long gown.[20]

The Sun Yat-sen jacket was maintained as official garb by the nationalist leadership. Even after his exile to Taiwan, Chiang Kai-shek wore the jacket, as a symbol of republican virtue, at least when he was not in his paraphernalia as a generalissimo.[21] Mao Tse-tung, too, came to wear a version of the jacket, and to promote it as proper proletarian wear. On his accession to power in 1949, he was pressured to put on a dark lounge suit and leather shoes, but resisted, apparently with the comment "We Chinese have our own customs. Why should we follow others?" Rather he chose a version of the Sun Yat-sen jacket.[22] This came to be known outside (though not in) China as the Mao jacket, and was most often made of thick cotton stuff, not of wool.

Through the period of Maoist rule in China, the ruling trope was austerity. A costume was developed which was one of the most uniform and androgynous that can be imagined. There were subtle differences, in hairstyle, in the way the trousers were opened and so forth, but these were subsumed under the generalized sameness, almost as if the leadership of the Communist Party wanted China's population to emulate Marx's famous description of the French peasantry as forming "a sack of potatoes".[23] Sun Yat-sen jackets in greys, blues and greens, above baggy and shapeless trousers, came to dominate dress. During the period of the Cultural Revolution, the wearing of dress which could be interpreted as bourgeois, decadent or individualistic was dangerous, and could lead to a show trial. The leaders of the Cultural Revolution did not always live up to the ideals they attempted to impose. After her fall, Jiang Qing, Mao's last wife and a member of the "Gang of Four", was accused, probably with reason, of having dresses made in which she would present herself as Empress.[24] Mao himself had his jackets specially tailored so as to conceal, as far as possible, his increasing corpulence.[25] For the masses, too, matters were never quite as totalitarian as they might be presented – in fact, of course, they never are. Even in posters, the gleaming peasants attending Chairman Mao on his tours of inspection were portrayed in much more variegated attire than might be supposed from the propaganda of the Revolution. Perhaps this was because such posters naturally enough depicted events in summer so women could display the cotton print and check blouses which could be legitimately worn under the jacket – men generally wore white shirts in such circumstances. Some individuality was always allowed.[26]

The sartorial steamroller that was Maoist China did have one major consequence for the post-Mao period. Now that it has become possible, the Chinese have taken to modern Western clothing virtually exclusively. The *qipao* is only seen among the diaspora, primarily among those who need to assert a Chinese identity in a multi-ethnic setting, and to some extent to demonstrate a specifically Hong Kong identity after the ending of British rule.[27] On the mainland, the country's leadership dared appear in Western suits and ties in 1985. Since then, the Sun Yat-sen, or Mao, jacket has more or less disappeared and men and women express themselves within much the same idiom as in Europe and North America, including by developing sartorial counter-cultures.[28] As China has become a major producer of clothing for the global market, so its citizens have come to take on the styles which that global market demands, albeit on occasion with local variations.[29]

The processes of sartorial politics in the various African states after independence took substantially different forms. As usual, the reactions were in some sense contradictory, or perhaps attempted to find the mean between various opposites. On the one hand there were repeated campaigns to require those people, in particular those men, whose dress was too scanty by the standard norms to cover up. In Ghana a variety of groups in the north of the country had long maintained their (semi-)nudity, as a way to distinguish themselves from the Muslims around them and from the Southerners, both of whom had in various ways exploited and enslaved the politically stateless peoples of the savanna. After independence in 1957, a variety of campaigns were launched in the name of "development" and "nation building" to dress the naked. Part of the problem was the idea that nakedness was a sign of savagery, and that Ghana should not allow itself to present any opportunity to be considered backward. First a number of Ghanaian and Afro-American women launched a campaign against nudity, which was to be taken over by the Government. As Hannah Kudjoe, the main spirit behind the campaigns, announced:

> As we are now one, our fashion, culture and way of life must also be identical. It [is] not good for some of us to prefer going out naked for some reasons. If it [is] due to custom, we should realise that such a custom is out-moded; and if it [is] due to poverty, we should all try to work hard to earn our living. . . . one expose[d] oneself to all sorts of dangers if one went about naked. The practice is also not in conformity with Ghanaian culture.

Even at the time, there were those who realized that the problem of nudity was above all in the eye of the beholder, those who were attempting to impose a national culture. The presence of "unclothed people" was said to "elicit ridicule and scorn from foreigners" – by no means evidently the case, as the number of foreigners in northern Ghana in the 1960s was fairly minimal. Rather, it was said that the whole question of nakedness was to be linked to the goal of female advancement, and the arguments around nudity were a way to debate questions of gender, which in the years after the deposition of the first President of the Republic, Kwame Nkrumah, tended to disappear out of public life.[30]

In other parts of the continent, similar campaigns were launched. In the north of Uganda in 1971, attempts to make the Karamajong wear shirts, trousers and shoes led to a riot as a result of which 120 were arrested and sentenced to six-month gaol sentences, no doubt in prison uniforms of shorts and shirt.[31] This, though, was only one part of the efforts of the Ugandan state, both colonial and independent, to control the pastoralists of the country's north, so far without evident success. The Tanzanian state's attempt to force the Maasai into clothes was more concerted, and more specifically concerned with their dress. It obviously formed part of the newly independent state's generalized attempt to bring about, in a way to impose, development on the country, one which was, at least for a time, notoriously heavy-handed.[32] With regard to the Maasai, questions of sympathetic magic were involved. For the administrators, the red ochre, bare buttocks and toga-like *lubega* cloth of the Maasai were signs of their backwardness – they were "ancient, unhealthy customs", and led to the equation of Tanzanians with wild animals, as part of the country's tourist attractions.[33] Operation Dress-Up, as it was called, was part of an attempt to bring the Maasai into the modern world, to force them to accept progress, and, in the rhetoric of the time, to become socialist revolutionaries. In this way, they would be brought under the control of the state bureaucracy. As part of the offensive to impose state control an Area Commissioner urged his subordinates that "It is *imperative*, I repeat again, *imperative*, that all Maasai in your divisions be ordered that they are not to be seen wandering about naked but they should instead wear normal clothes like other citizens." Those who disobeyed were likely to be denied access to medical care, bars, restaurants and buses.[34]

The Maasai did not, of course, see their attire as a problem. Maasai women began by cursing those of their kin who propagated the wearing of shirts and trousers – curses which could only be countered by the sacrifice of sufficient cattle. Red ochre was seen, in an area with little water, as an efficient way to control lice, which could gather on unwashed clothing. And anyway, for the Maasai, the use of soap, particularly of the popular Rexona brand, was detestable; just as Europeans and coastal Tanzanians often wanted to throw up in the presence of ochre-covered Maasai, so did the Maasai in the presence of their perfumed fellows.[35]

At the same time, and even more widely, there was a major assault by the governments of a variety of African states to impose what was considered to be seemly and modest dress on, in particular, young women. In a whole variety of African countries, the miniskirt was seen as a particularly heinous indication of the influence of the West and of the corruption of the modern world, although Afro hairstyles, flagrant lipstick, tight trousers – in some cases any sort of trousers worn by women – and skin-lightening cream were also part of the package of infamy. In Ethiopia, women wearing miniskirts were attacked in what led to a riot in which fifty people were injured and a hundred cars burnt. In Malawi, Dr Kamazu Banda, the country's long-term first president, once commented that "Mini-skirts and dresses are a diabolic fashion which must disappear from the country once and for all." It was, as signs in airports announced, "traditional for women not to appear in public in dresses that expose any part of the leg above the knee".[36] In Zambia, President Kaunda is said to have commented that the two things he hated most were apartheid and the miniskirt, a conflation which may seem excessive but is understandable in terms of the cultural and gender politics of the 1960s and 1970s. On Zanzibar, the revolutionary party had by the mid-1970s banned "for women, cosmetics, skin creams, long nails, wigs,

miniskirts, slacks, shorts and transparent blouses" and for men "slim
fitting shirts ... bell bottom pants ... shorts, big Afros, high-heeled
boots", and a variety of other ephemeral forms of trouser.[37] In mainland Tanzania, there was a major campaign, known as "Operation
Vijana", launched in 1968 by the Youth League of the ruling TANU
party attacking indecent dress. Women in the wrong sort of attire
were attacked at bus-stations, and at least one barmaid was reported
to have been stoned by a "mob of youngsters ... apparently incensed
at the shortness and tight fit of her miniskirt".[38] What women should
wear was thought to be the *kanga*, wrap-around cloths mainly made
of highly dyed cotton, which had developed in the later nineteenth
century as the height of (erotic) fashion,[39] but which by the period of
African independence had become the basis of modern dress, and to
some extent of a nationalist attempt to further economic development through local production.[40]

These attacks on the dress of young African women all occurred
in African cities. The city woman was seen by men as the antithesis
of all that was good about African womanhood, namely working hard
in the fields, bearing children and running a household, and generally
being subordinate to their menfolk. The young woman who went off
to town, who earned her own living and established her own independence, was a threat to social order as the men imagined it, and
indeed to their own possibilities of achieving adult masculinity, which
required being the head of a household. Moreover, women might see
the urban girls as threats to the income which men on migrant labour
were supposed to send home to their rural families. Even before the
advent of AIDS, in much of Africa the prostitute had come to be seen
as a witch, preying on the vital forces of society, and short skirts were
seen as a signal of prostitution. It was, of course, another instance of
sympathetic magic to hope that by banning the outward signs of a
particular way of behaviour the root cause would be extirpated, but
in the context of Africa since independence it was probably less irra-
tional than many such uses of magic.

Part of the rationale for these attacks was that the miniskirt was in
some sense un-African. The logic of this was that there had to be
some dress which was authentically African, which was difficult to
find. Only in those parts of West Africa where the weaving and dying
of cloth was an ancient craft could national or local costumes be
adopted which might claim a degree of authenticity, at least when, as
was usually not the case in Francophone West Africa, such was desired.
Even there, matters were complex. In Nigeria, in general, the Indian
pattern has been followed in that men dress in the costume appropriate to the region and religious group from which they come. In
Ghana, Nkrumah put his first cabinet in *Kente* cloth, at least to have

their photos taken, and on occasion other leading politicians have worn such attire.[41] They have to be careful, however, as dress and the politics of ethnicity are deeply intertwined. *Kente* is often seen as an Asante artefact, so that those governments which were seen as having an anti-Asante stance, such as those of J. J. Rawlings, president from 1979 to 2000, could wear *Kente* as a sign of pan-African nationalism; those such as that of John Kufuor, the current president, who was born in the Asante capital Kumasi, and who is seen as depending heavily on Asante support, have tended to revert to dark suits so as not to provide their opponents with unwanted ammunition. However, *Kente* cloth is very expensive, needs continual care and cannot really be tailored, so that it is much more usual for men and women to wear printed cotton. The best quality is still that produced by Vlisco at Helmond in the Netherlands, which is known in much of Africa as "real Dutch wax" and is a considerable status symbol.[42]

In eastern and southern Africa, such subtleties were rarely available. Presidents Nyerere and Kaunda, in Tanzania and Zambia, respectively, attempted to develop local styles, with jackets in some way related to that worn by Nehru, and to the *abacost* of Mobuto in Zaire (though they would have reeled at the thought of being associated with the latter). When they left office, though, the Western-style suit returned almost immediately.[43] In South Africa, since the *Wende* in 1994, there have been attempts to develop more "African" forms of fashion. This was not so much the highly admired and hardly imitated batik shirts worn by Nelson Mandela on all but the most formal occasions – famously, when rebuked by Archbishop Tutu for demeaning the dignity of the presidency, Mandela replied that this was rich coming from a man who wore long purple skirts. His action was clearly seen as the particular decision of a man whose stature allowed him the eccentricity of rejecting uniforms of which he had worn too many in gaol. Rather, designers have attempted to create outfits based on West African models, with Vlisco prints and often a cloth wrapped around the head in place of a hat, or on the Xhosa dresses which came out of the nineteenth-century encounter with the missionary. Although southern African dress is generally recognisable as specific to the region, such fashions are only for the upper end of the market. And as for men, it is only at the opening of Parliament that any appear, when being formal, in attire other than the dark suit, and this is little more than a fancy-dress parade.[44]

The ultimate irony was played out in Kenya. There, as a nationalist deed, a committee was appointed to create a national dress, and found it very difficult to produce anything which was acceptable. The only models on which they could have based their designs were either too nude or too evidently Islamic. The final answer – shirts with slashed collars for men, and ankle-length robes with a long cloak for women, all in the national flag's colours of red, green and black – failed to find favour among the general population. According to one trader, only whites buy national dress. "Mostly it's missionary people who like it."[45]

And then there is the veil, as Islamic headgear for women has come to be known, which in the early twenty-first century has become, if it was not already, the world's most controversial piece of clothing.

As was mentioned above, the veil was part of the clothing of Western Asia and the Mediterranean well before the advent of Islam. It was also one of the badges of honour and freedom; slave women, who had no honour and whose bodies were in principle fair game, were often forbidden to wear it.[46] There are also Koranic injunctions that have been interpreted as requiring a woman to wear the veil in the presence of men, except for her husband and close affines, as part of the modest behaviour enjoined upon her. What that veiling entailed varied considerably from one part of the Islamic world to another, finding its most extreme version in the Afghani *burqa*, in which women could only look out on the world through a mesh of threads, and outsiders could see nothing of her, not even her eyes. In general, veiling was far less extreme, and generally allowed an open face, although almost invariably the hair was covered and clothing was such as to hide rather than reveal the contours of the figure. In the context of global women's clothing before about 1800, there was nothing unusual in that, except in so far as stress placed on hair and hair covering was not common.

In the course of the twentieth century, however, the veil came to be politicized in a number of important ways. Colonial rulers, for instance in Egypt, pushed the same line, aiming for a change in women's rights which they were generally not prepared to countenance at home.[47] The French in Algeria also discouraged the headscarf, as a sign of Islam and as such a disqualification for moving out of the indigenat into French citizenship. However, the decline in the use of the veil was driven from within the Islamic lands, not from outside. In the first instance, it was the authoritarian modernizers of countries in the Middle East, notably Kemal Atatürk and Reza Shah, who came to see it as a symbol of backwardness. In Turkey the headscarf was long discouraged in the name of secularism. Entry into public buildings, including schools and universities, and employment in government offices, was forbidden to those wearing a headscarf, and those men whose wives did not bare their heads could not expect promotion, or government employment.[48] Equally, in Iran, the total ban on the headscarf and even more on the *chador*, the tent-like black dress which conservative Iranian women wore, was lifted after the fall of Reza Shah. Nevertheless, particularly after 1953 when his son Mohammed Reza Shah took power in a CIA-backed coup, wearing the *chador* was forbidden in many restaurants, actively discouraged in universities and schools and thoroughly disapproved of in social functions where women were increasingly expected to appear with their menfolk.[49]

Not all unveiling, though, was imposed. In particular in Egypt there was a steady move by upper- and middle-class women to move out of seclusion and to remove their veils when outside the home. This shadowed a move towards a much wider participation in economic life than had previously been the case. Certainly under Nasser, who promised a Government job to all those who graduated from university, increasing numbers of middle-class women were taking up outside jobs and were appearing on the streets with their faces and heads bared. They were nevertheless in danger of being the subject of unwelcome sexual comment, and forms of seclusion by class were not uncommon – unveiled women travelled in private and expensive buses, or in cars, and visited coffee bars and so forth which were out of reach for the common people – but there was from the 1920s (and to some extent there remains) a feminine space in which a degree of independence is signified by the Westernization of their outfits.[50]

In the course of the 1970s the trend began to change. New forms of Islamic dress came into use across the Middle East, and indeed beyond.[51] There were a number of reasons for this. In the first place, of course, there was the Islamic Revolution in Iran. In the latter years of the Shah's regime, a number of middle-class working women in Iran had taken to wearing various forms of headscarf as a protest against his increasingly disparaged government. After the Ayatollah Khomeini had taken over control in 1979, however, what had been an optional protest came to be imposed by law. It became illegal for any woman to appear in public with any part of her body other than her face exposed. In particular, all hair had to be hidden. The penalty for non-compliance was a beating, of up to seventy-four lashes. These regulations were enforced by a unit of the police which became known as the Vice Squad.[52] The control of women's dress has become a major part of state policy.[53]

It is important to realize that the impulses which had led some women to re-adopt headscarves, if not the full *chador*, before 1979, were replicated in many countries. At least two processes were going on. On the one hand, some women found in the donning of Islamic dress a way of maintaining a much desired form of privacy and personal space even when venturing onto the streets and the public arena of great cities.[54] At the same time, the later twentieth century saw a regeneration of confidence in Islam and a rejection of some parts at least of the power of the West. Beginning in Algeria during the war of liberation against the French, and clearly in Palestine during the Intifada, women have been taking on various forms of Islamic dress, which often had no "traditional" basis in the region in question, as a symbol of resistance to colonial rule. This has continued with the widespread solidarity with the struggle against Israel, seen as a Western intrusion into Arab lands. Later, individuals of the highest social class, in Turkey and in Egypt, took on the headscarf as an assertion of their Islamic commitment, and their appreciation that Islam and modernity were not incompatible. As if to signify this, the costume they have taken on has, in general, no specific precedent, and can certainly be worn with a considerable degree of flair, colour coordination and fashion sense.[55]

The justification for wearing the headscarf, and Islamic clothing in general, of course, goes back to the Koran, in which it is ordained that "believing women . . . should not display their beauty and ornaments except what ordinarily appear thereof; that they should draw their veils over their bosom and should not display their beauty to any but their husbands, their fathers" and other close relatives.[56] This is a text which, like so many scriptural utterances in many religions, can be interpreted to produce widely differing results in the world of today. It certainly can be seen as part of the justification of the unbridled oppression of women found in Afghanistan under the Taliban, or in Saudi Arabia, for instance. Even when taken in a looser way than

16 Girls in Islamic dress, Birmingham, 2002

under these regimes or in post-Khomeini Iran, it can certainly be seen as a limitation on women's control over their own bodies. However, particularly since similar injunctions are imposed by the Koran on men, there is a feminist interpretation which can be placed on the rule. It allows women to reject what is seen as the over-sexualized and commodified female body of Western consumerism. It is in this spirit that Leila Ahmed wrote that "Arab Muslim women need to reject, just as Western women are trying to reject, the androcentrism of whatever culture or tradition in which they find themselves, but that is quite different from saying that they need to adopt Western customs, goals, and life-styles."[57]

This, of course, is what makes Islamic dress worn by women so challenging when worn outside of majority Muslim countries. As so often, how women are dressed is a sharper commentary on the world than is the dress of men. Much more than the latter, which exhibits only minor deviations from the Western norms – the tie-less buttoned-up shirts of the Iranian leadership, Yasser Arafat's scarf – the wearing of what is seen, and is intended to be seen, as Islamic dress by women is a rejection of certain core values of Western society, and not necessarily those of which the West is most aware, or most proud. Such dress is in the first instance an assertion of Islam, which, since 11 September 2001 and the promulgation of the "War on Terror", is not something which the West can take lightly. It is also a rejection of secularism, and godlessness. This is a particular affront to parts of the French intellectual and political establishment, in that the modern French state was founded upon the rejection of a monarchy propped up by the (Catholic) church.[58] It can also be seen as an acceptance of the inequality of the sexes, a proposition which the Western world rejects in theory, if seldom in practice. It is often thought, by non-Muslims, that all women who wear headscarves or more all-covering forms of dress do so at the behest of some man, and would reject it if they had the chance, although there is no empirical justification for such a vision. At the same time, there is an appreciation that the headscarf, and body covering, is directed at the commercialization, sexualization and Americanization of the modern world. The idea that there can be an alternative modernity is something which is difficult for Westerners to accept. Europeans and North Americans have become too used to the rest of the world accepting, and wanting to accept, what the West has to offer, as symbolized in the clothing that the whole world now wears. The West is not prepared for there to be such a visible group, in the core of at least European society, who demonstratively put on markers of an identity at odds with what we have thought to be the pattern of history, and the way the world has come to be.

12

Conclusion

It is easy to explain away the processes described in this book as just so many examples of the pervading influence of the West, and of creeping Westernization. The corollary would then be to focus on the resistance of a whole range of societies to the processes of cultural imperialism which the imposition of Western dress entailed. Certainly, in individual studies there is a lot to be said for this approach. To most scholars, it is more satisfying to concentrate on the rejection, or at least the adaptation, of global norms than on what might be thought of as a slavish mimicry of those who are the imperial masters, not necessarily politically any more but certainly economically and culturally.[1]

As I have argued implicitly throughout this book, such an approach would be mistaken, for several reasons. First, it would tend to over-emphasize the exotic at the expense of those things which might, at first sight, seem to be normal, or at least familiar. The result of this might be to forget the exoticism of the ordinary, to fail to realize that all sorts of things which we take for granted were once exotic creations, certainly where they are now to be found. Historians, more than anyone else, should look in wonder at everyday things and habits, because they know, or should know, that matters were once different.

Secondly, it is important to treat those who wear European-style clothing with respect. It is important to allow the subjects of our enquiries the benefit of free will. In many cases, and within certain limits, people decide for themselves what clothes they will wear, which is why wearing clothes (and certainly not wearing them) is almost invariably a political act. Those who made particular decisions, to put on or not to put on European-style dress, did so with a clear idea of what they were doing, and for specific political reasons. There were moments when there were advantages to be gained from meeting the expectations of colonizers that their subjects would be dressed in a costume that they themselves would not put on, so that wearing something else than European clothing might be a form of conservatism, and thus a way of manipulating those same rulers in order to acquire power and prestige within a particular polity. There were certainly those times at which playing that role might have its definite benefits. There were also moments at which individuals could put on variants of indigenous dress as a form of resistance to imperial rule, as a nationalist statement that the tradition from which they derived was a good as any that the imperialists might themselves represent. These claims could be made towards outsiders, colonial rulers and their neo-imperialist successors, but they could also be made within a given society, as part of a strategy to gain a degree of popular legitimacy, as a genuine "man of the people". And then there were those who wore European clothes as an attempt to make clear that they were as good as anyone in the world, and certainly the equals of those who were perceived as looking down at the wearer of the suit. Particular forms of dress were used rhetorically, to make claims for equality, and above all of modernity, and it might also be imposed in the hope that the modernity they represented would be taken up by the subjects of those who were doing the imposing. It is not for the analyst, certainly not one who has grown up in what was once an imperial metropolis, and whose family had some connections with the imperial project, to decide which of these strategies was at any given moment acceptable and legitimate. It may not be everything to understand, but to condemn would be much worse. Historians do not need to judge.

Thirdly, and crucially, this is what the sartorial history of the world over the last century and a half has been about. Globalization dominates the world, and this, in our various ways, we have to accept, and perhaps even celebrate. The great economist Joan Robinson is said once to have commented that the only thing worse than being exploited was not being exploited at all. Equally, it is easy to see that the only thing worse than suffering under globalization is being entirely free from it. People across the world have developed strategies for negotiating their own relationships to the global economy, to the global international order and to the global cultural regime. For some this may entail falling back on traditions which they, or their forebears, have invented. For many more, cultural globalization allows them to behave as modern members of international society, to think of themselves as modern people, and in this way to believe that they matter to others, and to themselves. These sorts of statement are made in many ways, but clothing is always one of the most salient media. It is one of the most public ways by which people can announce to their fellows who they are, or at least, remembering Umberto Eco's definition of the sign as something with which people can lie, who they would like to be, or who they would like to be thought to be.

The question does still remain, however, how completely Western forms of dress have taken over the whole of the world. What is most important to realize is that dress is inevitably highly gendered. Women are likely to have taken on Western dress at a different tempo to that of the men of their society, usually slower. Again there are a whole variety of reasons for this, both in terms of the sexual morality which the West is thought to bring with it, at times restricting but also being seen as providing women with opportunities to escape from male domination. The struggle about women's dress was often part of the broader sexual politics of a given society. It may be that men attempted to keep women in "traditional" dress, or in more acceptable forms of Western attire, as part of a generalized attempt to maintain patriarchal control, but there were other possibilities. For a man to allow, or even more to require, that the women whom he believed to be under his control dress as Westerners, and to parade themselves in ways to which they were not accustomed, was one of the most potent ways in which he could demonstrate his own, and his family's, modernity. Women, too, might want to be "modern" or "new" women, or they might reject the exploitation which was seen as accompanying such an imposition of a specific form of modernity, and seek to develop other types of modernity, which might accept, or might reject, that which global society and culture has been trying to foist on them. Respect, honour and, consequently, independence might depend on such claims in ways which from the outside might seem demeaning, but to the individuals themselves would signify their freedom.

The gendered aspects of clothing thus emphasize one, perhaps two, of clothing's prime functions. Modesty – *Scham* – and to a lesser extent ornament – *Schmuck* – are more clearly related to the questions of identity and gender construction than is the protection against the elements – *Schutz* – which clothing also provides. Nevertheless, as this book has shown, none of these three are absolutes. All have been interpreted in a multitude of different ways over the course of the last few centuries. In this way they have been used to mark the ever-shifting identities of the world as they have developed. But clothing has done more than that. The very mutability of clothing has driven the world economy to a degree probably unequalled by any other class of commodity. The production of clothing, in the whole process from fleece, flax or cotton plant to suit, skirt and shirt, and above all the distribution of clothing have driven the economy of the world to its current state. The homogenization of clothing may be a symptom of globalization, but at the same time the profits deriving from the clothing industry have made that globalization possible. Regions have been incorporated into the world economy, at differential rates and at different times, precisely because of their position in the economy of dress. The exploitation of workers in China and elsewhere in Asia, and the disastrous non-exploitation of Africans, as Joan Robinson would have said, are results of this. We are a dressed species, because we are a species of cultures, and the consequence of this has made the world what it is today.

Notes

NOTES TO CHAPTER 1

1　Ali A. Mazrui, "The Robes of Rebellion: Sex, Dress, and Politics in Africa", *Encounter*, 34, 1970, 22.

2　For some comments on this phenomenon, see C. A. Bayly, *The Birth of the Modern World, 1780–1914*, Oxford, Blackwell, 2004, 12–19; see also Wilbur Zelinsky, "Globalization Reconsidered: The Historical Geography of Modern Western Male Attire", *Journal of Cultural Geography*, 22, 2004.

3　In this book, I take these phenomena for granted, and do not, except incidentally, expand on them, or attempt to provide explanations for them. Places to start which are as good as any, and much better than most, would include Bayly, *Birth of the Modern World* and A. G. Hopkins (ed.), *Globalization in World History*, London, Pimlico, 2002.

4　Max Beerbohm, "Dandies and Dandies", in *The Incomparabel Max Beerbohm*, London, Icon, 1964, 18, cited in Michael Carter, *Fashion Classics: From Carlyle to Barthes*, Oxford and New York, Berg, 2003, 10.

5　Our father worked in the Natural History Museum, next door, and we were thus frequent visitors to the South Kensington Museum complex.

6　Even Margaret Maynard, *Dress and Globalisation*, Manchester, Manchester UP, 2004, tends in fact to stress difference, rather than the basic convergence which lies at the heart of globalization.

7　Lou Taylor, *The Study of Dress History*, Manchester, Manchester UP, 2002, 116. James Laver, long curator of clothing at the Victoria and Albert Museum, London, and one of the founders of costume studies, wrote that he was drawn to the subject because "I wanted to date the pictures". Cited in Carter, *Fashion Classics*, 121.

8   Petr Bogatyrev, *The Functions of Folk Costume in Moravian Slovakia*; translated by Richard G. Crum, The Hague, Mouton, 1971.

9   Cited by Charles Bremner, article entitled "Chirac's Monument for Paris", in *Times Online*, 17.6.2006.

10   These can be found, for instance, in Mary Ellen Roach-Higgins and Joanne B. Eicher, "Dress and Identity", first published in *Clothing and Textiles Research Journal*, 10, 1992, 1–8, and conveniently found in Mary Ellen Roach-Higgins, Joanne B. Eicher and Kim K. P. Johnson, *Dress and Identity*, New York, Fairchild Publications, 1995, 9–11.

11   For an idea of how things have changed even in North America, Peter N. Stearns, *Fat History: Bodies and Beauty in the Modern West*, New York and London, New York University Press, 1997. For similar analysis in the world of high fashion, see Valerie Steele, *Fashion and Eroticism: Ideals of Feminine Beauty from the Victorian Era to the Jazz Age*, New York and Oxford, Oxford University Press, 1985, esp ch. 11.

12   Umberto Eco, *A Theory of Semiotics*, Bloomington and London, Indiana UP, 1976, 7.

13   Famously, Roland Barthes, *The Fashion System*, New York, Hill and Wang, 1983 (translation of *Système de la mode*, Paris, Seuil, 1967); also Marshall Sahlins, *Culture and Practical Reason*, Chicago and London, Chicago UP, 1976, esp. ch. IV.

14   *Finnegan's Wake* might, I suppose, be an exception.

15   In the Oxford UP edition (Oxford, 1987), 30.

16   First published by Macmillan in New York, 1899, and reprinted with great frequency ever since.

17   *Distinction: A Social Critique of the Judgement of Taste*, trans. Richard Nice, Cambridge, Mass., Harvard UP, 1984.

18   Mary Douglas and Baron Isherwood, *The World of Goods*, New York, Basic Books, 1979.

NOTES TO CHAPTER 2

1   This is a contrast which occurs, for instance, in modern Tanzania.

2   G. R. Driver and John C. Miles, *The Assyrian Laws*, Oxford, Clarendon Press, 1935, 126–34.

3   Sarah B. Pomeroy, *Goddesses, Whores, Wives and Slaves: Women in Classical Antiquity*, New York, Schocken Books, 1975, 57, 180–2; T'ung-tsu Ch'ü, *Law and Society in Traditional China*, Paris and The Hague, Mouton, 1961, 137–41.

4   Isaiah 3: 16–18.

5   Satire II, in *The Sixteen Satires*, cited by Aileen Ribeiro, *Dress and Morality*, London, Batsford, 1986, 22.

6   John V. Murra, "Cloth and its Functions in the Inca State", *American Anthropologist*, 64, 1962, 710–23; Penny Dransart, "Pachamama: The Inka Earth Mother of the Long Sweeping Garment", in Ruth Barnes and Joanne B. Eicher (eds), *Dress and Gender: Making and Meaning*,

Oxford, Berg, 1992, 149–54; Armin Bollinger, *So kleideten sich die Inka*, Zurich, 1983, esp. 130–8; Rosaleen Howard, personal communication; Mariselle Meléndez, "Visualizing Difference: The Rhetoric of Clothing in Colonial Spanish America", in Regina A. Root (ed.), *The Latin American Fashion Reader*, Oxford and New York, Berg, 2005, 18–24.

7   Ann Pollard Rowe, "Inca Weaving and Costume", *Textile Museum Journal*, 34 & 35, 1995–6, 32; ead., *Costume and Identity in Highland Ecuador*, Washington, DC, Seattle and London, The Textile Museum, and University of Washington Press, 1998, 44; Murra, "Cloth and its Functions", 721.

8   Inga Clendinnen, *Aztecs: An Interpretation*, Cambridge, Cambridge University Press, 1991, 33–4, 40–1, citing Fr. Diego Durán, *Historia de las Indias de Nueva España e Islas de la Tierra Firme*, 2 vols, edited by Angel María Garibay, Mexico City, Porrúa, 1967, II, 209–10; Patricia Anawalt, "Costume and Control: Aztec Sumptuary Laws", *Archeology*, 33, 1980.

9   Clendinnen, *Aztecs*, 114–21, citing, on areas further north, George Catlin, *Letters and Notes on the Manners, Customs, and Conditions of the North American Indians*, 2 vols, New York, Dover, I, 145–54.

10 R. S. Rattray, *Religion and Art in Ashanti*, Oxford, Clarendon Press, 1927, 236–50.

11 Robin Law, *The Slave Coast of West Africa, 1550–1750*, Oxford, Oxford UP, 1991, 78.

12 Paula Gerschick Ben-Amos, *Art, Innovation and Politics in Eighteenth-Century Benin*, Bloomington and Indianapolis, Indiana University Press, 1999, 124.

13 Patricia L. Baker, "The Fez in Turkey: A Symbol of Modernization?", *Costume*, 20, 1986, 72.

14 John Norton, "Faith and Fashion in Turkey", in Nancy Lindisfarne-Tapper and Bruce Inham (eds), *Languages of Dress in the Middle East*, London, Curzon in association with the Centre of Near and Middle Eastern Studies, SOAS, 1997, 150; Donald Quaraert, "Clothing Laws, State, and Society in the Ottoman Empire, 1720–1829", *International Journal of Middle East Studies*, 29, 1997, 403–25.

15 J. Forbes Watson, *The Textile Manufactures and the Costumes of the People of India*, London, Eyre and Spottiswood, 1866, 11, cited in B. N. Goswamy, *Indian Costumes in the Collection of the Calico Museum of Textiles*, Ahmedabad, Calico Museum, 1993, 17.

16 Stanley Lane-Poole, *Aurangzib and the Decay of the Mughal Empire*, Oxford, Clarendon Press, 1908, 19, cited in William Dalrymple, *White Mughals: Love and Betrayal in Eighteenth-Century India*, London, HarperCollins, 2002, 10.

17 Baker, "The Fez", 73.

18 Zhou Xun and Gao Chunming, *Le Costume chinois*, Fribourg, Office du Livre, 1984, 146.

19 Valery M. Garrett, *Chinese Clothing: An Illustrated Guide*, Hong Kong, Oxford and New York, Oxford University Press, 1994, 12.

20 Those who wore clothing to which they were not entitled would receive 100 strokes with a heavy bamboo, and be banned from office. William

C. Jones (ed. and trans.), *The Great Qing Code*, Oxford, Clarendon Press, 1994, 180.

21   Garrett, *Chinese Clothing*, 30, 127.
22   A form of unbleached Chinese silk made from the pupae of wild silkworms.
23   A textile made of yarn spun from a species of nettle.
24   Donald H. Shively, "Sumptuary Regulation and Status in Early Tokugawa Japan", *Harvard Journal of Asiatic Studies*, 25, 1964–5, 126.
25   Ibid., 146.
26   Ibid., 133, 139.
27   Ibid., 134.
28   Michel de Montaigne, "Of Sumptuary Laws", in *The Complete Works of Montaigne*, trans. D. M. Frame, London, Hamish Hamilton, 1958, 196, cited in Alan Hunt, *Governance of the Consuming Passions: A History of Sumptuary Law*, Houndmills and London, Macmillan, 1996, 102.
29   Dale Carolyn Gluckman, "Towards a New Aesthetic: The Evolution of the Kosode and its Decoration", in Dale Carolyn Gluckman and Sharon Sadako Takeda (eds), *When Art Became Fashion: Kosode in Edo-Period Japan*, Los Angeles, Los Angeles Country Museum of Art, 1992, 79–80.
30   Cited in Fernand Braudel, *Capitalism and Material Life, 1400–1800*, trans. Miriam Kochan, London, Weidenfeld and Nicolson, 1973, 235.
31   Gluckman and Takeda, "Introduction", *When Art Became Fashion*, 40, citing Jacob Raz, *Audience and Actors: A Study of their Interaction in the Japanese Traditional Theatre*, Leiden, Brill, 1983.
32   Monica Bethe, "Reflections on *Beni*: Red as a Key to Edo-Period Fashion", in Gluckman and Takeda (eds), *When Art Became Fashion*, 133–49.
33   This is a technique by which the strings of a tie-dye are released before the dye has fully dried, thus producing a dappled effect.
34   Cited in Shively, "Sumptuary Regulation and Status", 124–5.
35   Hunt, *Governance of the Consuming Passions*, ch. 2; Diane Owen Hughes, "Sumptuary Law and Social Relations in Renaissance Italy", in John Bossy (ed.), *Disputes and Settlements: Law and Human Relations in the West*, Cambridge, Cambridge UP, 1983, 72 and further; Liselotte Constanze Eisenbart, *Kleiderordnungen der deutschen Städte zwischen 1350 und 1700: Ein Betrag zur Kulturgeschichte des deutschen Bürgertums*, Göttingen, Berlin and Frankfurt, Musterschmidt, 1956, 6–7; Cathering Kovesi Killerby, *Sumptuary Law in Italy, 1200–1500*, Oxford, Clarendon Press, 2002.
36   Hughes, "Sumptuary Law", 75–6; N. B. Harte, "State Control of Dress and Social Change in Pre-industrial England", in D. C. Coleman and A. H. John (eds), *Trade, Government and Economy in Pre-Industrial England: Essays Presented to F. J. Fisher*, London, Weidenfeld and Nicolson, 1976, 148 (I have modernized the spelling of the Scots law).
37   Martin A. S. A. Hume, "A Fight against Finery", in *The Year after the Armada and Other Historical Studies*, London, T. Fisher Unwin, 1896, 250–3.

38 Diane Owen Hughes, "Distinguishing Signs: Ear-rings, Jews and Franciscan Rhetoric in the Italian Renaissance City", *Past and Present,* 112, 1986.

39 Hughes, "Sumptuary Law", 83–7; the Bernese figures are from John Martin Vincent, *Costume and Conduct in the Laws of Basel, Bern and Zurich, 1370–1800,* Baltimore, Johns Hopkins Press, 1935, 104.

40 Cited in Louise Godard de Donville, *Signification de la Mode sous Louis XIII,* Aix-en-Provence, Edisud, 1978, 208.

41 Eisenbart, *Kleiderordnungen,* 86.

42 Frances Elizabeth Baldwin, *Sumptuary Legislation and Personal Regulation in England,* Baltimore, Johns Hopkins Press, 1926, 30–1, 112, 115, 131, 142, 149, 159–61; Reed Benhamou, "The Restraint of Excessive Apparel: England 1337–1604", *Dress,* 15, 1989, 32–3.

43 C. W. Cole, *Colbert and a Century of French Mercantilism,* II, New York, Columbia UP, 1939, cited in Harte, "State Control of Dress", 151.

44 Hume, "Fight against Finery", 205–60.

45 J. H. Elliott, *The Count-Duke of Olivares: The Statesman in an Age of Decline,* New Haven and London, Yale University Press, 1986, 100, 105, 111.

46 Hughes, "Sumptuary Laws", 99.

47 See Hunt, *Governance of the Consuming Passions,* 122–3; Kim M. Philipls, "Masculinities and the Medieval English Sumptuary Laws", *Gender and History,* 19, 2007.

48 Hughes, "Sumptuary Law", 74–5.

49 Harte, "State Control of Dress", 133.

50 Eisenbart, *Kleiderordnungen,* 14; Hans Medick, *Weben und Überleben in Laichingen, 1650–1900: Lokalgeschichte als Allgemeine Geschichte,* Göttingen, Vandenhoeck & Ruprecht, 1996, ch. 5; see also Medick, "Une culture de la considération. Les vêtements et leur couleur à Laichingen entre 1750 et 1820", *Annales, Histoire, Science Sociales,* 50, 1995, 753–74; Neithard Bulst, "Kleidung als sozialer Konfliktstoff: Probleme kleidergesetzlicher Normierung im soziale Gefüge", *Saeculum,* 44, 1993, 33.

51 Eisenbart, *Kleiderordnungen,* 84; Godard de Donville, *Signification de la Mode,* 20.

52 Published in L. Gilliodts-van Severen, *Inventaire de la Ville de Bruges, Section I: Inventaire des Chartres,* VI, Bruges, Edward Gaillard sous les auspices de l'Administration Communale, 1876, 481–2. I owe this reference to Wim Blockmans, with thanks.

53 A. T. van Deursen, *Mensen van Klein Vermogen: Het 'kopergeld' van de Gouden Eeuw,* Amsterdam, Bert Bakker, 1992, 218, citing the archive of the Staten van Holland, 2600d.

54 Joan R. Kent, "Attitudes of Members of the House of Commons to the Regulation of 'Personal Conduct' in Late Elizabethan and Early Stuart England", *Bulletin of the Institute of Historical Research,* 46, 1973.

55 *Areopagitica,* paragraph beginning "next what of more national corruption".

56 Cited in Christopher J. Berry, *The Idea of Luxury: A Conceptual and Historical Investigation,* Cambridge, Cambridge UP 1994, 111–12.

57   Rudolf Dekker, "'Private Vices, Public Virtues' Revisited: The Dutch Background of Bernard Mandeville", *History of European Ideas,* 14, 1992, 481–98.

58   Bernard Mandeville, "Remark M", in *The Fable of the Bees*, edited with an introduction by Philip Harth, Harmondsworth, Penguin, 1970, 150–4.

59   Sir William Temple cited in Berry, *Idea of Luxury*, 107.

60   Simon Schama, *The Embarrassment of Riches: An Interpretation of Dutch Culture in the Golden Age*, London, Collins, 1987.

61   Jan de Vries, "Luxury in the Dutch Golden Age in Theory and Practice", in Maxine Berg and Elizabeth Eger, *Luxury in the Eighteenth Century: Debates, Desires and Delectable Goods*, Houndmills and New York, Palgrave Macmillan, 2003; the quotation is from p. 53.

62   Smith was of course brought up in the Calvinist faith of the Church of Scotland, as might be expected on the basis of the anti-Weberian correlation I am proposing here.

63   I. Hont and M. Ignatieff (eds), *Wealth and Virtue: The Shaping of Political Economy in the Scottish Enlightenment*, Cambridge, Cambridge UP, 1983.

64   Cited in Berry, *Idea of Luxury*, 115.

NOTES TO CHAPTER 3

1   N. B. Harte, "The Economics of Clothing in the Late Seventeenth Century", *Textile History*, 22/2, 1991.

2   David Corner, "The Tyranny of Fashion: The Case of the Felt-Hatting Trade in the Late Seventeenth and Eighteenth Centuries", *Textile History*, 22/2, 1991; for a useful survey of the North American (and other) fur trades, see John F. Richards *The Unending Frontier: An Environmental History of the Early Modern World*, Berkeley, Los Angeles and London, University of California Press, 2003.

3   This is the description of the current state of play given by Maxine Berg, "New Commodities, Luxuries and their Consumers in Eighteenth-Century England", in Maxine Berg and Helen Clifford (eds), *Consumers and Luxury: Consumer Culture in Europe, 1650–1850*, Manchester and New York, Manchester UP, 1999. I should point out that she, like me, is essentially disappointed in her findings. For an aggressive assertion of the primacy of demand, in the context of (British) North America, see Cary Carson, "The Consumer Revolution in Colonial British America: Why Demand?" in Cary Carson, Ronald Hollman and Peter J. Albert (eds), *Of Consuming Interest: The Style of Life in the Eighteenth Century*, Charlottesville and London, University Press of Virginia for the United States Capitol Historical Society, 1994.

4   Harte, "Economics of Clothing".

5   The first patents were taken out in 1842.

6 Cited in Daniel Roche, *The Culture of Clothing: Dress and Fashion in the Ancien Regime*, trans. Jean Birrell, Cambridge, Cambridge UP, 1994, *Culture of Clothing*, 301.

7 Beverly Lemire, *Dress, Culture and Commerce: The English Clothing Trade before the Factory, 1660–1800*, Houndmills and London, Macmillan, 1997, 20.

8 Ibid., 70–1.

9 P. Earle, "The Female Labour Market in London in the Late Seventeenth and Early Eighteenth Centuries", *Economic History Review*, 2nd series, 42, 1989; L. D. Schwarz, *London in the Age of Industrialization: Entrepreneurs, Labour Force and Living Conditions, 1700–1850*, Cambridge, Cambridge UP, 1992, 19.

10 Stanley Chapman, *Hosiery and Knitwear: Four Centuries of Small-Scale Industry in Britain, c.1589–2000*, Oxford, Oxford UP for the Pasold Research Fund, 2002, 10.

11 Cissie Fairchilds, "The Production and Marketing of Populuxe Goods in Eighteenth-Century Paris", in John Brewer and Roy Porter (eds), *Consumption and the World of Goods*, London, Routledge, 1993, 232; the sample on which this figure is based was drawn primarily from lower-middle and lower-class decedents.

12 Lemire, *Dress, Culture and Commerce*, 39, 98.

13 Margaret Spufford, *The Great Reclothing of Rural England: Petty Chapmen and their Wares in the Seventeenth Century*, London, Hambledon Press, 1984, 123–5. There are indications as early as the 1680s of travelling salesmen selling outer garments of wool off the peg, but these are rare.

14 *The Art of Love*, cited in Neil McKendrick, "The Commercialization of Fashion", in Neil McKendrick, John Brewer and J. H. Plumb, *The Birth of a Consumer Society: The Commercialization of Eighteenth-Century England*, London, Europa Publications, 1982, 34.

15 See e.g. Thera Wijsenbeek-Olthuis, *Achter de Gevels van Delft: Bezit en bestaan van rijk en arm in een periode van achteruitgang (1700–1800)*, Hilversum, Verloren, 1987, 281.

16 David Kuchta, *The Three-Piece Suit and Modern Masculinity in England, 1550–1850*, Berkeley, Los Angeles and London, University of California Press, 2002, 1–3; both of the Restoration's prime diarists, Samuel Pepys and John Evelyn, were at court to witness the transformation. The quotations are from Evelyn, as cited in Lemire, *Fashion's Favourite: The Cotton Trade and the Consumer in Britain, 1600–1800*, Oxford, Oxford UP, 1991, 11.

17 Anne Hollander, *Sex and Suits: The Evolution of Modern Dress*, New York, Alfred A. Knopf, 1994, 65, 80–3.

18 Lemire, *Fashion's Favourite*, 12; Kuchla, *Three-Piece Suit*, 77–84.

19 Lemire, *Fashion's Favourite*, 29–41.

20 D. C. Coleman, "An Innovation and its Diffusion: The 'New Draperies'", *Economic History Review*, 22, 1969, 417–29.

21 Roche, *Culture of Clothing*, 127, 138.

22 Aileen Ribeiro, *Dress and Morality*, London, Batsford, 1986, 100.

23 Lemire, *Fashion's Favourite*, 168–76; Amanda Vickery, *The Gentleman's Daughter: Women's Lives in Georgian England*, New Haven and London, Yale University Press, 172–7.

24 Daniel Defoe, *The Complete English Tradesman*, 1727, 332, cited in Anne Buck, "Variations in English Women's Dress in the Eighteenth Century", *Folk Life*, 9, 1971, 7.

25 Cited in Corner, "Tyranny of Fashion", 173–4.

26 Valerie Steele, "The Social and Political Significance of Macaroni Fashion", *Costume: the Journal of the Costume Society*, 19, 1985. Orice, more usually spelt orris, was a form of gold lace.

27 Except, in satire, by Yankie Doodle.

28 John Mackay, *A Journey through England*, London, J. Pemberton, 1722, II, 238, cited in Kuchta, *Three-Piece Suit*, 122.

29 Cited in Steele, "Macaroni Fashion", 101.

30 On the process as a whole see Linda Colley, *Britons: Forging the Nation, 1707–1837*, New Haven and London, Yale University Press, 1992.

31 Roche, *Culture of Clothing*, 109. A *sétier* was approximately 150 litres by volume.

32 Madeleine Delpierre, "Rose Bertin, les marchandes de modes et la Révolution", in *Modes et Révolutions,* Paris, Editions Paris-Musées, 1989, 21–6; Hollander, *Sex and Suits*, 12.

33 Roche, *Culture of Clothing*, Fairchilds, "Populuxe Goods"; Jennifer Jones, "*Coquettes* and *Grisettes*: Women Buying and Selling in Ancien Régime Paris", in Victoria de Grazia (ed.), *The Sex of Things: Gender and Consumption in Historical Perspective*, Berkeley, Los Angeles and London, University of California Press, 1996.

34 Françoise Vittu, "1780–1804 ou vingt ans de 'Révolution des Têtes Françaises'", in *Modes et Révolutions*, 54.

35 Jean Marc Devocelle, "D'un costume politique à une politique du costume: approches théoriques et idéolgiques du costume pendant la Révolution française", in *Modes en Révolutions*, 84, 99 (for the text of the order.)

36 Aileen Ribeiro, *The Art of Dress: Fashion in England and France 1750–1820*, New Haven and London, Yale UP, 1995, 82–4; Lynn Hunt, "Freedom of Dress in Revolutionary France", in Sara E. Melzer and Kathryn Norberg (eds), *From the Royal to the Republican Body: Incorporating the Political in Seventeenth- and Eighteenth-Century France*, Berkeley, Los Angeles and London, University of California Press, 1998, 228–31.

37 Hunt, "Freedom of Dress", 228–30, and various citations there.

38 See Annemarie Kleinert, "La Mode, miroir de la Révolution française", in *Modes et Révolutions*, 60–1; Daniel Roche, "Apparences révolutionnaires ou révolution des apparences", ibid., 118.

39 François-Xavier Mercier, *Comment m'habillerai-je? Réflexions politiques et philosophiques sur l'habillement français et sur la nécessité d'un costume nationale*, Paris, 1793, cited in Roche, "Apparences révolutionaires", 122.

40 Hunt, "Freedom of Dress", 241–2; Roche, "Apparences révolutionaires", 126; Aileen Ribeiro, *Fashion in the French Revolution*, London, Batsford, 1988, 115–17.

41 See the famous paintings by David, reproduced for instance in Ribeiro, *Art of Dress*, 158–9.

42 Hunt, "Freedom of Dress", 242. She claims, not implausibly, that Napoleon dressed thus to camouflage his increasing portliness.

43 Madeleine Delpierre, "Le Retour aux costumes de cour sous le Consulat et l'Empire", in *Modes et Révolutions*, 35.

44 Hunt, "Freedom of Dress", 242.

45 J. C. Flügel, *The Psychology of Clothes*, London, Hogarth Press, 1930, 111; Flügel's comments surely underestimate the degree to which male tailoring has striven for elegance, if within a limited range of form and colour.

46 Colley, *Britons*, 187.

47 John Harvey, *Men in Black*, London, Reaktion Books, 1995.

48 Kuchta, *Three-Piece Suit*, 165–6.

49 Cited ibid, 167.

50 Colley, *Britons*, 187.

51 Philippe Perrot, *Fashioning the Bourgeoisie: A History of Clothing in the Nineteenth Century*, trans. Richard Bienvenu, Princeton, Princeton UP, 1994, 112–13.

NOTES TO CHAPTER 4

1 Cited in Willard J. Peterson, "What to wear? Observation and Participation by Jesuit Missionaries in late Ming society", in Stuart B. Schwartz (ed.), *Implicit Understandings: Observing, Reporting and Reflecting on the Encounters between Europeans and Other Peoples in the Early Modern Era*, Cambridge, Cambridge UP, 1994, 409.

2 Cited ibid., 414; Peterson also points out that at this era there was no specific Jesuit habit.

3 Information from Rudy Kousbroek; the women's roles were taken by young boys.

4 William Dalrymple, *White Mughals: Love and Betrayal in Eighteenth-Century India*, London, HarperCollins, 2002, 12–13.

5 J. A. de Mandelslo, *The Voyages and Travels of J. A. de Mandelslo . . . into the East-Indies. Begun in the year 1638 and finish'd in 1640. Containing a particular description of the great Mogul's empire, the kingdoms of Decan, . . . Zeilon, Coromandel, Pegu, . . . Japan, the great kingdom of China. . . . Rendered into English, by J. Davies, etc.*, London, no publisher given, 1662, cited in Dalrymple, *White Mughals*, 22.

6 Hobson-Jobson, 65, cited in E. M. Collingham, *Imperial Bodies: The Physical Experience of the Raj, c.1800–1947*, Cambridge, Polity, 2001, 41.

7   Dalrymple, *White Mughals*, particularly 34–54.
8   James Johnson, *The Influence of Tropical Climates, More Especially the Climate of India, on European Constitutions*, London, Stockdale, 1813, cited in Collingham, *Imperial Bodies*, 41.
9   F. de Haan, *Oud-Batavia*, 2 vols, Batavia, Kolff, 1922, II, 138.
10 Leonard Blussé, *Bitters Bruid: een koloniaal huwelijksdrama in de gouden Eeuw*, Amsterdam, Balans, 1997; idem, *Strange Company: Chinese Settlers, Mestizo Women and the Dutch in VOC Batavia*, Leiden, KITLV, 1986, 171; Jean Gelman Taylor, *The Social World of Batavia: European and Eurasian in Dutch Asia*, Madison and London, University of Wisconsin Press, 1983, 37–42, 66, 100–1.
11 Cited in Taylor, *Social World*, 39.
12 Anthony Reid, *Southeast Asia in the Age of Commerce, 1450–1680, vol. I: The Lands below the Winds*, New Haven and London, Yale UP, 1988, 85.
13 De Haan, *Oud-Batavia*, I, 467.
14 J. J. Ras (ed.), *Babad tanah Djawi*, trans. W. L. Olthof, Dordrecht and Providence, Foris, 1987, 208–9, cited in Kees van Dijk, "Sarong, Jubbahs, and Trousers: Appearance as Means of Distinction and Discrimination", in Henk Schulte Noordholt (ed.), *Outward Appearances: Dressing State and Society in Indonesia*, Leiden, KITLV, 1997, 48.
15 Van Dijk, "Sarong, Jubbahs, and Trousers", 70.
16 Ibid., 46–7. How successful the Dutch were in keeping the various ethnic groups of colonial Batavia apart is open to question; it is probable that those who now claim to be indigenous Jakartans (Orang Batavi) in fact descend in large part from the immigrants of seventeenth- and eighteenth-century Batavia, of numerous origins. Information from Leonard Blussé.
17 J. A. van der Chijs (ed.), *Nederlansch-Indisch plakaatboek, 1602–1811*, 17 vols, Batavia Landsdrukkerij, 1885–1900, VI, 784–7.
18 Taylor, *Social World*, 99–101, 116; De Haan, *Oud-Batavia*, II, 148.
19 Arnold J. Bauer, *Goods, Power, History: Latin America's Material Culture*, Cambridge, Cambridge UP, 2001, 71.
20 James Lockhart, *The Nahuas after the Conquest: A Social and Cultural History of the Indians of Central Mexico, Sixteenth through Eighteenth Century*, Stanford, Stanford UP, 1992, 200.
21 Ibid., 199.
22 Nancy M. Farriss, *Maya Society under Colonial Rule: The Collective Enterprise of Survival*, Princeton, Princeton UP, 1984, 94; Matthew Restall, *The Maya World: Yucatec Culture and Society, 1550–1850*, Stanford, Stanford UP, 1997, 184.
23 A similar process went on in Amazonia, but perhaps the institutions created were less total.
24 The expulsion from Portuguese territories, i.e. Brazil, was three years later.
25 Maxime Haubert, *La Vie quotidienne au Paraguay sous les jésuites*, Paris, Hachette, 1967, 205–9.

26 Farriss, *Maya Society,* 97, 110.

27 Cited in Bauer, *Goods, Power, History,* 110.

28 Cited ibid., 111.

29 Cited ibid., 112.

30 Stuart B. Schwartz and Frank Salomon, "New Peoples and New Kinds of People: Adaptation, Readjustment and Ethnogenesis in South American Indigenous Societies (Colonial Era)", in Frank Salomon and Stuart B. Schwartz (eds), *The Cambridge History of the Native Peoples of the Americas, vol. III: South America,* Cambridge, Cambridge UP, 1999, part II, 490.

31 Mariselle Meléndez, "Visualizing Difference: The Rhetoric of Clothing in Colonial Spanish America", in Regina A. Root (ed.), *The Latin American Fashion Reader,* Oxford and New York, Berg, 2005, 24–9.

32 Ann Pollard Rowe (ed.), *Costume and Identity in Highland Ecuador,* Washington, DC, Seattle and London, Textile Museum and University of Washington Press, esp. 49; George M. Foster, *Culture and Conquest: America's Spanish Heritage,* New York, Wenner-Gren Foundation for Anthropological Research, 1960, 87. Ruth Corcuera, "Ponchos of the River Plate: Nostalgia for Eden", in Root (ed.), *Latin American Fashion Reader,* 169–74.

33 Marshall Joseph Becker, "Matchcoats: Cultural Conservatism and Change in One Aspect of Native American Clothing", *Ethnohistory,* 52, 2005; Dorothy Downs, "British Influences on Creek and Seminole Men's Clothing, 1733–1858", *Florida Anthropologist,* 33, 1980; Timothy J. Shannon, "Dressing for Success on the Mohawk Frontier: Hendrick, William Johnson and the Indian Fashion", *William and Mary Quarterly,* 53, 1996.

34 Bianca Tovías, "Power Dressing on the Prairies: The Grammar of Blackfoot Leadership Dress 1750–1930", in Louise Edwards and Mina Roces (eds), *The Politics of Dress in Asia and the Americas,* Eastbourne, Sussex Academic Press, 2007; Sandra Lee Evenson and David J. Trayte, "Dress and the Negotiation of Relationships between the Eastern Dakota and Euroamericans in Nineteenth-Century Minnesota", in Linda B. Arthur (ed.), *Religion, Dress and the Body,* Oxford and New York, Berg, 1999.

35 Carolyn R. Shine, "Scalping Knives and Silk Stockings: Clothing the Frontier, 1780–1795", *Dress,* 14, 1988.

36 Cited in Rhys Isaac, *The Transformation of Virginia: 1740–1790,* Chapel Hill, University of North Carolina Press, 1982, 44.

37 Cited in C. Dallett Hemphill, *Bowing to Necessities: A History of Manners in America, 1620–1860,* New York and Oxford, Oxford UP, 1999, 18, 232. In the event, many of those charged under the edict were able to prove that they, their husbands or their fathers were worth above £200, or that they were sufficiently educated to be granted exemptions. See Karin Calvert, "The Function of Fashion in Eighteenth Century America", in Cary Carson, Ronald Hollman and Peter J. Albert (eds), *Of Consuming Interest: The Style of Life in the Eighteenth Century,* Charlottesville and London, University Press of Virginia for the United States Capitol Historical Society, 1994, 259.

38   Richard L. Bushman, *The Refinement of America: Persons, Houses, Cities*, New York, Alfred A. Knopf, 1992, 69–74; Isaac, *Transformation of Virginia*, 44.

39   Shane White and Graham White, "Slave Clothing and African-American Culture in the Eighteenth and Nineteenth Centuries", *Past and Present*, 148, 1995, 154–6.

40   Hugh Trevor-Roper, "The Invention of Tradition: The Highland Tradition of Scotland", in Eric Hobsbawm and T. O. Ranger (eds), *The Invention of Tradition*, Cambridge, Cambridge UP, 1983, 30.

41   Helen Bradley Foster *'New Raiments of Self': African American Clothing in the Antebellum South*, Oxford and New York, Berg, 1997, ch. 3.

42   Cited in White and White, "Slave Clothing", 156; see also Jonathan Prude, "To Look upon the 'Lower Sort': Runaway Ads and the Appearance of Unfree Laborers in America, 1750–1800", *Journal of American History*, 78, 1991.

43   White and White, "Slave Clothing", citations at 156, 161, 176; Foster *"New Raiments of Self"*, 187.

44   See e.g. Beth Graybill and Linda B. Arthur, "The Social Control of Women's Bodies in Two Mennonite Communities", and Jean A. Hamilton and Jana M. Hawley, "Sacred Dress, Public Worlds: Amish and Mormon Experience and Commitment", both in Linda B. Arthur (ed.), *Religion, Dress and the Body*, Oxford, Berg, 1999.

45   George Fox, the founder of the Society of Friends, famously announced that "When the Lord sent me forth in the world, he forbade me to put off my hat to any, high or low . . . neither might I bow or scrape with my leg to any one." *The Journal of George Fox*, ed. J. L. Nickalls, Cambridge, Cambridge UP, 1952, 36, cited in Penelope J. Corfield, "Dress for Deference and Dissent: Hats and the Decline of Hat Honour", *Costume: the Journal of the Costume Society*, 23, 1989, 72.

46   Leigh Eric Schmidt, "'A Church-going people are a dress-loving people': Clothes, Communication and Religious Culture in Early America", *Church History*, 58, 1989, citations at 40–1, 48, 49; Philip Greven, *The Protestant Temperament: Patterns of Child-Rearing, Religious Experience and the Self in Early America*, New York, Alfred A. Knopf, 1977, 45; see also Bushman, *Refinement of America*, 315–20; Isaac, *Transformation of Virginia*, 164.

47   Cited in T. H. Breen, "An Empire of Goods: The Anglicisation of Colonial America", *Journal of British Studies*, 25, 1986, 498; see also idem, "Narrative of Commercial Life: Consumption, Ideology, and Community on the Eve of the American Revolution", *William and Mary Quarterly*, 3rd series, 50, 1993, 484.

48   Cited in T. H. Breen, "'Baubles of Britain': The American and Consumer Revolutions of the Eighteenth Century", *Past and Present*, 119, 1988.

49   Calvert, "Function of Fashion", 281–3; David Yosifon and Peter N. Stearns, "The Rise and Fall of American Posture", *American Historical Review*, 103, 1998, 1058–60.

50   Breen, "Empire of Goods".

51 Richard L. Bushman, "American High-Style and Vernacular Cultures", in Jack P. Greene and J. R. Pole (eds), *Colonial British America: Essays in the New History of the Early Modern Era*, Baltimore, Johns Hopkins University Press, 1984, 359–60.
52 Greven, *Protestant Temperament*, 358.
53 Breen, "Baubles of Britain", 92–4.
54 Cited in Michael Zakim, "Sartorial Ideologies: From Homespun to Ready-Made", *American Historical Review*, 106, 2001, 1558–9.
55 Cited ibid., 1567; see further, Kate Haulman, "Fashion and the Culture Wars of Revolutionary Philadelphia", *William and Mary Quarterly*, 62, 2005.

NOTES TO CHAPTER 5

1 Logically, the production of synthetic fibres fits in this list, but this was a twentieth-century innovation.
2 For reasons which I do not understand, the proportion of wool which was exported from South Africa in a washed state declined sharply in the later part of the nineteenth century. William Beinart, *The Rise of Conservation in South Africa: Settlers, Livestock, and the Environment, 1770–1950*, Oxford, Oxford UP, 2003, 13–14.
3 Claudia B. Kidwell, *Cutting a Fashionable Fit: Dressmakers' Draftmaking Systems in the United States*, Washington, DC, Smithsonian Institution Press, 1979.
4 Cited in Claudia Kidwell and Margaret C. Christman, *Suiting Everyone: The Democratization of Clothing in America*, Washington, DC, Smithsonian Institution Press for the National Museum of History and Technology, 1974, 52.
5 Michael Zakim, *Ready-Made Democracy: A History of Men's Dress in the American Republic*, Chicago, University of Chicago Press, 2003, esp. 50–3, 64–72.
6 Stanley Chapman, "The Innovating Entrepreneurs in the British Ready-Made Clothing Industry", *Textile History*, 24, 1993.
7 They probably only meant 80 per cent of adult British men.
8 Chapman, "Innovating Entrepreneurs", 22; *Oxford Dictionary of National Biography*, article on Elias Moses; Pamela Sharpe, "'Cheapness and Economy': Manufacturing and Retailing Ready-Made Clothing in London and Essex, 1830–1850", *Textile History*, 26, 1995; Sarah Levitt, "Cheap Mass-Produced Men's Clothing in the Nineteenth and Early Twentieth Centuries", *Textile History*, 22, 1991.
9 Philippe Perrot, *Fashioning the Bourgeoisie: A History of Clothing in the Nineteenth Century*, trans. Richard Bienvenu, Princeton, Princeton UP, 1994, 54.
10 Gisela Krause, "Altpreußische Uniformfertigung als Vorstufe der Bekleidungsindustrie", in *Forschungen und Urkunde zur Heeresgeschichte*, II, Hamburg, 1965; Jochen Krengel, "Das Wachstum der

Berliner Bekleidungsindustrie vor dem Ersten Weltkrieg", *Jahrbuch für die Geschichte Mittel- und Ost Deutschlands*, 27, 1978.

11   K. P. C. de Leeuw, *Kleding in Nederland 1813–1920: van een traditioneel bepaald kleedpatroon naar een begin van modern kleedgedrag*, Hilversum, Verloren, 1991, 116–17.

12   Zakin, *Ready-Made Democracy*, 156–84; Sally Alexander, "Women's Work in Nineteenth Century London: A Study of the Years 1820–60s", in *Becoming a Woman and Other Essays in 19th and 20th Century Feminist History*, New York, New York University Press, 1995, figures on p. 15.

13   Karl Marx, *Capital*, vol. I, Penguin Edition, London, 1976, 601.

14   Zakin, *Ready-Made Democracy*, 134.

15   Chapman, "Innovating Entrepreneurs"; *Oxford Dictionary of National Biography*, entry on the Barran family. There was of course another side to this; certainly in France there was the tendency for clothing manufacturing to be relocated into "family" shops in an attempt to evade the restrictions on hours of employment for women and children. See Judith G. Coffin, *The Politics of Women's Work: The Paris Garment Trades, 1750–1915*, Princeton, Princeton UP, 1996, esp. ch. IV.

16   Kidwell and Christman, *Suiting Everyone*, 94–5.

17   On the spread of sewing machines, see also Coffin, *Politics of Women's work*, ch. 3; ead., "Consumption, Production, and Gender: The Sewing Machine in Nineteenth-Century France", in Laura L. Frader and Sonya O. Rose (eds), *Gender and Class in Modern Europe*, Ithaca and London, Cornell UP, 1996; Karin Hausen, "Technical Progress and Women's Labour in the Nineteenth Century: The Social History of the Sewing Machine", in Georg Iggers (ed.), *The Social History of Politics: Critical Perspectives in West German Historical Writing since 1945*, Leamington Spa, Dover, NH, and Heidelberg, Berg 1985.

18   Hausen, "Technical Progress and Women's Labour", 264; Krengel, "Das Wachstum der Berliner Bekleidungsindustrie".

19   J. C. Flügel, *The Psychology of Clothes*, London, Hogarth, 1930.

20   Michael Carter, *Fashion Classics: From Carlyle to Barthes*, Oxford and New York, Berg, 2003, 97–120; Barbara Burman and Melissa Leventon, "The Men's Dress Reform Party 1929–1923", *Costume*, 21, 1987; Barbara Burman, "Better and Brighter Clothes: The Men's Dress Reform Party, 1929–1940", *Journal of Design History*, 8/4, 1995; Joanna Bourke, "The Great Male Renunciation: Men's Dress Reform in Inter-war Britain", *Journal of Design History*, 9, 1996.

21   Anne Hollander, *Sex and Suits*, New York, Alfred A. Knopf, 1994.

22   Zakin, *Ready-Made Democracy*, ch. 7; Christopher Breward, *The Hidden Consumer: Masculinities, Fashion and City Life, 1860–1914*, Manchester and New York, Manchester UP, 1999, ch. 2.

23   Kimberly Chrisman, "*Unhoop* the Fair Sex: the Campaign against the Hoop Petticoat in Eighteenth-Century England", *Eighteenth-Century Studies*, 30, 1996, 5–23.

24   The *New Oxford Dictionary of English* defines this as the "accumulation of large amounts of fat on the buttocks, especially as a normal

condition in the Khoikhoi and other peoples of arid parts of southern Africa".

25 Philip Mansel, *Dressed to Rule: Royal and Court Costume, from Louis XIV to Elizabeth II*, New Haven and London, Yale UP, 2005, 135.

26 Leigh Summers, *Bound to Please: A History of the Victorian Corset*, Oxford and New York, Berg, 16.

27 This changed around 1900, when suspender belts came to be added to the corset, so that the corset itself was kept in place by stockings under the women's feet.

28 Summers, *Bound to Please*, 10.

29 Mel Davies, "Corsets and Conception: Fashion and Demographic Trends in the Nineteenth Century", *Comparative Studies in Society and History*, 24, 1982, 628–30.

30 For the controversy, see Helene E. Robert, "The Exquisite Slave: The Role of Clothes in the Making of the Victorian Woman", and David Kunzle, "Dress Reform as Antifeminism: A Response to Helene E. Robert's 'The Exquisite Slave: The Role of Clothes in the Making of the Victorian Woman' ", both in *Signs: Journal of Women in Culture and Society*, 2, 1977; Perrot, *Fashioning the Bourgeoisie*, 150–9.

31 Cited in Elizabeth Ewing, *Dress and Undress: A History of Women's Underwear*, London, Batsford, 1978, 93.

32 Gayle V. Fischer, *Pantaloons and Power: A Nineteenth-Century Dress Reform in the United States*, Kent, Ohio, and London, Kent State University Press, 2001, 20.

33 Cited in Zakin, *Ready-Made Democracy*, 201.

34 On this see Amy Kesselman, "The 'Freedom Suit': Feminism and Dress Reform in the United States, 1848–1875", *Gender and Society*, 5, 1991; Fischer, *Pantaloons and Power*, *passim*.

35 "The woman shall not wear that which pertaineth to the man, neither shall a man put on a woman's garment: for all that do so are abomination unto the Lord thy God." Deut. 22: 5.

36 Aileen Ribeiro, *Dress and Morality*, London, Batsford, 1986, 133.

37 Kesselman, "Feminism and Dress Reform", 500–3.

38 Deborah Jean Warner, "Fashion, Emancipation, Reform, and the Rational Undergarment", *Dress: Journal of the Costume Society of America*, 4, 1978.

39 Jill Field, "Erotic Modesty: (Ad)ressing Female Sexuality and Propriety in Open and Closed Drawers, USA, 1800–1930", *Gender and History*, 14, 2002.

40 Diana de Marly, *Worth: Father of Haute Couture*, London, Elm Tree, 1980; Valerie Steele, *Paris Fashion: A Cultural History*, New York and Oxford, Oxford UP, 1988.

41 Elizabeth Wilson, *Adorned in Dreams: Fashion and Modernity*, London, Virago, 1985, 146.

42 Chapman, "Innovating Entrepreneurs", 11.

43 In general, see Geoffrey Crossick and Serge Jaumain (eds), *Cathedrals of Consumption: The European Department Store, 1850–1939*, Aldershot: Ashgate, 1999; Michael B. Mille, *The Bon Marché: Bourgeois*

Culture and the Department Store, 1869–1920, Princeton, Princeton UP, 1981; William R. Leach, "Transformations in a Culture of Consumption: Women and Department Stores, 1890–1925", *Journal of American History*, 71, 1984.

44   Wilson, *Adorned in Dreams*, 150.

45   Erika Diane Rappaport, *Shopping for Pleasure: Women in the Making of London's West End*, Princeton, Princeton UP, 2000; Elaine Abelson, *When Ladies Go A-thieving: Middle-Class Shoplifters in the Victorian Department Store*, Oxford and New York, Oxford UP, 1989; Patricia O'Brien, "The Kleptomania Diagnosis: Bourgeois Women and Theft in Late Nineteenth-Century France", *Journal of Social History*, 17, 1983; Ann-Louise Shapiro, *Breaking the Codes: Female Criminality in Fin-de-Siècle Paris*, Stanford, Stanford UP, 1996.

46   Alicia Foster, "Dressing for art's sake: Gwen John, the Bon Marché and the spectacle of the women artist in Paris", in Amy de la Haye and Elizabeth Wilson (eds), *Defining Dress: Dress as object, meaning and identity*, Manchester, Manchester UP, 1999.

47   Kidwell and Christman, *Suiting Everyone*, 115, 162–4.

48   Andrew Godley, "Singer in Britain: The Diffusion of Sewing Machine Technology and its impact on the Clothing Industry in the UK, 1860–1905", *Textile History*, 27, 1996; idem, "Homeworking and the Sewing Machine in the British Clothing Industry, 1850–1905", in Barbara Burman (ed.), *The Culture of Sewing: Gender, Consumption and Home Dressmaking*, Oxford, Berg, 1998.

49   Margaret Walsh, "The Democratization of Fashion: The Emergence of the Women's Dress Pattern Industry", *Journal of Americal History*, 66, 1979.

50   Walsh, "Democratization of Fashion"; Christopher Breward, "Patterns of Respectability: Publishing, Home Sewing and the Dynamics of Class and Gender, 1870–1914", in Burman (ed.), *Culture of Sewing*.

51   Kenneth Hudson, *The Archaeology of the Consumer Society: The Second Industrial Revolution in Britain*, London, Heinemann, 1983, 69. He also commented that no examples of the dry cleaning machines from the 1930s and earlier had survived.

NOTES TO CHAPTER 6

1   Marx *Capital*, Penguin edition, I, 601.

2   For compositional reasons, the sartorial history of the authochthonous Australians will be covered later in this chapter.

3   Robert Hughes, *The Fatal Shore*, New York, Alfred A. Knopf, 1987, 139. The use of clothing uniforms to demoralize the inmates of total institutions is well known. See e.g. Erving Goffman, *Asylums*, Garden City, NY, Doubleday, 1961, 20–1, anthologized in Mary Ellen Roach and Joanne Bubolz Eicher, *Dress, Adornment and the Social Order*, New York, London and Sydney, John Wiley & Sons, 1965, 246–7.

4   Jane Elliott, "Was there a Convict Dandy? Convict Consumer interests in Sydney", *Australian Historical Studies*, 25, 1995, 373–92.

5   Margaret Maynard, *Fashioned from Penury: Dress as Cultural Practice in Colonial Australia*, Cambridge, Cambridge UP, 1994, 16–27. Most of information and interpretation in the following paragraphs derive from this work.

6   Penny Russell, *A Wish of Distinction: Colonial Gentility and Femininity*, Melbourne, Melbourne UP, 1994.

7   It should not be thought that the wearing of white was not in itself a statement, particularly given the costs of laundering and otherwise maintaining white clothing.

8   On colonial mores in general, see Kirsten McKenzie, *Scandal in the Colonies, Sydney and Cape Town, 1820–1850*, Melbourne, Melbourne UP, 2004.

9   Regina A. Root, "Introduction", in Regina A. Root (ed.), *The Latin American Fashion Reader*, Oxford and New York, Berg, 2005, 3.

10 Regina A. Root, "Fashioning Independence: Gender, Dress and Social Space in Postcolonial Argentina", ibid., 31–44.

11 Arnold J. Bauer, *Goods, Power, History: Latin America's Material Culture*, Cambridge, Cambridge UP, 2001, 130.

12 Patricià Vera Jiménez, "From Benches to Sofas: Diversification of Patterns of Consumption in San José (1857–1961)", in Benjamin Orlove (ed.), *The Allure of the Foreign: Imported Goods in Postcolonial Latin America*, Ann Arbor, University of Michigan Press, 1997, 79.

13 Jeffrey D. Needell, *A Tropical Belle Epoque: Elite Culture and Society in Turn-of-the-Century Rio de Janeiro*, Cambridge, Cambridge UP, 1987, 140, cited in Bauer, *Goods, Power, History*, 158.

14 Bauer, *Goods, Power, History*, 136–7, citing Manuel Antonio Carreño, *Manual de urbanidad y buenas maneras*, 41st edn, Mexico City, 1987, and Beatriz González Stephan. "Escritura y modernización: la domesticación de la barbarie", *Revista Iberoamericana*, 60, 1994.

15 Thomas Krüggeler, "Changing Consumption Patterns and Everyday Life in Two Peruvian Regions: Food, Dress, and Housing in the Central and Southern Highlands (1820–1920)", in Orlove (ed) *Allure of the Foreign*, 31–67; Erich Langer, "Foreign Cloth in the Lowland Frontier: Commerce and Consumption of Textiles in Bolivia, 1830–1930", ibid., 97, 102.

16 This was part of a long debate, which led the great French historian Lucien Febvre, the founder of the *Annales* school, to wish that historians applied themselves to problems "such as the origin and distribution of the button". This comment was reported by Claude Lévi-Strauss, "Histoire et Ethnologie", *Annales ESC*, 38/2, 1983, 1217, who continued to explain that the button demarcated two major regimes, that of the *drapé* and that of the *cousu*, with consequences which extended to the differentiation of civilizations.

17 Mukulika Banerjee and Daniel Miller, *The Sari*, Oxford and New York, Berg, 27, 85; but see Emma Tarlo, *Clothing Matters: Dress and Identity in India*, London, Hurst, 1996, 28.

18   Bernard S. Cohn, "Cloth, Clothes and Colonialism: India in the Nineteenth Century", in Annette B. Weiner and Jane Schneider, *Cloth and Human Experience*, Washington, DC, and London, Smithsonian Institution Press, 1989, 332.

19   Kees van Dijk, "Sarong, Jubbah, and Trousers: Appearance as a Means of Distinction and Discrimination", in Henk Schulte Noordholt (ed.), *Outward Appearances: Dressing State and Society in Indonesia*, Leiden, Koninklijk Instituut voor Taal-, Land- en Volkenkunde, 1997, 49.

20   It is uncertain whether the baring of the breast entailed the signalling of sexual availability. Given the fear of pollution, this seems relatively unlikely. See Eliza F. Kent, *Converting Women: Gender and Protestant Christianity in Colonial South India*, Oxford and New York, Oxford UP, 2004, 212–16; see also Robert L. Hardgrave, *The Nadars of Tamilnad: The Political Culture of a Community in Change*, Berkeley and Los Angeles, University of California Press, 1969, 56–7.

21   Cited in E. M. Collingham, *Imperial Bodies: The Physical Experience of the Raj, c.1800–1947*, Cambridge, Polity, 2001, 61.

22   Cited ibid., 65, also 176.

23   Cohn, "Cloth, Clothes and Colonialism", 310, 336–7.

24   One of the exceptions, remarkably, was Gandhi, while recruiting for the army in 1917. In general, see Collingham, *Imperial Bodies*, 89–91; for a later comment by Gandhi extolling the virtues of the topi and explaining why it nevertheless could not become the Indian national headdress, see Tardo, *Clothing Matters*, 87.

25   This paragraph is based primarily on Dorine Brinkhorst and Esther Wils, *Tropenecht: Indische en Europese kleding in Nederlands-Indië*, The Hague, Stichting Tong Tong, 1994.

26   J. M. J. Catenius-van der Meijden, *Ons huis in Indië: handboek bij de keuze, de inrichting, de bewoning ende verzorging van het huis met bijgebouwen en erf, naar de eischen der hygiëne, benevens raadgevingen en wenken op huishoudelijk gebied*, Semarang, Masman & Stroink, 1908, cited in Brinkhorst and Wils, *Tropenecht*, 46.

27   Jean Gelman Taylor, "Costume and Gender in Colonial Java, 1800–1940", in Schulte Noordholt (ed.), *Outward Appearances*, 101–8.

28   Cited in Collingham, *Imperial Bodies*, 65.

29   Jayne Shrimpton, "Dressing for a Tropical Climate: The Role of Native Fabrics in Fashionable Dress in Early Colonial India", *Textile History*, 23, 1992, 55–70, esp. 59.

30   Collingham, *Imperial Bodies*, 62.

31   Ibid., 214.

32   See e.g. Nandi Bhatria, "Fashioning Women in Colonial India", *Fashion Theory*, 7, 2003, 327–44.

33   Dick Kooiman, *Conversion and Social Equality in India: The London Missionary Society in South Travancore in the 19th Century*, New Delhi, Manohar, 1989, 148–52; idem, "Christelijke zending, sociale mobiliteit en geweld: een klerenconflict in Travancore", *Sociologische Gids*, 30, 1983; Clifford G. Hospital, "Clothes and Caste in Nineteenth-Century

Kerala", *Indian Church History Review*, 13, 1979; Robert L. Hardgrave, "The Breast-cloth Controversy: Caste Consciousness and Social Change in Southern Travancore", *Indian Economic and Social History Review*, 5, 1968.

34 Cited in Hardgrave, *Nadars of Tamilnad*, 60.

35 Kooiman, *Conversion and Social Equality*, 173.

36 Ibid., 159; Eliza F. Kent, "Books and Bodices: Material Culture and Protestant Missions in Colonial South India", in Jamie S. Scott and Gareth Griffiths (eds), *Mixed Messages: Materiality, Textuality, Missions*, New York, Palgrave Macmillan, 2005, 77.

37 Travancore was a theoretically independent Indian state, covering much of modern Kerala, and thus my comments on colonial change are strictly speaking inaccurate. However, by this stage Travancore was unable to take important measures without the approval of a British resident; on the other hand, successive British residents were primarily concerned to preserve peace and order in the state.

38 Cited in Hardgrave, *Nadars of Tamilnad*, 67, 69.

39 Thomas Abler, *Hniterland Warriors and Military Dress: European Empires and Exotic Uniforms*, Oxford and New York, Berg, 1999; Cohn, "Cloth, Clothes and Colonialism", 322–6.

40 C. A. Heshusius, "Het Schoeisel van de KNIL-militair", *Stabelan*, 17. 1991, 32–42, cited in Van Dijk, "Sarong, Jubbah and Trousers", 53.

41 Nirad Chaudhuri, *Culture in the Vanity Bag*, Bombay, Jaico, 1976, 6, cited in Tardo, *Clothing Matters*, 50. A dhoti is the draped loincloth of general wear among Hindu men.

42 Photo in Van Dijk, "Sarong, Jubbah and Trousers", 66.

43 Ibid., 63.

44 Rudolf Mrázek, "Indonesian Dandy: The Politics of Clothes in the Late Colonial Period, 1893–1942", in Schulte Noordholt (ed.), *Outward Appearances*, 117–50.

45 As the last British soldiers to leave India after independence in 1947 passed through Port Said, they ceremonially threw their topis into the Mediterranean, Tardo, *Clothing Matters*, 57.

46 M. Ramanujan, "The Language of Clothes: An Indian Perspective", *Media Perspective*, 4, 1984, 32, cited in Tardo, *Clothing Matters*, 53.

47 M. Nehru, *Selected Works of Motilal Nehru*, ed. R. Kumar, 4 vols, Delhi, Vikas, 1982, I, 91, cited in Tardo, *Clothing Matters*, 61.

NOTES TO CHAPTER 7

1 For one example, see William J. F. Keenan, "Clothed with Authority: The Rationalization of Marist Dress-Culture", in Linda B. Arthur (ed.), *Undressing Religion: Commitment and Conversion from a Cross-Cultural Perspective*, Oxford and New York, Berg, 2000, 83–100.

2 My thanks to Mw. Nettie Tichelaar for information on this point; see also M. J. Aalders, *De komst van de toga: een historisch onderzoek naar*

het verdwijnen van mantel en bef *en de komst van* toga *op de Neder-landse kansels, 1796–1898*, Delft, Eburon, 2001.

3   Susan Thorne "'The Conversion of Englishmen and the Conversion of the World Inseparable': Missionary Imperialism and the Language of Class in Early Industrial Britain", in Frederick Cooper and Ann Laura Stoler (eds), *Tensions of Empire: Colonial Cultures in a Bourgeois World*, Berkeley, Los Angeles and London, University of California Press, 238–62.

4   M. J. D. Robert, *Making English Morals: Voluntary Association and Moral Reform in England, 1787–1886*, Cambridge, Cambridge UP, 2004.

5   Cf. Ryan Dunch, "Beyond Cultural Imperialism: Cultural Theory, Christian Missions, and Global Modernity", *History and Theory*, 41, 2002; Andrew N. Porter, "'Cultural Imperialism' and Protestant Missionary Enterprise", *Journal of Imperial and Commonwealth History*, 25, 1997.

6   Bernhard Krüger, *The Pear Tree Blossoms: A History of the Moravian Mission Stations in South Africa, 1737–1869*, Genadendal, Genadendal Printing Works, 1967, 80; A. M. Lewin Robinson with Margaret Lenta and Dorothy Driver (eds), *The Cape Journals of Lady Anne Barnard, 1797–1798*. Cape Town, Van Riebeeck Society, 1994, 339; see also John Barrow, *An account of travels into the interior of Southern Africa in the years 1797 and 1798: including cursory observations on the geology and geography . . . with a map constructed entirely from actual observations*, London: Cadell and Davies, 2 vols, 1801–4, I, 352–3.

7   C. I. Latrobe, *Journal of a Visit to South Africa in 1815 and 1816, with Some Account of the Missionary Settlements of the United Brethren near the Cape of Good Hope*, New York, James Eastburn & Co., 1818, 74.

8   F. A. Steytler (ed.), "Minutes of the First Conference held by the African Missionaries at Graaff Reinet in August 1814", *Hertzog-Annale van die Suid-Afrikaanse Akademie vir Wetenskap en Kuns*, III, 1956, 111; a *kaross* is a fur cloak, which was the standard dress of the Khoekhoe.

9   Eugene Casalis, *My Life in Basutoland: A Story of Missionary Enterprise in South Africa*, trans. J. Brierley, London, Religious Tract Society, 1889. Casalis is here recounting what he had heard on his visit to Bethelsdorp in 1832.

10 John Philip, "A Narrative written for Buxton", LMS archives, School of Oriental and African Studies, London, Africa Odds, Philip Papers, Box 3, folder 5.

11 John Philip, *Researches in South Africa, Illustrating the Civil, Moral and Religious Condition of the Native Tribes*, 2 vols, London, James Duncan, 1828, I, 219.

12 Ibid., 210–11.

13 Ibid., 222.

14 Journal of Samuel Rolland, 17.2.1830, Archives of the Paris Evangelical Missionary Society, Bibliothèque nationale, Paris; *Journal des missions évangeliques*, V, 1830, 241–4.

15   E.g. John Garrett, *To Live among the Stars: Christian Origins in Oceania*, Geneva and Suva, World Council of Churches in association with the Institute of Pacific Studies, University of the South Pacific, 1982.

16   Margaret Maynard, *Fashioned from Penury: Dress as Cultural Practice in Colonial Australia*, Cambridge, Cambridge UP, 1994, 61–2.

17   Lancelot Threlkeld, *Australian Reminiscences and Papers of L. E. Threlkeld, Missionary to the Aborigines*, ed. Neil Gunson, Canberra, Australian Institute of Aboriginal Studies, 1974, 44, cited in Anna Johnston, *Missionary Writing and Empire, 1800–1860*, Cambridge, Cambridge UP, 2003, 167.

18   Maynard, *Fashioned from Penury*, 61–8.

19   Louise Meredith, *Notes and Sketches of New South Wales during a Residence in that Colony, 1839–44*, reprinted Harmondsworth, Penguin, 1973, 99–100, cited in Maynard, *Fashioned from Penury*, 72.

20   See e.g. Nicholas Thomas, Anna Cole and Bronwen Douglas (eds), *Tattoo: Bodies, Art and Exchange in the Pacific and the West*, London, Reaktion, 2005.

21   Lissant Bolton, "Gender, Status and Introduced Clothing in Vanuatu", in Chloë Colchester (ed.) *Clothing the Pacific*, Oxford, Berg, 2003, 120.

22   Anne D'Alleva, "Elite Clothing and the Social Fabric of Pre-Colonial Tahiti", in Susanne Küchler and Graeme Were (eds), *The Art of Clothing: A Pacific Experience*, London, UCL Press, 2005, 53.

23   Linda B. Arthur, "Hawaiian Women and Dress: The *Holukū* as an Expression of Ethnicity", *Fashion Theory*, 2, 1998, 270.

24   Serge Tcherkézoff, "Of Cloth, Gifts and Nudity: Regarding some European Misunderstandings during Early Encounters in Polynesia", in Colchester (ed.), *Clothing the Pacific*, 72.

25   See e.g. the image of the arrival of the Rev. John Williams in southern Vanuatu, published in Nicholas Thomas, "Technologies of Conversion: Cloth and Christianity in Polynesia", in Artah Brah and Anne E. Coombes (eds), *Hybridity and its Discontents: Politics, Science, Culture*, London and New York, Routledge, 2000, 206. Williams, incidentally, was one of the very few missionaries actually to have been eaten, as the archivist of the London Missionary Society, Miss Irene Fletcher, once informed me with gusto. There is no apparent truth in the famous joke that the cannibals found his boots too tough to consume.

26   John Williams, *Missionary Enterprises in the South Sea Islands*, London, J. Snow, 1837, 582, cited in Johnston, *Missionary Writing and Empire*, 147.

27   Johnston, *Missionary Writing and Empire*, 147–8.

28   Williams, *Missionary Enterprises*, 114, cited ibid., 148.

29   William Gill, *Gems from the Coral Islands; or Incidents of Contrast between Savage and Christian Life of the South Sea Islanders*, vol I: *Western Polynesia*; vol. II: *Eastern Polynesia*, London, Presbyterian Board of Publication, 1856, II, 96, cited in Niel Gunson, *Messengers of Grace: Evangelical Missionaries in the South Seas, 1797–1860*,

Melbourne, Oxford UP, 1979, 275–6.

30   J. Waterhouse, *The King and the People of Fiji: Containing a life of Thakombau ... previous to the Great Religious Transformation in 1854*, New York, AMS Press, 1866, 258–61, cited in Chloë Colchester, "Objects of Conversion: Concerning the Transfer of *Sulu* to Fiji", in Küchler and Were (eds), *The Art of Clothing*, 40–1.

31   R. Moyle (ed.), *The Samoan Journals of John Williams, 1830 and 1832*, Canberra, Australian National University Press, 1984, 68, 237, cited in Thomas, "Technologies of Conversion", 207.

32   Charles W. Forman, *The Island Churches of the South Pacific: Emergence in the Twentieth Century*, Maryknoll, New York, Orbis, 1982, cited in Johnston, *Missionary Writing and Empire*, 147.

33   Patrick O'Reilly and Jean Poirier, "L'Évolution du costume", *Journal de la Société des Océanistes*, 9, 1953, 152.

34   Cited in Bolton, "Gender, Status and Introduced Clothing in Vanuatu", 129.

35   Garrett, *To Live among the Stars*, 47.

36   See in general Margaret Jolly, "'To Save the Girls for Brighter and Better Lives': Presbyterian Missions and Women in the South of Vanuatu: 1848–1870", *Journal of Pacific History*, 26, 1991, 27–48; Richard Eves, "Colonialism, Corporeality and Character: Methodist Missions and the Refashioning of Bodies in the Pacific", *History and Anthropology*, 10. 1996, 85–138.

37   D'Alleva, "Elite Clothing", 47, 55–6.

38   Tcherkézoff, "Of Cloths, Gifts and Nudity", 66, 73.

39   Letter from Charles Barff to the LMS, 26.7.1865, cited in Gunson, *Messengers of Grace*, 275.

40   Thomas, "Technologies of Conversion", 205–1; Susanne Küchler, "The Poncho and the Quilt: Material Christianity in the Cook Islands", in Colchester (ed.), *Clothing the Pacific*, 99.

41   Küchler, "The Poncho and the Quilt", 104.

42   Colchester, "Objects of Conversion", 34–5.

43   See e.g. the photograph accompanying the obituary of Ratu Sir Kamisese Mara, *Guardian*, 23.4.2004.

44   Sally Engle Merry, *Colonizing Hawai'i: The Cultural Power of Law*, Princeton, Princeton UP, 2000, 61, citing *Missionary Herald*, 1821, 115.

45   Patrick V. Kirch and Marshall Sahlins, *Anahulu: The Anthropology of History in the Kingdom of Hawaii*, vol. I: *Historical Ethnography*, Chicago and London, University of Chicago Press, 1992, 57–82.

46   Ibid., 78.

47   Linda B. Arthur, "Cultural Authentication Refined: The Case of the Hawaiian Holokū", *Clothing and Textiles Research Journal*, 15, 1997, 131–2.

48   Linda B. Arthur, "Fossilized Fashion in Hawai'i", *Paideusis: Journal for Interdisciplinary and Cross-cultural Studies*, 1, 1998, A-15-28; ead., "Hawaiian Women and Dress: The *Holokū* as an Expression of Ethnicity", *Fashion Theory*, 2, 1998, 269–86.

49   Alan Lester, *Colonial Discourse and the Colonisation of Queen Adelaide Province, South Africa,* London, Historical Geography Research Series, no. 34, 1998, 44–54.

50   J. Tyler, 1868, cited in Norman Etherington, "Outward and Visible Signs of Conversion in Nineteenth-Century KwaZulu-Natal", *Journal of Religion in Africa,* 32, 2002, 435.

51   Linda Roodenburg, *De Bril van Anceaux: volkenkundige fotografie vanaf 1860,* Zwolle, Waanders for the Rijksmuseum voor Volkenkunde, Leiden, 2002.

52   Kirsten Rüther, *The Power Beyond: Mission Strategies, African Conversion and the Development of a Christian Culture in the Transvaal,* Münster, Lit Verlag, 2001, 108.

53   John Comaroff and Jean Comaroff, *Of Revelation and Revolution: The Dialectics of Modernity on a South African Frontier,* II, Chicago and London, University of Chicago Press, 244. Wittingly or otherwise, the missionary Robert Moffat, who in many ways set himself up as a Tswana chief, also on occasion went about in a leopard-skin waistcoat, ibid., 249.

54   The missionary has explained that the baptized are generally young and cattleless.

55   Cited in Rüther, *The Power Beyond,* 204–5; unfortunately Rüther does not state which of the four Hermannsburg missionaries named Behrens was the author of this passage.

56   Ibid., 205–6.

57   Peter Delius, "Migrant Labour and the Pedi, 1840–1880", in Shula Marks and Anthony Atmore (eds), *Economy and Society in Pre-Industrial South Africa,* London, Longmans, 1980, 292–313.

58   Patrick Harries, *Work, Culture, and Identity: Migrant Laborers in Mozambique and South Africa, c.1860–1910,* London, James Currey, 1994, 60, 176.

59   Brian Willan, "An African in Kimberley: Sol. T. Plaatje, 1894–1898", in Shula Marks and Richard Rathbone (eds), *Industrialisation and Social Change in South Africa: African Class Formation, Culture and Consciousness, 1870–1930,* London, Longmans, 1982, 254, citing the *Diamond Fields Advertiser,* 26.1.1898.

60   C. B. Richter in the *Berliner Missionberichte,* 1882, 57–8, quoted (and translated) in Rüther, *The Power Beyond,* 215.

61   Rüther, *The Power Beyond,* 199; by 1875, crinolines had been out of fashion in Europe for some years, but apparently neither the missionaries nor the African women of Pretoria were aware of this.

62   Ibid., 218. cf. Philip Prein, "Guns and Top Hats: African Resistance in German South West Africa, 1907–1915", *Journal of Southern African Studies,* 20, 1994.

63   Kirch and Sahlins, *Analulu,* I, 163–5, citing a report from the Rev. John C. Emerson, in 1848; Haula should be spelled Haole.

64   In time, the mission theorists developed a a fascinating distinction between "Zivilization" which was universal, and "Kultuur", which was

ethno-specific, and could be encouraged, so long as it did not conflict with "Zivilization". See Birgit Meyer, "Christianity and the Ewe Nation: German Pietist Missionaries, Ewe Converts and the Politics of Culture", *Journal of Religion in Africa*, 32, 2002, 167–99.

65   Birgit Meyer, "Christian Mind and Worldly Matters: Religion and Materiality in Nineteenth-Century Gold Coast", *Journal of Material Culture*, 2, 1998, 311–37, quotation at 328. For more on the mission, see ead., *Translating the Devil: Religion and Modernity among the Ewe in Ghana*, Edinburgh, Edinburgh UP, 1999.

66   Hildi Hendrickson, "The 'Long' Dress and the Construction of Herero Identities in Southern Africa", *African Studies*, 53, 1994.

67   Hildi Hendrickson, "Bodies and Flags: The Representation of Herero Identity in Colonial Namibia", in Hildi Hendrickson (ed.), *Clothing and Difference: Embodied Identities in Colonial and Post-Colonial Africa*, Durham, NC, and London, Duke University Press, 1996, 213–44.

68   Deborah Durham, "The Predicament of Dress: Polyvalency and the Ironies of Cultural Identity", *American Ethnologist*, 26, 1999, 389–411.

69   See e.g. the photos in Comaroff and Comaroff, *Of Revelation and Revolution*, II, 261, 265.

70   Jan-Bart Gewald, *Herero Heroes: A Socio-Poiltical History of the Herero of Namibia, 1890–1923*, Oxford, James Currey, 1999; idem, *"We Thought We Would be Free": Socio-Cultural Aspects of Herero History in Namibia, 1915–1940*, Cologne, Rüdiger Köppe, 2000.

71   Wolfgang Werner, "'Playing Soldiers': The Truppenspieler Movement among the Herero of Namibia", *Journal of Southern African Studies*, 16, 1990, 485–502; Hendrickson, "Bodies and Flags".

72   Prein, "Guns and Top Hats", 99–100.

73   Personal communication, Jan-Bart Gewald.

NOTES TO CHAPTER 8

1   Geoffrey Parker, *The Military Revolution: Military Innovation and the Rise of the West, 1500–1800*, Cambridge, Cambridge UP, 1988, 70–1.

2   W. M. McNeill, *Keeping Together in Time: Dance and Drill in Human History*, Cambridge MA, Harvard UP, 1995; Olaf van Nimwegen, *Deser landen crijchsvolk: het Staatse leger en de militaire revoluties,1588–1688*, Amsterdam, Bert Bakker, 2006. The double meaning of *corps* in this context – both body in the literal sense and body of soldiers – is at least suggestive.

3   Daniel Roche, *The Culture of Clothing: Dress and Fashion in the Ancien Regime*, trans. Jean Birrell, Cambridge, Cambridge UP, 1994, 233. This section relies to a considerable extent on ch. 9 of this magnificent book.

4   Symptomatically, the foreign legions of the French army – Irish, Swiss and so forth – each had their own specific colour; ibid., 247.

5   Richard Hellie, *The Economy and Material Culture of Russia, 1600–1725*, Chicago and London, University of Chicago Press, 1999, 355–8.

6   Cited in Lindsay Hughes, *Peter the Great: A Biography*, New Haven and London, 2002, 53–4.

7   Cited in Christine Ruane, "Subjects into Citizens: The Politics of Clothing in Imperial Russia", in Wendy Parkins (ed.), *Fashioning the Body Politics: Dress, Gender, Citizenship*, Oxford and New York, Berg, 2002, 49.

8   Lindsey Hughes, "From Caftans into Corsets: The Sartorial Transformation of Women during the Reign of Peter the Great", in Peter I. Barta (ed.), *Gender and Sexuality in Russian Civilisation*, London, Routledge, 2001; Hughes, *Peter the Great*, 59–60.

9   Orlando Figes, *Natasha's Dance: A Cultural History of Russia*, London, Allen Lane, 2001, 18.

10 Cited in Ruanne, "Subjects into Citizens", 62–3.

11 Cited ibid., 62.

12 Cited in Figes, *Natasha's Dance*, 108.

13 Ibid., 124.

14 Keiichirō Nakagawa and Henry Rosovsky, "The Case of the Dying Kimono: The Influence of Changing Fashions on the Development of the Japanese Woolen Industry", *Business History Review*, 37, 1963.

15 Cited ibid., 62.

16 Hirakawa Sukehiro, "Japan's turn to the West", in Marius Jansen (ed.) *Cambridge History of Japan*, V, Cambridge, Cambridge UP, 1989, 471; Ildiko Klein-Bednay, "Kimono und Cul de Paris: der Einfluss des Westens auf die japanische Kleidung im 19. Jahrhundert", *Waffen- und Kostümkunde: Zeitschrift der Gesellschaft für Historische Waffen- und Kostümkunde*, 1996, 46–8.

17 Satsuki Kawano, "Japanese Bodies and Western Ways of Seeing in the Late Nineteenth Century", in Adeline Masquelier (ed.), *Dirt, Undress and Difference: Critical Perspectives on the Body's Surface*, Bloomington and Indianapolis, Indiana UP, 2005, 150.

18 Nakagawa and Rosovsky, "Case of the Dying Kimono", 63; Brian McVeigh, *Wearing Ideology: State, Schooling as Self-Preservation in Japan*, Oxford, Berg, 2000, 105–8.

19 Klein-Bednay, "Kimono und Cul de Paris", 54.

20 Nakagawa and Rosovsky, "Case of the Dying Kimono", 63.

21 Edward Seidensticker, *Low City, High City: Tokyo from Edo to the Earthquake*, New York, Alfred A. Knopf, 1983, 277–8; apparently nurses were the first substantial group of working women to take to Western-style attire.

22 Brian McVeigh, "Wearing Ideology: How Uniforms Discipline Minds and Bodies in Japan", *Fashion Theory*, 1, 1997, 191.

23 Personal communication, Anna Beerens; see also Masami Suga, "Exotic West to Exotic Japan: Revival of Japanese Tradition in Modern Japan", in Joanne B. Eicher (ed.), *Dress and Ethnicity: Change across Space and Time*, Oxford and Washington, DC, Berg, 1995, 96–8; Klein-Bednay, "Kimono und Cul de Paris", 66; McVeigh, "Wearing Ideology", 191.

24 Millie R. Creighton, "The Depâto: Merchandising the West while Selling Japaneseness", in Joseph J. Tobin (ed.), *Re-made in Japan: Everyday Life and Consumer Taste in a Changing Society*, New Haven and London, Yale UP, 1992, 54, cited in Suga, "Exotic West to Exotic Japan", 98.

25 Maurizio Peleggi, *Lords of Things: the fashioning of the Siamese Monarchy's modern Image*, Honolulu, University of Hawaii Press, 2002, 62–9.

26 Personal communication, Bas Terwiel.

27 Patricia L. Baker, "The Fez in Turkey: A Symbol of Modernization?", *Costume*, 20, 1986, 74, 81.

28 C. E. Padwick, *Call to Istanbul*, London, Longmans, Green, 1958, 49, cited in John Norton, "Faith and Fashion in Turkey", in Nancy Lindisfarne-Tapper and Bruce Ingham (eds), *Languages of Dress in the Middle East*, London, Curzon in association with the Centre of Near and Middle Eastern Studies, SOAS, 1997, 160.

29 Donald Quataert, "Clothing Laws, State, and Society in the Ottoman Empire", *International Journal of Middle East Studies*, 29, 1997, 405–6.

30 Ibid., 408–9.

31 Fatma Müge Göçek, *Rise of the Bourgeoisie, Demise of Empire: Ottoman Westernization and Social Change*, New York, Oxford UP, 1996, 83.

32 Baker, "Fez in Turkey", 73–5; Quataert, "Clothing Laws", 413–14.

33 Quataert, "Clothing Laws". In the nature of things, this desired inclusiveness was mitigated by the need of successive rulers to maintain their power by fostering, and festering, divisions among their subjects, so that the history of the late Ottoman empire was punctuated by ethnic violence and, indeed, genocidal massacres.

34 Selçuk Esenbel, "The Anguish of Civilized Behavior: The Use of Western Cultural Forms in the Everyday Lives of the Meiji Japanese and the Ottoman Turks during the Nineteenth Century", *Japan Review: Bulletin of the International Research Center for Japanese Studies*, 5, 1994, 170–1; Göçek, *Rise of the Bourgeoisie*, chs. 2 and 3; Nancy Micklewright, "Tracing the Transformations in Women's Dress in Nineteenth-Century Istanbul", *Dress*, 13, 1987, 33–43.

35 Esenbel, "The Anguish of Civilized Behavior", 180.

36 Cited in Houchang Chehabi, "Dress Codes for Men in Turkey and Iran", in Touraj Atabake and Erik J. Zürcher (eds), *Men of Order: Authoritarian Modernization under Atatürk and Reza Shah*, London, I. B. Taurus, 2004, 213; see also Norton, "Faith and Fashion", 157–62.

37 Chehabi, "Dress Codes for Men", 214; in this, he was following the opinion of the modernist Great Mufti of Egypt, Muhammed 'Abduh, in what became known as the "Transvaal fatwa" of 1903. For text and context, see Charles C. Adams, "Muhammed 'Abduh and the Transvaal Fatwa", in *The Macdonald Presentation Volume*, Princeton, Princeton UP, 1933, esp. p. 17.

38 Houchang E. Chehabi, "Staging the Emperor's New Clothes: Dress codes and Nation-Building under Reza Shah", *Iranian Studies*, 26, 1993, 209, 223–4. There is of course some irony in this, as the European three-

piece suit was seen at the time of its introduction, under Charles II of England, as Persian costume. See above.

39 Patricia L. Baker, "Politics of Dress: The Dress Reform Laws of 1920s/30s Iran", in Lindisfarne-Tapper and Ingham (eds), *Languages of Dress*, 179–80.

40 Ali Akbar Siassi, *La Perse au contact de l'occident: étude historique et sociale*, Paris, Ernest Leroux, 1931, 205–6, cited in Chehabi, "Dress Codes for Men", 227.

41 Chehabi, "Staging the Emperor's New Clothes", 213–15, 221.

42 Norton, "Faith and Fashion", 157–8.

43 Ibid., 163.

44 Cited in H. E. Chehabi, "The Banning of the Veil and its Consequences", in Stephanie Cronin (ed.), *The Making of Modern Iran: State and Society under Riza Shah, 1921–1941*, London, Routledge Curzon, 2003, 200; see also Jamine Rostam-Kolayi, "Expanding Agendas for the 'New' Iranian Woman: Family Law, Work and Unveiling", and Shireen Mahdavi, "Reza Shah Pahlavi and Women: A Re-evaluation", both in the same volume.

45 Chehabi, "Banning of the Veil", 201–2.

46 Chehabi, "Dress Codes for Men", 230; for the subsequent sartorial history of Iran, and the controversies around the veil, see below, ch. 11.

NOTES TO CHAPTER 9

1 Monica Hunter, *Reaction to Conquest: Effects of Contact with Europeans on the Pondo of South Africa*, 2nd edn, 1960, Oxford, Oxford UP, 1960 [1936], 10.

2 Ibid., 101–2, 542, 486.

3 Godfrey Wilson, *An Essay on the Economics of Detribalization in Northern Rhodesia, Part II*, Livingstone, Rhodes Livingstone Institute, 1942, 16–20.

4 Karen Tranberg Hansen, *Salaula: The World of Secondhand Clothing and Zambia*, Chicago and London, University of Chicago Press, 2000, 29–36; citation from J. Merle Davis, *Modern Industry and the Africa: An Enquiry into the Effect of the Copper Mines of Central Africa upon Native Society and the Work of the Christian Missions*, London, Macmillan, 1933, 42.

5 For two exceptions, see Timothy Burke, *Lifebuoy Men, Lux Women: Commodification, Consumption, and Cleanliness in Modern Zimbabwe*, Durham, NC, Duke UP, 1996; Michael Rowlands [strictly an anthropologist], "The Consumption of an African Modernity", in Mary Jo Arnoldi, Christraud M. Geary, and Kris L. Hardin (eds), *African Material Culture*, Bloomington and Indianapolis, Indiana UP, 1996, 188–213. See also the work of Margaret Jean Hay, referred to below.

6 Eugene C. Burt, "Bark-Cloth in East Africa", *Textile History*, 26, 1995.

7   Patricia Davison and Patrick Harries, "Cotton-Weaving in South-East Africa: Its History and Technology", in Dale Idiens and K. G. Ponting (eds), *Textiles of Africa*, Bath (UK), Pasold Research Fund, 1980; Jeremy G. Prestholdt, *As Artistry Permits and Custom May Ordain: The Social Fabric of Material Consumption in the Swahili World, circa 1450 to 1600*, Programme of African Studies, Northwestern University, Evanston, Ill., Working Paper 3, 1998; Edward Alpers, "*Futa Benaadir*: Continuity and Change in the Traditional Cotton Textile Industry of Southern Somalia, c.1840–1980", in *Actes du Colloque Entreprises en Entrepreneurs en Afrique (XIXe et XXe siècles)*, I, Paris, L'Harmattan, 1981, 77–98.

8   Prestholdt, *As Artistry Permits*, esp. 24–33; Laura Fair, *Pastimes and Politics: Culture, Community and Identity in Post-Abolition Urban Zanzibar, 1890–1945*, Athens, Ohio UP, and Oxford, James Currey, 2001, 64–74.

9   Jeremy Prestholdt, "On the Global Repercussions of East African Consumerism", *American Historical Review*, 109, 2004.

10   David Parkin, "Textile as Commodity, Dress as Text: Swahili *Kanga* and Women's Statements", in Ruth Barnes (ed.), *Textiles in Indian Ocean Societies*, London and New York, Routledge Curzon, 2005; R. M. Beck, "Aesthetics of Communciation: Texts on Textiles ('*Leso*') from the East-African Coast (Swahili)", *Research in African Literatures*, 31, 2000, 104–24; R. M. Beck, "Ambiguous Signs: The Role of the *Kanga* as a Medium of Communication", *Afrikanistische Arbeitspapiere*, 68, 2001; Marloes van der Bijl, "*Mafumbo na Kininja:* Dress Utterances of Young Zanzibari Women", MA thesis, Leiden University, 2006.

11   Atieno Odhimabo, "From Warriors to Jonanga: The Struggle of Nakedness by the Luo of Kenya", in Werner Graebner (ed.), *Sokomoko: Popular Culture in East Africa*, Amsterdam, Rodopi, 1992, 15; Margaret Jean Hay, "Hoes and Clothes in a Luo Household: Changing Consumption in a Colonial Economy, 1906–1936", in Mary Jo Arnoldi, Christraud M. Geary, and Kris L. Hardin (eds), *African Material Culture*, Bloomington and Indianapolis, Indiana UP, 1996, 251.

12   Margaret Jean Hay, *Western Clothing and African Identity: Changing Consumption Patterns among the Luo*, Discussion Papers in the African Humanities, 2, African Studies Centre, Boston, 1989; Hay, "Changes in Clothing and Struggles over Identity in Colonial Western Kenya", in Jean Allman (ed.), *Fashioning Africa: Power and the Politics of Dress*, Bloomington, Indiana UP, 2004, 69.

13   Cited in Hay, "Changes in Clothing", 77.

14   Atieno Odhiambo, "From Warriors to Jonanga", esp. 16–17; Hay, "Changes in Clothing", 78; Hay, *Material Culture and the Shaping of Consumer Society in Colonial Western Kenya*, Working Papers in African Studies, 179, African Studies Centre, Boston, 1994, 16.

15   Cited in David William Cohen and E. W. Atieno Odhiambo, *Siaya: The Historical Anthropology of an African Landscape*, London, James Currey, 1989, 111.

16   There is a large literature which shows that these ideas were in essence spurious. The classic text on the matter is probably ch. 10, "The Creation

of Tribes", in John Iliffe, *A Modern History of Tanganyika*, Cambridge, Cambridge UP, 1979, 318–42.

17 Cape Town and Johannesburg, David Philip, 1984.

18 Only one woman appears in the gallery, Elizabeth Plaatje, who in a previous chapter was being awaited on the platform of Kimberley station, before her marriage. In the photograph which Odendaal reproduces, she is suitably dressed in blouse, skirt, bonnet and what appear to be short boots.

19 Jeff Guy, "Subject or Object: The Photographic Image and the Struggle for Power in Colonial Natal", paper presented to the Conference of the Historical Association of South Africa, June 2006.

20 Christopher Fyfe, *A History of Sierra Leone*, Oxford, Oxford UP, 1962, 379.

21 John Parker, *Making the Town: Ga State and Society in Early Colonial Accra*, Oxford, James Currey, 2000, 136.

22 Cited in J. F. Ade Ajayi, *Christian Missions in Nigeria, 1841–1891: The Making of a New Elite*, London, Longmans Green, 1965, 236.

23 Betty M. Wass, "Yoruba Dress in Five Generations of a Lagos Family", in Justine Cordwell and Ronald A. Schwarz (eds), *The Fabrics of Culture: The Anthropology of Clothing and Adornment*, The Hague, Mouton, 1979, 333–5; Kristen Mann, *Marrying Well: Marriage, Status and Social Change among the Educated Elite in Colonial Lagos*, Cambridge, Cambridge UP, 1985, 33.

24 For descriptions of three different weddings, from the Lagos press, see Titilola Euba, "Dress and Status in 19th Century Lagos", in B. A. Agiri et al. (eds), *History of the Peoples of Lagos State*, Ikeja Lagos, Lantern Books, 1987, 153–4; Judith Byfield, *"Unwrapping" Nationalism: Dress, Gender, and Nationalist Discourse in Colonial Lagos*, Discussion Papers in the African Humanities, 30, African Studies Centre Boston, 2000, 6; Mann, *Marrying Well*, 56–7.

25 Cited in Euba, "Dress and Status", 159.

26 On this, see esp. Vivian Bickford-Smith, "The Betrayal of Creole Elites, 1880–1920", in Philip Morgan and Sean Hawkins (eds), *Black Experience and the Empire*, Oxford History of the British Empire Companion Series, Oxford, Oxford UP, 2004, 194–227.

27 Helen Callaway, "Dressing for Dinner in the Bush: Rituals of Self-Definition and British Imperial Authority", in Ruth Barnes and Joanne B. Eicher (eds), *Dress and Gender: Making and Meaning*, Oxford Berg, 1992, 232–47; Andreas Eckert, "Making African Bureaucrats: Colonial Education, 'Character Training' and African Agency in Tanzania, 1920s to 1960s", unpublished seminar paper, Afrika-Studiecentrum Leiden, 2004.

28 F. D. Lugard, *The Dual Mandate in Tropical Africa*, London, Blackwood, 589, cited in Judith A. Byfield, *The Bluest Hands: A Social and Economic History of Women Dyers in Abeokuta (Nigeria), 1890–1940*, Oxford, Portsmouth, NH, and Cape Town, James Currey, Heinemann and David Philip, 2002, 68.

29 E.g. Terence Ranger, *Are We Not Also Men? The Samkange Family and African Politics in Zimbabwe, 1920–1964*, London, James Currey, 1995; Michael O. West, *The Rise of an African Middle Class: Colonial Zimbabwe, 1898–1965*, Bloomington, Indiana UP, 2002.

30 *New York Times Style*, 27.7.1997, cited in Sandra Klopper, "Re-dressing the Past: The Africanisation of Sartorial Style in Contemporary South Africa", in Avtah Brah and Annie E. Coombes, *Hybridity and its Discontents: Politics, Science, Culture*, London, Routledge, 2000, 218.

31 For instance, he opened parliament, and received honorary degrees, in a suit.

32 Fyfe, *History of Sierra Leone*, 468.

33 Richard Burton, *Abeokuta and the Cameroons Mountain: An Exploration*, I, London, Tinsley Brothers, 1863, 102, cited in Byfield, *The Bluest Hands*, 3.

34 Byfield, *Bluest Hands*, 4–6, citing Samuel Johnson, *The History of the Yorubas from the Earliest Times to the Beginning of the British Protectorate*, 6th edn, London, Routledge & Kegan Paul, 1973 (original edition 1921, written by 1897), 110–12.

35 For Nigerian cloth, see e.g. Judith Perani and Norma H. Wolff, *Cloth, Dress and Art Patronage in Africa*, Oxford and New York, Berg, 1999; for *kente*, see Doran H. Ross, *Wrapped in Pride: Ghanaian Kente and African American Identity*, Los Angeles, UCLA Fowler Museum of Cultural History, 1998; Malika Kramer, "Colourful Changes: Two Hundred Years of Social and Design History in the Handwoven Textiles of the Ewe-Speaking Regions of Ghana and Togo (1800–200)", Ph.D. thesis, SOAS, 2005.

36 Ruth Nielsen, "The History and Development of Wax-Printed Textiles intended for West Africa and Zaire", in Justine Cordwell and Ronald A. Schwarz (eds), *The Fabrics of Culture: The Anthropology of Clothing and Adornment*, The Hague, Mouton, 1979, 467–98.

37 Byfield, *"Unwrapping" Nationalism*, 11–12. Michael J. C. Echeruo, *Victorian Lagos: Aspects of Nineteenth Century Lagos Life*, London and Basingstoke, Macmillan, 1977, 39.

38 *Lagos Weekly Record*, March 1896, cited in Echeruo, *Victorian Lagos*, 39.

39 Euba, "Dress and Status", 160.

40 Agneta Pallinder, "Adegboyega Edun: Black Englishman and Yoruba Cultural Patriot", in P. F. de Moraes Farias and Karin Barber (eds), *Self-Assertion and Brokerage: Early Cultural Nationalism in West Africa*, Birmingham, Centre of West African Studies, 1990, 13; this article, incidentally, includes a wonderful photograph of the Alake of Abeokuta, in full ethnic dress, next to the Governor of Lagos colony, Sir William MacGregor, also in full ethnic dress, with kilt, sporran and tam o'shanter.

41 Wass, "Yoruba Dress".

42 Information from the family, relayed to me by Michel Doortmont.

43 Ross, *Wrapped in Pride*, 165–8; Barbara S. Monfils, "A Multifaceted Image: Kwame Nkrumah's Extrinsic Rhetorical Strategies", *Journal of Black Studies*, 7, 1977, 313–30.

44 E.g. Victoria L. Rovine, "Fashionable Traditions; the Globalization of an African Textile", in Allman, *Fashioning Africa*; Leslie W. Rabine, *The Global Circulation of African Fashion*, Oxford and New York, Berg, 2002; Perani & Wolff, *Cloth, Dress and Art Patronage.*

45 Cited in Byfield, *Bluest Hands*, 210, from *West Africa*, 20.3.1937.

46 Byfield, *Bluest Hands*, 211.

47 This account follows in particular Tardon, *Clothing Matters*, chs 3 and 4; see also, in particular, C. A. Bayly, "The Origins of Swadeshit (home industry): Cloth and Indian Society, 1700–1930", in A. Appadurai (ed.) *The Social Life of Things: Commodities in Cultural Perspective*, Cambridge, Cambridge UP, 1986; Susan Bean, "Gandhi and Khadi: The Fabric of Independence", and Bernard S. Cohn, "Cloth, Clothes and Colonialism: India in the Nineteenth Century", both in Annette B. Weiner and Jane Schneider, *Cloth and Human Experience*, Washington and London, Smithsonian Institution Press, 1989.

48 Nurad C. Chauduri, *Culture in the Vanity Bag, being an Essay on Clothing and Adornment in Passing and Abiding India*, Bombay, Jailo, 1976, 161–2; Emma Tarlo, *Clothing Matters: Dress and Identity in India*, London, Hurst, 1996, 123.

49 Mukulika Banerjee and Daniel Miller, *The Sari*, Oxford, Berg, 2003, esp. 238–46.

50 This section follows the fascinating, and neglected, work of Nira Wickramasinghe, *Dressing the Colonised Body: Politics, Clothing and Identity in Sri Lanka*, New Delhi, Orient Longman, 2003.

51 Reprinted ibid., 130–4.

52 Roger Lipsey, *Coomaraswamy*, vol. II: *His Life and Work*, Princeton, Princeton UP, 1977, 17–19.

53 A loose-fitting long jacket.

54 A. Guruge (ed.), *Anagarika Dharmapala: Return to Righteousness*, Colombo, Government Press, 1965, 509, cited in Wickramasinghe, *Dressing the Colonised Body*, 14.

55 Wickramasinghe, *Dressing the Colonised Body*, 22.

56 Ibid., 125–8.

57 This section depends on Mina Roces, "Gender, Nation and the Politics of Dress in Twentieth-Century Philippines", in Louise Edwards and Mina Roces (eds), *The Politics of Dress in Asia and the Americas*, Brighton, Sussex UP, 2007; ead., "Women, Citizenship and the Politics of Dress in Twentieth-Century Philippines", in Wil Burghoorn et al. (eds), *Gender Politics in Asia: Women Manoeuvring with Dominant Gender Orders*, Copenhagen, NIAS press, forthcoming (I am most grateful to Dr Roces for letting me see these articles in advance of publication); B. Lynne Milgram, "Piña cloth, Identity and the Project of Philippine Nationalism", *Asian Studies Review*, 29, 2005.

58 The best general study is Thomas Hylland Eriksen, *Ethnicity and Nationalism*, London, Pluto Press, 1993, reprinted 2002.

59 Such distinctions need not, of course, be on the basis of what is perceived as ethnicity. Religious affiliation, for instance, can be marked in much the same way. Orthodox Jews form one obvious such example, as do the Mennonites – on whom see e.g. Beth Graybill and Linda B. Arthur, "The Social Control of Women's Bodies in two Mennonite Communities", and Jean A. Hamilton and Jana M. Hawley, "Sacred Dress, Public Worlds: Amish and Mormon Experience and Commitment", both in Linda B. Arthur (ed.), *Religion, Dress and the Body*, Oxford, Berg, 1999. For Islamic dress as an expression of commitment, see below, ch. 11.

60 Carola Lentz, "Ethnic Conflict and Changing Dress Codes: A Case Study of an Indian Migrant Village in Highland Ecuador", in Joanne B. Eicher, *Dress and Ethnicity: Change across Space and Time*, Oxford, Berg, 1995, 280.

61 E.g. Ann Pollard Rowe (ed.), *Costume and Identity in Highland Ecuador*, Washington, DC, Seattle and London, Textile Museum and University of Washington Press, 1998.

62 Lentz, "Ethnic Conflict".

63 Blenda Femenías, *Gender and the Boundaries of Dress in Contemporary Peru*, Austin, University of Texas Press, 2005, 184, 230.

64 Dakar, Rufisque, Gorée and St Louis.

65 Leslie W. Rabine, *The Global Circulation of African Fashion*, Oxford and New York, Berg, 2002, 33–4; Hudiata Nura Mustafa, "Sartorial Ecumenes: African Styles in a Social and Economic Context", in *The Art of African Fashion*, The Netherlands and Eritrea [sic], Prince Claus Fund and Africa World Press, 1998, 13–48; Deborah Heath, "Fashion, Anti-Fashion, and Heteroglossia in Urban Senegal", *American Ethnologist*, 19, 1992.

66 Jan Vansina, *The Tio Kingdom of the Middle Congo, 1880–1892*, London, Oxford UP, 1973, 151–3.

67 Joseph C. Miller, *Way of Death: Merchant Capitalism and the Angolan Slave Trade, 1730–1830*, London, James Currey, 1988, 79–82; F. Pigafetta, *A Report of the Kingdom of Congo and of the Surrounding Countries, Drawn out of the Writings and Discourses of the Portuguese Duarte Lopez*, reprinted London, Cass, 1970, 109, cited in Jonathan Friedman, "The Political Economy of Elegance: An African Cult of Beauty", *Culture and History*, 7, 1990, 107.

68 Jehan de Witte, *Les deux Congo*, Paris, Plon, 1913, 164, cited in C. Didier Gondola, "Dream and Drama: The Search for Elegance among Congolese Youth", *African Studies Review*, 42/1, 1999, 26.

69 Cited in Phyllis M. Martin, "Contesting Clothes in Colonial Brazzaville", *Journal of African History*, 35, 1994, 418–19.

70 Gondola, "Dream and Drama", 32–3; no doubt there have been continual changes as to the brands which are the most desired and prestigious.

71 Kenneth Lee Adelman, "The Recourse to Authenitciy and Negritude in Zaire", *Journal of Modern African Studies*, 13, 1975, 134–5.

NOTES TO CHAPTER 10

1 "On the Disappearance of Knickers: Hypotheses for the Functional Analysis of the Psychology of Clothing", *Journal of Social Psychology*, 51, 1960, 359–66, citation at 362.

2 Aileen Ribeiro, *Dress and Morality*, London, Batsford, 1986, 134; Elizabeth Wilson, *Adorned in Dreams: Fashion and Modernity*, London, Virago, 1985, 162–3. The same strictures were applied to the wearing by women of drawers in which the seam at the gusset was not left open. See Jill Fields, "Erotic Modesty: (Ad)dressing Female Sexuality and Propriety in Open and Closed Drawers, USA, 1800–1930", *Gender and History*, 14, 2002, 492–515.

3 Cherryl Buckley, "'De-Humanised Females and Amazonians'; British Wartime Fashion and its Representation in *Home Chat, 1914–1918*", *Gender and History*, 14, 2002, 516–36, quotations at 529. See also Susan Voso Lab, "'War' Drobe and World War I", in Patricia A. Cunningham and Susan Voso Lab (eds), *Dress in American Culture*, Bowling Green, Bowling Green State University Popular Press, 1991.

4 Christopher Sladen, *The Conscription of Fashion: Utility Cloth, Clothing and Footwear, 1941–1952*, Aldershot, Scolar Press, 1995.

5 Valerie Steele, "Dressing for Work", in Claudia Brush Kidwell and Valerie Steele (eds), *Men and Women: Dressing the Part*, Washsington, DC, Smithsonian Institute Press, 1989, 78–82.

6 See, among many places, Valerie Steele, *Fifty Years of Fashion: New Look to Now*, New Haven, Yale UP, 1997. See also Kurt Lang and Gladys Lang, "Fashion: Identification and Differentiation in Mass Society", in Mary Ellen Roach and Joanne Bubolz Eicher (eds), *Dress, Adornment, and the Social Order*, London, New York and Sydney, John Wiley and Sons, 1965, 323–6.

7 Ribeiro, *Dress and Morality*, 161.

8 Kathy Lee Peiss, *Hope in a Jar: The Making of America's Beauty Culture*, New York, Metropolitan Books, 1998; ead., "Making Up, Making Over: Cosmetics, Consumer Culture and Women's Identity", in Victoria de Grazia (ed.), *The Sex of Things: Gender and Consumption in Historical Perspective*, Berkeley, University of California Press, 1996, 311–37; Wilson, *Adorned in Dreams*, 109–11.

9 Ribeiro, *Dress and Morality*, 145.

10 Helena Rubinstein, *My Life for Beauty*, New York, paperback 1972 [originally published in 1965], 61, cited in Jennifer Craik, *The Face of Fashion: Cultural Studies in Fashion*, London, Routledge, 1994, 160.

11 In *Strong Poison* (London, Victor Gollancz, 1930), a novel by Dorothy L. Sayers published four years before *It Happened One Night*, Lady Mary Wimsey appears so clad. Patricia Campbell Warner, "The Americanisation of Fashion: Sportswear, the Movies and the 1930s", in Linda Welters and Patricia A. Cunningham (eds), *Twentieth-Century American Fashion*, Oxford and New York, Berg, 2005, 87, sees the moment in

Susan Lenox, Her Fall and Rise (1931) when Greta Garbo puts on Clark Gable's pyjamas as more crucial.

12   Philip Magnus, *King Edward VII*, London, John Murray, 1964, ch. 19.

13   Illustrated in Alison Lurie, *The Language of Clothes*, New York, Random House, 1981, 121.

14   Joanna Bourke, "The Great Male Renunciation: Men's Dress Reform in Inter-War Britain", *Journal of Design History*, 9, 1996, 30.

15   Laura Ugolini, "Ready-to-Wear or Made-to-Measure? Consumer Choice in the British Menswear Trade, 1900–1939", *Textile History*, 34, 2003; Brent Shannon, *The Cut of his Coat: Men, Dress, and Consumer Culture in Britain, 1860–1914*, Athens, Ohio UP, 2006, esp ch. 5.; Katrina Honeyman, *Well Suited: A History of the Leeds Clothing Industry 1850–1990*, Oxford, Oxford UP for the Pasold Research Fund, 2000; Paul Jobling, "'Virility in Design': Advertising Austin Reed and the 'New Tailoring' during the Interwar Period in Britain", *Fashion Theory*, 9, 2005.

16   *Sunlight*, December 1929, cited in Barbara Burman, "Better and Brighter Clothes: The Men's Dress Reform Party, 1929–1940", *Journal of Design History*, 8, 1995, 277.

17   "The King's Bodyguard", *Tailor and Cutter*, 5.6.1931; "Slackness and Fitness", ibid., 25.12.1931, both cited in Bourke, "Great Male Renunciation", 29.

18   Helen Callaway, "Dressing for Dinner in the Bush: Rituals of Self-Definition and British Imperial Authority", in Ruth Barnes and Joanne B. Eicher (eds), *Dress and Gender: Making and Meaning in Cultural Contexts*, New York and Oxford, Berg, 1992. On p. 243 she cites from Constance Larymore, *A Resident's Wife in Nigeria*, 2nd edn, London, Routledge, 1911, 288, the advice to her fellows: "*Always* wear corsets, even for a *tête-à-tête* home dinner on the warmest evenings; there is something about their absence almost as demoralizing as hair in curling-pins." Mrs Larymore recommended that a woman take at least six corsets with her when setting out to aid in the ruling of Africa.

19   Michael Carter, "J. C. Flügel and the Nude Future", *Fashion Theory*, 7, 2003.

20   See notes to ch. 5, n. 35.

21   Warner, "Americanisation of Fashion", 87–9.

22   Wilson, *Adorned in Dreams*, 164.

23   Ibid., 165.

24   Queen Juliana of the Netherlands did wear trousers to welcome the winner of the Eleven Towns skating race in 1963; the temperature was probably 10 degrees below freezing and a gale was blowing.

25   Steele, "Dressing for Work", 70–1.

26   Resolution, South Carolina House of Representatives, 10 March 1987, adopted by 105 votes to 2.

27   Steele, "Dressing for Work", 84–6.

28   Eventually, this came to mark secretaries, and was thus avoided by those who wished to be considered professionals.

29 Steele, "Dressing for Work", 86–9; Patricia A. Cunningham, "Dressing for Success: The Re-suiting of Corporate America in the 1970s", in Welters and Cunningham (eds), *Twentieth-Century American Fashion*, 201–5. Both cite John Molloy, *The Women's Dress for Success Book*, New York, Warner Books, 1977.

30 Farid Chenoune, *A History of Men's Fashion*, Paris, Flammarion, 1993.

31 Cunningham, "Dressing for Success", 198–201.

32 T. L. Lennon, S. J. Lennon and K. K. P. Johnson, "Is Clothing Probative of Attitude or Intent? Implications for Rape and Sexual Harassment Cases", *Law & Inequality: A Journal of Theory and Practice*, 11 (1993), 391–415; Kim K. P. Johnson, Jane E. Hegland and Nancy A. Scholfield, "Survivors of Rape: Functions and Implications of Dress in a Context of Coercive Power", in Kim K. P. Johnson and Sharon J. Lennon (eds), *Appearance and Power*, Oxford and New York, Berg, 1999, 11–32.

33 A very similar trajectory, for instance, was followed by the T-shirt.

34 Dick Scheuring, "Heavy Duty Denim: 'Quality never dates' ", in Angela McRobbie (ed.), *Zoot Suits and Second-Hand Dresses: An Anthology of Fashion and Music*, Houndmills and London, Macmillan, 1989; Jennifer Craik, *The Face of Fashion: Cultural Studies in Fashion*, London, Routledge, 1994, 194–6; Djurdja Bartlett, "Let Them Wear Beige: The Petit-bourgeois World of Official Socialist Dress", *Fashion Theory*, 8, 2004; Judd Stitziel, *Fashioning Socialism: Clothing Politics and Consumer Culture in East Germany*, Oxford and New York, Berg, 2005.

35 www.benetton.com, accessed 30.5.2007. It is notable and not surprising that Benetton's only outlets on the continent of Africa are in Egypt, South Africa and – perhaps no more – in Ivory Coast.

36 Christopher M. Moore, John Fernie and Steve Burt, "Brands without Boundaries: The Internationalization of the Designer Retailer's Brand", *European Journal of Marketing*, 34, 2000.

37 In this section, I am following Karen Tranberg Hansen, *Salaula: The World of Secondhand Clothing and Zambia*, Chicago and London, University of Chicago Press, 2000.

NOTE TO CHAPTER 11

1 Information from Dr Anjana Singh.

2 Fernand Braudel, *Capitalism and Material Life, 1400–1800*, trans. Miriam Kochan, London, Weidenfeld and Nicolson, 1973, 227, cited in Antonia Finnane, "Yangzhou's 'Modernity': Fashion and Consumption in the Early Nineteenth Century", *Positions*, 11, 2005, 396.

3 Suzanne E. Cahill, "'Our Women are Acting like Foreigners': Western Influences on Tang Dynasty Women's Fashion", in Valerie Steele and John S. Major (eds), *China Chic: East meets West*, New Haven and

London, Yale UP, 1999, 103–18. In this case, of course, the West is Central Asia.

4 Cited in Steele and Major (eds), *China Chic*, 24.

5 Finnane, "Yangzhou's 'modernity' ", 401.

6 The reference is of course to Tennyson's *Locksley Hall.*

7 Steele and Major (eds), *China Chic*, 34.

8 Ibid., 42–4; Dorothy Ko, "Bondage in Time: Footbinding and Fashion Theory", *Fashion Theory*, 1, 1997; ead., *Cinderella's Sisters: A Revisionist History of Footbinding*, Berkeley, University of California Press, 2005. The defenders of footbinding, incidentally, had not unreasonably compared the practice to the contemporary European donning of the corset.

9 Michael Godley, "The End of the Queue: Hair as a Symbol in Chinese History", *East Asian History*, 8, 1994.

10 Cited in Paul Carroll, "Refashioning Suzhou: Dress, Commodification, and Modernity", *Positions*, 11, 2003, 444.

11 Ibid., 453.

12 Louise Edwards, "Dressing for Power: Scholars' Robes, School Uniforms and Military Attire in China", in Louise Edwards and Mina Roces, *The Politics of Dress in Asia and the Americas*, Eastbourne, Sussex Academic Press, 2007; Carroll, "Refashioning Suzhou", esp. 455–7; Ellen Johnston Laing, "Visual Evidence for the Evolution of 'Politically Correct' Dress for Women in Early Twentieth Century Shanghai", *Nan Nü*, 5, 2003, 69–114. In general for the phenomenon of commercial nationalism, see Karl Gerth, *China Made: Consumer Culture and the Creation of the Nation*, Cambridge, Mass., and London, Harvard UP, 2003.

13 The former is the Mandarin term, the latter the Cantonese, for the same garment. The term means "banner dress", thus stressing its derivation from the attire of the Manchu banner troops.

14 Cited, apparently with a mistaken reference, in Antonia Finnane, "What Should Chinese Women Wear? A National Problem", *Modern China*, 22, 1996, 115–166.

15 For brief comments on the anti-breast binding movements, see Antonia Finnane, "Military Culture and Chinese Dress in the Early Twentieth Century", in Steele and Major (eds), *China Chic*, 127; for similar changes in Japan, see Laura Miller, "Mammary Mania in Japan", *Positions*, 11, 2003.

16 Finnane, "What Should Chinese Women Wear?", 118–20; Laing, "Visual Evidence", 101–11; Valery M. Garrett, "The Cheong san: Its Rise and Fall", *Costume*, 29, 1995; Naomi Yin-yin Szeto, "*Cheungsam*: Fashion, Culture and Gender", in Claire Roberts (ed.), *Evolution and Revolution: Chinese Dress, 1700s–1990s*, Sydney, Powerhouse Publishing, 1999. For a fascinating insider's view of these matters, see Eileen Chang, "A Chronicle of Changing Clothes", *Positions*, 11, 2003; this article is a compilation of the text which Eileen Chang (Zhang Ailing) first published, in slightly different English and Chinese versions, in the 1940s.

17 *Zhongshan* is the mandarin version of Sun's personal name.

18 Robert E. Harrist, Jr., "Clothes Make the Man: Dress, Modernity and Masculinity in China, ca. 1912–1937", in Wu Hung and Katherine R. Tsiang, *Body and Face in Chinese Visual Culture*, Cambridge, Mass., and London, Harvard UP, 2005, 184.

19 Carroll, "Refashioning Suzhou", 465–70 (citation at 468); Verity Wilson, "Dressing for Leadership in China: Wives and Husbands in an Age of Revolutionaries", *Gender and History*, 14, 2002, 608–14.

20 Harrist, "Clothes Make the Man", 179–85.

21 Wilson, "Dressing for Leadership", 615–19.

22 Finnane, "What Should Chinese Women Wear?", 99.

23 The reference is, of course, to "The Eighteenth Brumaire of Louis Napoleon", in the Penguin edition of Karl Marx, *Surveys from Exile*, Harmondsworth, 1973, 239.

24 Antonia Finnane, "Looking for the Jiang Qing Dress: Some Preliminary Findings", *Fashion Theory*, 9, 2005.

25 Wilson, "Dressing for Leadership", 620.

26 Tina Mai Chen, "Proletarian White and Working Bodies in Mao's China", *Positions*, 11, 2003; ead., "Dressing for the Party: Clothing, Citizenship, and Gender-Formation in Mao's China", *Fashion Theory*, 5, 2001; Verity Wilson, "Dress and the Cultural Revolution", in Steele and Major (eds), *China Chic*, particularly the illustration at p. 180; Finnane, "What Should Chinese Women Wear?", 120–3.

27 Chua Beng-huat, "Postcolonial Sites, Global Flows and Fashion Codes: A Case Study of power *cheongsams* and other clothing styles in modern Singapore", *Postcolonial Studies*, 3, 2000; Hazel Clark and Agnes Wong, "Who Still Wears the *Cheongsam*?", in Roberts (ed.), *Evolution and Revolution*.

28 Xiaoping Li, "Fashioning the Body in Post-Mao China", in Anne Brydon and Sandra Niessen (eds), *Consuming Fashion: Adorning the Transnational Body*, Oxford, Berg, 1998.

29 Matthew Chew, "The Dual Consequences of Cultural Localization: How Exposed Short Stockings Subvert and Sustain Global Cultural Hierarchy", *Positions*, 11, 2003.

30 Jean Allman, "'Let your Fashion be in Line with our Ghanaian Costume': Nation, Gender and the Politics of Clothing in Nkrumah's Ghana", in Jean Allman (ed.), *Fashioning Africa: Power and the Politics of Dress*, Bloomington and Indianapolis, Indiana UP, 2004, citation at 144; Esther Goody and Jack Goody, "The Naked and the Clothed", in John Hunwick and Nancy Lawler (eds), *The Cloth of Many Colored Silks: Papers on History and Society Ghanaian and Islamic in Honor of Ivor Wilks*, Evanston, Ill., Northwestern University Press, 1996.

31 *Time*, 2.8.1971, cited in Audrey Wipper, "African Women, Fashion, and Scapegoating", *Canadian Journal of African Studies*, 6, 1972, 335–6.

32 This culminated in the policy of villagization known as Ujamaa. There are many descriptions of this; for the most famous, see James C. Scott,

Seeing Like a State: How Certain Schemes to Improve the Human Condition have Failed, New Haven and London, Yale UP, 1998.

33   Given the image of the Maasai in the advertising media, this is not entirely without foundation.

34   Leander Schneider, "The Maasai's New Clothes: A Developmentalist Modernity and its Exclusions", *Africa Today*, 53, 2006. The citation, from the Tanzanian National Archives, is on p. 106.

35   Ibid., 109–10.

36   Wipper, "African Women, Fashion and Scapegoating", 329–30, 332, 339; Karen Tranberg Hansen, "Dressing Dangerously: Miniskirts, Gender Relations, and Sexuality in Zambia", in Allman (ed.), *Fashioning Africa*, 166–87.

37   Thomas Burgess, "Cinema, Bell Bottoms, and Miniskirts: Struggles over Youth and Citzenship in Revolutionary Zanzibar", *International Journal of African Historical Studies*, 26, 2002, 307.

38   Andrew M. Ivaska, "'Anti-mini Militants meet Modern Misses': Urban Style, Gender and the Politics of 'National Culture' in 1960s Dar es Salaam, Tanzania", in Jean Allman (ed.), *Fashioning Africa*, quotation at 113.

39   Sheryl McCurdy, "Fashioning Sexuality: Desire, Manyema Ethnicity and the Creation of the *Kanga, ca.* 1880–1900", *International Journal of African Historical Studies*, 29, 2005.

40   Karen Tranberg Hansen, *Salaula: The World of Secondhand Clothing and Zambia*, Chicago and London, University of Chicago Press, 2000, esp. 83–7. In Zambia, the material is known as *chitenge*.

41   Allman, "'Let your Fashion be in Line with our Ghanaian Costume'", 145.

42   *Kente* cloth, often printed to resemble the strip weave of the Ghanaian original, has become a sartorial symbol for Afro-Americans, who might be surprised to see it thought of as a metonym for a slave-trading kingdom. See Doran H. Ross, *Wrapped in Pride: Ghanaian Kente and African American Identity*, Los Angeles, UCLA Fowler Museum of Cultural History, 1998.

43   On Tanzania, information from Jan-Kees van Donge; on Zambia, Hansen, *Salaula*, 92–4.

44   Sandra Klopper, "Re-dressing the Past: The Africanisation of sartorial style in Contemporary South Africa", in Artah Brah and Annie E. Coombes, *Hybridity and its Discontents: Politics, Science, Culture*, London and New York, Routledge, 2000.

45   Jeevan Vasagar, "Kenyans say No Thanks to National Dress", *Guardian*, 25.10.2004.

46   See above, ch. 2.

47   Dawn Chatty, "The Burqa Face Cover: An Aspect of Dress in Southeastern Arabia", in Nancy Lindisfarne-Tapper and Bruce Ingham (eds), *Languages of Dress in the Middle East*, London, Curzon in association with the Centre of Near and Middle Eastern Studies, SOAS, 1997, 133,

where she notes that the Viceroy most eager to unveil Egyptian women, Lord Cromer, was a founder member of the (British) Men's League for Opposing Women's Suffrage.

48 Norton, "Faith and Fashion", 162–5; Emelie A. Olson, "Muslim Identity and Secularism in Contemporary Turkey: 'The Headscarf Dispute'", *Anthropological Quarterly*, 54, 1985, 162–5.

49 Ziba Mir-Hosseini, "Women and Politics in Post-Khomeini Iran: Divorce, Veiling and Emerging Feminist Voices", in Haleh Afshar, *Women and Politics in the Third World*, London and New York, Routledge, 1996, 153.

50 Beth Baron, "Unveiling in Early Twentieth Century Egypt: Practical and Symbolic Considerations", *Middle Eastern Sudies*, 25, 1989; Leila Ahmed, *Women and Gender in Islam: Historical Roots of a Modern Debate*, New Haven and London, Yale UP, 1992, esp. chs 8–10; Anouk de Koning, "Embodiment and Public Space in Up-Market Cairo", unpublished paper, Amsterdam School for Social Research, 2007.

51 For an Indonesian example, see Suzanne Brenner, "Reconstructing Self and Society: Javanese Muslim Women and 'the Veil'", *American Ethnologist*, 23, 1996.

52 Its actual title translates as "promoter of virtue".

53 Mir-Hosseini, "Women and Politics", 153–8; Faegheh Shirazi, "Islamic Religion and Women's Dress Code: The Islamic Republic of Iran", in Linda B. Arthur (ed.), *Undressing Religion: Commitment and Conversion from a Cross-Cultural Perspective*, Oxford and New York, Berg, 2000; ead., *The Veil Unveiled: The Hijab in Modern Culture*, Gainesville, University Press of Florida, 2001, esp. 88–109.

54 Arlene Elowe MacLeod, "Hegemonic Relations and Gender Resistance: The New Veiling as Accommodating Protest in Cairo", *Signs*, 17, 1993.

55 In general, Fadwa El Guindi, *Veil: Modesty, Privacy and Resistance*, Oxford and New York, Berg, 1999, esp. 161–78. El Guindi argues that the two explanations used in this paragraph are incompatible, which seems mistaken. See further, Olson, "Muslim Identity and Secularism"; Alexandru Balasescu, "Tehran Chic: Islamic Headscarves, Fashion Designers and the new geographies of modernity", *Fashion Theory*, 7, 2003; Özlem Sandıkı and Güliz Ger, "Aesthetics, Ethics and Politics of the Turkish Headscarf", in Susanne Küchler and Daniel Miller (eds), *Clothing as Material Culture*, Oxford and New York, Berg, 2005.

56 Koran, 24: 30, 31.

57 Ahmed, *Women and Gender*, 245.

58 On this see John R. Bowen, *Why the French don't Like Headscarves: Islam, the State, and Public Space*, Princeton and Oxford, Princeton UP, 2007; Malcolm D. Brown, "Multiple Meanings of the 'Hijab' in Contemporary France", in William J. F. Keenan (ed.), *Dressed to Impress: Looking the Part*, Oxford and New York, Berg, 2001.

NOTE TO CHAPTER 12

1   There has been a considerable literature on colonial mimicry and its
ambiguities. See for instance Homi Bhabha, "Of Mimicry and Men: The
Ambivalence of Colonial Discourse", in Homi Bhabha, *The Location
of Culture*, London, Routledge, 1994, 85–92; Michael Taussig, *Mimesis
and Alterity: A Particular History of the Senses*, New York and London,
Routledge, 1993; but also James Ferguson, "Of Mimicry and Member-
ship: Africans and the 'New World Society' ", *Cultural Anthropology*, 17,
2002, 551–69.

Index